JACK
AND THE
THAMES
TORSO
MURDERS

JACK
AND THE
THAMES
TORSO
MURDERS
A NEW RIPPER?

DREW D. GRAY AND ANDREW WISE

AMBERLEY

Dr Drew Gray is a Senior Lecturer in the History of Crime at the University of Northampton and has published three books and several articles on crime and violence in eighteenth- and nineteenth-century London, including *London Shadows* (Bloomsbury). He has been lecturing on the Whitechapel murders and the social history of East London for twelve years.

Andrew Wise is a history graduate with a research background in crime and espionage. He is a former police officer and private investigator.

First published 2019

Amberley Publishing
The Hill, Stroud
Gloucestershire, GL5 4EP

www.amberley-books.com

Copyright © Drew D. Gray and
Andrew Wise, 2019

The right of Drew D. Gray and Andrew Wise
to be identified as the Authors of this work has
been asserted in accordance with the Copyrights,
Designs and Patents Act 1988.

ISBN 978 1 4456 8776 6 (paperback)
ISBN 978 1 4456 8777 3 (ebook)

British Library Cataloguing in Publication Data.
A catalogue record for this book is available
from the British Library.

Typesetting by Aura Technology and Software
Services, India. Printed in Great Britain.

CONTENTS

ACKNOWLEDGEMENTS

Writing a book like this is a long process and it involves many people at different stages. The authors would therefore like to thank to several people who have made this easier, more fun, or indeed, possible at all. Firstly, Rob Hills because without his initial investigation into the candidacy of James Hardiman we wouldn't have had the springboard for our own research. Hopefully Rob will be pleased to see the results of this in print today.

Getting the story out there also means we need to salute Amberley's Shaun Barrington for recognising that we had a story worth telling and for taking a punt on us in a market already saturated with books on the 'Ripper' case. We would also like to thank Cathy Stagg and others in the Amberley family for helping get this off the drawing board and into print.

We owe a massive debt to the legion of Ripperologists who have come before us in researching, debating, and detailing the history of the Whitechapel murders and the lives of the women who were murdered. It isn't fair to say that the histories of these women had never been told before 2019, they have, but it was certainly enlightening to speak to Haille Rubenhold and get a sense of her research prior to its publication in March. Likewise conversations with Charlotte Mallinson have helped us consider some aspects of this case that are not always covered, explicitly at least, by previous studies. Our clear debt, however, is to the giants of Ripperology who have provided the detail and the narrative that has framed all subsequent books on the subject. So we would like to say thank you to Phillip Sugden, Donald Rumbelow and, most of all, to Paul Begg for their work over many years. Paul has also been very helpful and generous with his time in discussing the case and its place in popular culture. With some trepidation we sent a draft version of this book to Neil Bell, himself the author of an excellent study of the policing of the Whitechapel murder series. Neil's comments were positive, encouraging and helpful in pointing out some obvious flaws in our narrative. Naturally, any mistakes that remain are our own and we take responsibility for them. There is an oft-maligned group of amateurs that study the 'Ripper' and the area he terrorised in 1888, and we would like to thank the very many of them who have debated with us at talks and conferences, online and by email. Ripperology deserves to be seen as a legitimate and entirely honest sub-section of local history and 'true crime' but certain elements have exploited the case for financial gain and they continue to undermine the good name of those who simply want to understand the past a little better. We have been critical of some of the ways in which the case has been exploited but we are not out to attack Ripperology or demean those with an interest in it. We just ask for a little understanding of those who hold different opinions and who come to the case from outside 'the club' so to speak.

We would also like to thank the very many Northampton University students of criminology and history who have studied with Drew over the years. Education is not a one-way street and many of the ideas shared in seminars have helped frame the content and style of this book. Asking why we study the murders is a more important question than who 'Jack' was, because it demands that we think about the whole process of studying and writing history itself. In an age of 'fake news' and instant-access to 'facts', careful consideration of historical method, bias, and construction is more important than ever.

Finally we would like to thank our families and friends for their support in undertaking what has been a journey of several years. Colleagues at Northampton, particularly Caroline Nielsen and Robert Farmer, have tramped around Whitechapel with us and friends have listened as we outlined our ideas and made us reflect on them. As we said at the start, writing a book isn't easy and it isn't achieved in isolation, so thanks again to everyone involved.

This book is about how one man – an ordinary, insignificant and deeply troubled man – brutally ended the lives of at least 13 women. His victims deserve to be remembered as human beings, as women who lived, loved and worked in London in the 1880s. They are symbolic however of all women who have been abused, hurt or killed by men. We dedicate this book to them and their families and hope one day our society will have the decency to erect a monument to the victims (and survivors) of male violence. We think that Whitechapel would be a fitting location for just such a memorial.

FOREWORD

A PECULIAR ENCOUNTER IN SPITALFIELDS

In the early hours of Sunday 30 September 1888, PC Robert Spicer (101 H Division) turned into Heneage Street from Brick Lane, as he perambulated his beat. Today, this area is part of the bustling heart of Banglatown, where curry houses vie with sari shops and visitors who are interested in dark tourism are regaled with stories of the 'Ripper' and his crimes. The Pride of Spitalfields pub serves up Truman ales and salt beef sandwiches and there is hardly a thought to the street's history. Indeed no one propping up the bar at the Pride is likely to be aware that this street once played a pivotal role in one of the darkest mysteries that London, or any city, has known. Most of the clientele at this East End pub are still locals – while the tourists tend to frequent the much trendier Ten Bells opposite Spitalfields Market – and they have far more pressing things to worry about than a 130-year-old-unsolved murder.

In 1888 there was a brewery to the rear of where the current pub now stands. At some point in the late 1800s or early twentieth century, a pub was built there (named the Romford Arms) but in 1888 there was probably just a beer shop, a place for locals to buy and take out a jug of ale.[1] A few doors down from the brewery, an alley led into a large courtyard which is now the smart home of a firm of architects. Another pub, the Osborne Arms, used to stand at the end of the road, as the Ordnance Survey map for 1873 shows. This was an area well supplied with places to drink yourself into a stupor if you wanted to but as Charles Booth, who documented working-class life in London at the end of the nineteenth century, observed, most of these were actually relatively sober establishments that provided an important network of community support and cohesion.[2] You went to the pub to talk out your troubles as well as to forget them, and you'd usually find someone to listen.

After PC Spicer had walked about 50 yards along Heneage Street, he turned into a court and found a man chatting to a well-known local prostitute named 'Rosy'. The man, although apparently 'respectably' dressed, had blood on his shirt cuffs and carried a brown bag. Not surprisingly, this aroused the constable's suspicions because by the time PC Spicer entered Heneage Court in the autumn of 1888, a serial killer had already struck several times in the area and the Metropolitan Police were engaged in a manhunt for the character who was to become notorious to contemporaries and future generations alike as 'Jack the Ripper'. When Spicer questioned the man he was evasive, refusing to answer him satisfactorily and so Spicer had little choice but to ask him to accompany him to the nearest police station. Back at Commercial Street 'nick' the unnamed man gave an address in Brixton (which was a long way south from Whitechapel) and claimed to be a medical doctor. Much to the policeman's disgust, the mystery 'doctor', having given his word that he would happily return later for questioning, was released without even having his bag searched. PC Spicer later claimed to have seen the man several times afterwards at Liverpool Street station, always dressed similarly and pestering women, before walking off quickly when he approached him. But where had the 'good doctor' gone on his release in the early hours of that late autumn evening – and what, if anything, did he have in his bag?

PC Spicer waited until 1931 to tell his 'Ripper' story and so we should necessarily be cautious of the 'evidence' he has left us.[3] But the date is significant because 29/30 September 1888 was the night of the so-called 'double event' when two local women

(Elizabeth 'Long Liz' Stride and Catherine 'Kate' Eddowes) were brutally murdered within an hour of each other, barely a short walk from Heneage Street. Spicer described the man he saw with 'Rosy' as 5 foot 8 inches tall, about 12 stone in weight, with a high forehead and a fair moustache; he also noticed that he had 'rosy cheeks'. He was dressed in a black suit with a high hat and sported a gold watch and chain.[4] Had Spicer brought in 'Jack the Ripper', only for the desk sergeant to let him go again? Or was the constable, many years afterwards, merely attempting to profit from his connection with the case? For how Heneage Street looks today, *see* plate insert.

Several researchers into the case, now collectively known as 'Ripperologists', have dismissed PC Spicer's story as mere fabrication, concocted to garner fame and fortune, especially given that it surfaced so long after the event. The notion that Spicer's suspect was a doctor certainly rings alarms bells because the idea that 'Jack' was a medical man, complete with top hat and Gladstone bag, is a well-worn trope that was first suggested in 1888 and now seems risible. Maybe Spicer over-egged the pudding and gave the public what he thought they wanted to hear. But what if, beneath the embroidery, there had been a kernel of truth in the copper's story?

Why does this matter? Well, because in the small hours of that night, someone had murdered Kate Eddowes in Mitre Square and seems to have managed to escape back into Spitalfields, at some stage leaving a bloodied piece of the victim's apron underneath a message chalked on the entrance to a block of dwellings in Goulston Street. Did the same man rest in Heneage Court that night and, if so, was it because it was close to his home where he felt safe? According to Spicer's letter to the *Daily Express* in 1931, the Heneage Court encounter had taken place at 1.45 that morning, although author Christopher J. Morley suggests a rather later time of 3 a.m.[5] Whatever the exact timing was, we believe that the man found chatting to an unknown streetwalker named Rosy was actually the most notorious serial killer in history – and Rosy herself believed it.[6] We hope to convince you to at least give this version of events your consideration.

INTRODUCTION

SETTING THE SCENE

Between 11 May 1887 and 13 February 1891, a succession of horrific murders shook Victorian London. Over a period of three years and nine months, sixteen women were attacked – of whom only three survived. At the time, the police believed these atrocities comprised two or more distinct and unrelated sets of assaults, with several of the killings becoming known as the 'Thames Torso Murders' and some of the remainder, with varying degrees of consensus, the infamous 'Whitechapel Murders'. Despite the best attempts of contemporary detectives, no individual was ever formally charged or prosecuted for these crimes. As a result, an entire sub-genre of 'true crime' (dubbed 'Ripperology') has arisen as countless researchers and armchair sleuths have attempted to solve the 130-year-old mystery: Who was 'Jack the Ripper'?

This new book will offer what we believe is a plausible solution to these unsolved mysteries and argue that the two sets of murders were connected and that one individual alone was responsible for the awful attacks on these women. In doing so, we have built on some previous suggestions while pursuing radically different lines of enquiry suggested by new information. While we believe that we have been able to present a convincing case and a plausible candidate for these killings, we recognise that after 130 or more years of trying, it is unlikely anyone will be able to conclusively prove who the killer was. The benchmark for those attempting to solve the mystery may well be to establish a case that would hold up to scrutiny in a late nineteenth-century court of law. There the niceties of modern rules of evidence did not apply in the way they do today, and circumstantial evidence was not so easily dismissed. One of the authors has spent considerable time looking at the operation of the Victorian court system in London, from the forerunners of modern magistrate courts (the Metropolitan Police courts) to the Central Criminal Court at Old Bailey. It is reasonable to suggest that the level of proof supplied by forensic evidence in today's justice system was not always required to get a conviction in the 1880s.[7] The police of late-Victorian London did not possess the forensic armoury that the modern service enjoys: no DNA, fingerprinting, offender profiling, CCTV, squad cars or mobile phones. They had to rely on witness statements, circumstantial evidence, interviews and confessions.[8] They still sought, however, to establish the three key elements that might identify a potential suspect: means, motive and opportunity. Our candidate, as we will demonstrate, possessed all of these in abundance. We will also answer the off-asked question of why he stopped killing without being caught, something that serial killers supposedly do not do. Unlike many, or even most, previous 'solution studies' of the 'Ripper' we have built our case by looking at the geography of late nineteenth-century London and at the ways in which its inhabitants experienced and interacted with the city. Previous attempts to solve the case have presented characters (such as the Duke of Clarence and Avondale, Queen Victoria's physician, or a Liverpudlian businessman) who would have had little personal relationship or knowledge of the capital and its transport networks. We believe the killer not only knew his way around the city but that his working practices, and the routes he used for them, played a vital role in determining the pattern of the crimes he committed. His work, in fact, and the locations to which it took him, afforded him the means and opportunity to kill and evade justice.

Whoever 'Jack the Ripper' was, he was not someone who stood out in the dark streets of East London. A real-life aristocrat in top hat and cape was unlikely to have passed unnoticed in the early hours of a Whitechapel morning. Similarly, a 'crazed' immigrant fleeing from the scene of a crime would also have drawn the attention of the many locals who were making their way to and from work. London in the late 1880s was a busy, vibrant and active city. The East End itself was crowded, there were potential witnesses everywhere and while people often kept themselves to themselves (and certainly didn't willingly talk to the police) they would have noticed 'strangers' and those who looked out of place in their community, particularly at a time when the newspapers were filled with speculation about the sort of person the 'Whitechapel fiend' might have been. So we believe that the killer had to be someone relatively ordinary and perhaps quite familiar, someone people were used to seeing, someone who did not need an explanation for being where they were, while carrying odd bundles, or occasionally being soiled with blood.

For all these reasons, and those put forward by Christopher Frayling who was commissioned by the BBC to make the 1988 documentary *Shadow of the Ripper*, we reject the idea that 'Jack the Ripper' was a 'decadent milord', a 'mad doctor' or an immigrant 'anarchist or socialist'.[9] These stereotypes have largely been created by the clamour of the nineteenth-century press, contemporary concerns about the 'other', as well as the desperate responses of the Metropolitan Police, and modern attempts to solve the mystery using false trails somehow taken as reality. Moreover, much of the evidence that has been used to try to discover the identity of 'Jack the Ripper' is based on recycled accounts that owe their origin to contemporary witness statements and news reports. So how reliable are these?

In the case of the Whitechapel series, it is certainly true that we have many reports of dubious credibility, such as that of the man seen loitering outside Miller's Court of the night of Mary Kelly's murder.[10] Mistakes aside, witnesses are well known for deliberately embroidering the truth or fabricating their accounts. Why do they do this? In many instances it is to attract attention, to make themselves feel more important, or simply to reinforce the accepted norms of the society in which they exist. Put another way, people sometimes see what they want to see purely because they believe that is what they are *expected* to have seen. Conversely, however, we also have a good number of credible sightings of men with some of the victims shortly before their assaults and careful analysis of these has enabled us to offer something approaching a rough photo-fit of the killer. It has been a case of sorting the wheat from the chaff when dealing with the facts – rejecting the unreliable in favour of the credible. Eyewitnesses are problematic, but they are often all we have to go on, especially in respect to a murder series that took place more than 100 years ago.

Similarly, because we don't have a murder weapon, and as very little that is material from the case survives, researchers have fallen back on more eclectic sources. In recent years a shawl, supposedly found at the scene of Katherine Eddowes' murder, was presented as the solution to the case.[11] Previously, the killer's supposed diary has been put forward as 'evidence', and a knife and a series of medical slides have also formed the basis on which suspects have been nominated.[12] This book, however, offers no such sleights of hand or revelations of new forensic material because, frankly, none is ever likely to come to light. Forensic material such as DNA will have been degraded in the years since the murders occurred and corrupted by the hundreds, if not thousands, of hands through which they might have passed, so we seriously doubt whether a 'smoking gun' (or a dripping knife) will help to solve this case. Instead we believe we can piece together what would seem to be the most likely scenario and present a suspect who should bear close examination.

In doing so we will explore the murky world of London's slaughterhouses and the meat trade it supplied. We will look at the dreadful effects of sexually transmitted diseases and the ways in which they have blighted the lives of ordinary people in a period before antibiotics. We will tell the social history of Whitechapel and Spitalfields and look at the curious geography of its streets and alleys, and explain how they and London's wider transport network are intimately connected with the murders of 1887–1891. Last of all, we will outline the tragic personal history of one man and show how he interconnects with all of the themes outlined in this book. In so doing, we hope to convince you that we have presented a case for solving the Whitechapel and Thames Torso Murders. Ultimately, of course, you will form the jury for his trial, and judge him on the merits of the case before you.

One final point before we start our journey back through time needs addressing as it is something that is constantly asked: Why do we need to know who 'Jack the Ripper' was? Well, apart from the obvious desire to solve the most intriguing 'cold case' in history, it is our belief that we owe it to the victims. We believe at least thirteen women were murdered in the space of just four years and, like the victims of serial killers Peter Sutcliffe and Stephen Wright, they have a right to a justice of sorts. There should be a memorial in East London to remind us that society does care about what happens to even its most desperate members and by framing this account around the reality of what might have occurred (instead of some fantasy about mad doctors and royal conspiracies) we acknowledge that this one man was likely responsible for the brutal murders of numerous defenceless women. Understanding why he did what he did will not bring them back, but it might help their relatives to think that we do at least care. Much has been said recently about the inherent misogyny in 'Ripperology' and this will be addressed in some depth at the end of this book but perhaps we can make a brief case for what we are doing here. We don't offer up a suspect as a heroic figure; this is no crusading Dr Gull or criminal mastermind. Our candidate is a deeply flawed and disturbed individual who chose to project his personal tragedy onto the environment in which he grew up and worked. Instead of recognising his own part in what happened to him and his loved ones, he decided to take it out on some of the most vulnerable members of that community. He was not a mythical monster, he was a very ordinary, if troubled, working-class man – and given that violence towards women remains endemic in our modern society, and was arguably even more widespread in the 1880s, we think it fitting that we present him as one extreme example of cruelty among many in the period. This story then is not intended as a celebration of his life or a justification for what he did, it is instead a reminder that serial killers (who are invariably male and kill the vulnerable, many of whom are women) can emerge anywhere in society, and can be anyone. They are not 'special' or 'anti-heroes' they are, like modern terrorists, merely ordinary, misguided, unpleasant and inhuman people.

So this book also aims to do a little more than merely rehash the case or offer an updated contextual history of 1880s Whitechapel and London. At the close of this case, we will also consider the present state of Ripperology and the industry that has grown up around the murders. Perhaps the best legacy we can offer the victims of the man we believe was responsible is to separate myth and exploitative voyeurism from historical reality and attempt to provide a serious analysis of motive and consequence. There was no person named 'Jack the Ripper' and the mask that has concealed him has largely been created by those who wish to profit from his crimes rather than hold him responsible for them. It is high time that mask was wrenched away so that history recognises him for what he was: a disturbed and mentally unbalanced individual overwhelmed by a hatred of women and those he believed to be street prostitutes (what has recently been termed 'whorephobia')[13] because of the life choices he'd made and the awful consequences that resulted from them.

I

WHITECHAPEL AND ITS GEOGRAPHIES

From the moment the very first 'Ripper' victim was discovered, the London press, and then their regional and international counterparts, recommenced a process of characterising the East End as a place of 'social danger'.[14] Reporters soon infested the streets, courts and alleys of Whitechapel, looking for any new or original angle on the killings.[15] They were not alone of course – social investigators, 'slum' priests and moral reformers tripped over each other as they vied to explore this 'heart of darkness' at the centre of the British Empire. So, it is important for us to remember that Whitechapel and the wider East End is just as much a product of myth-creation as was 'Jack the Ripper' himself. If the murders themselves were 'a media event'[16] that hatched a mythology that has been sustained to the present day, then it is equally true that the streets on which they occurred have passed into legend.

If you leave the London Underground at Aldgate East and take the exit for the Whitechapel Gallery, you will find yourself at the entrance to the maze of alleyways and streets that once formed one of the poorest quarters of Queen Victoria's empire. Most 'Ripper' tours choose the entrance to Gunthorpe Street, close by the White Hart pub, as a suitably authentic place to begin. Gunthorpe Street today is framed by an archway that acts as portal into what one contemporary author described as the 'abyss', and thousands of feet trudge along this cobbled pathway on a weekly basis.[17] The White Hart is infamous as the site of the one-time home of Severin Klosowski (also known as George Chapman) who was hanged for murder in 1903 and continues to command attention as a possible 'Ripper' suspect.[18] Outside, the pub proudly declaims its association with both Chapman and the Whitechapel murders, one of relatively few public displays of linkage to the killings. Indeed, one of the perhaps remarkable aspects of modern Whitechapel and Spitalfields is just how absent the 'Ripper' is today, despite it being one of the first things tourists associate with the area.

In 1888 Gunthorpe Street was called George Yard and at the point that the road met Wentworth Street, George Yard Buildings provided cheap housing for the area's poor.[19] A nearby ragged school attempted to give the local children a basic education and Toynbee Hall (on Commercial Street) overlooked the area, as the middle-class beacon of light its founders intended. George Yard Buildings had been opened in the mid-1870s as one of many 'model dwellings' in the capital but by 1888, there were complaints that the behaviour of some of the tenants was far below the standard expected of them. The model dwelling movement had started in the 1840s with the lofty aim of 'providing the labouring man with an increase in comforts and conveniences of life, with full compensation to the capitalist.'[20] In 1863 the architect Henry Darbishire had published what amounted to a manifesto for social housing that was both affordable and improving. By building homes with the emphasis on fresh air, cleanliness and order, Darbishire hoped to combine entrepreneurship with moral reformation. Backed by the wealthy American philanthropist George Peabody, he set about an extensive building programme in London.[21] Many Peabody homes have survived into the twenty-first century, a tribute to the building materials and skills of those who constructed them, but not all model dwellings lived up to the aspirations of their creators. At the Rothschild Buildings, in Flower and Dean Street, the rules effectively excluded the very poorest in society. Tenants could not fall behind with their rents, and charity visitors such as the women of Octavia Hill's Charity Organisation Society (hereafter COS) called regularly to make sure that husbands were sober and in work, homes were clean and tidy, and the children were going to school – failure in any of these areas might result in eviction.[22] The model dwellings on George Yard fell well below the standards of the COS and in 1888 its superintendent, Francis Fisher, was obliged to issue a denial that beds in the property were being used for prostitution.[23] He may have been correct in his robust denial but the accusations stuck.

On the morning of 7 August 1888, the body of Martha Tabram was found on the first floor; she had been stabbed 39 times by an unknown assailant.[24] Circumstantial evidence suggests that Martha was a local prostitute – if only on a part-time basis – and that at least one other murder victim that summer, Emma Smith, had also been living in the property in the weeks and months before she died. In 1890 George Yard buildings were converted into accommodation for the imported and well-heeled students at Toynbee Hall, and Gunthorpe Street, while it retains some of the atmosphere of the old East End, now provides homes for much wealthier occupants than it did in the 1880s.

To the right of Gunthorpe Street, and accessible via a cobbled yard to the rear of some modern buildings, lies Angel Alley, a narrow passageway that once linked Whitechapel High Street to Wentworth Street. At the time of the Whitechapel and Torso murder series, there was a pub at the High Street end, the Angel Inn, which gave the alley its name, and a number of cheap lodging houses were situated near the Wentworth Street exit. Local prostitutes used Angel Alley as a location for sex, as it was conveniently close to two pubs and the busy high street. For centuries London's sex workers had deployed the tactic of soliciting 'business' by asking passing strangers if they'd like to buy them a drink or keep them company. On the night of 6 August 1888, it was to Angel Alley that Mary Ann Connelly (more colourfully known as 'Pearly Poll') allegedly brought a soldier client for sex, having spent the evening drinking with him. Poll later testified that she and Martha Tabram had picked up two guardsmen earlier that night but recent research has thrown some doubt on her evidence.[25] Whatever the truth, Angel Alley was exactly the sort of place where such liaisons would have occurred. Nowadays the alley is home to the radical bookshop of the Freedom Press and the Whitechapel Gallery's side entrance, but no such cultural institutions existed here in 1888.[26]

The streets that emanate from Gunthorpe Street and Angel Alley give little impression these days of the dark and concentrated dwellings of the late Victorian capital. Slum clearance, improvement schemes and the ravages of the Luftwaffe mean that only occasional pockets of buildings remain from the 1880s, and while the street pattern has largely been retained, this too has been transformed by electric street lighting and the motor car. You have to use your imagination if you want to see Whitechapel and Spitalfields as it was in the 1880s. One of the ways to do this is to view it through the eyes of those journalists and social commentators who etched a vision of the East End before, during, and after the 'autumn of terror'. Their view is pretty much all we have to go on and so, while we must remember that it is a vision that is presented from an exclusively middle-class perspective, it is as close as we are likely to get.

In 1883 William Stead, the campaigning editor of the newspaper *The Pall Mall Gazette,* promoted a shocking exposé of working-class living conditions in the East End. Andrew Mearns' *Bitter Cry of Outcast London* echoed the work of earlier social commentators (such as Henry Mayhew in the 1850s) and those who had been working among the poor of Spitalfields for years, like Canon Samuel Barnett (1844–1913) who had moved to the parish of St Jude's in 1873. Andrew Mearns (1837–1925) was himself a Congregationalist minister, born and educated in Scotland, who moved to London to work among the poorest in society. Mearns painted a picture of desperate poverty, overcrowded lodging houses, and (more controversially) rampant immorality.

The *Bitter Cry* could be purchased for a penny and it must have provided a sensational and sobering read in middle-class drawing rooms. Mearns claimed that because working-class families were crammed in so close to each other and forced to share beds within communal rooms, 'incest was common.' 'Immorality,' wrote Mearns, 'is but the natural outcome of conditions like these.'[27] Octavia Hill (1838–1912) chipped in with a new edition of her 1875 publication, *The Homes of the London Poor*, which 'drew on her own extensive experience of visiting the poorer classes' of the capital.[28] Hill, backed by her long-standing friend the art critic John Ruskin, had sought to improve the lives of working men and women through contact with her army of lady visitors and by helping to fund the building of affordable housing. William Stead used Mearns and Hill as part of his campaign to force the government of Lord Salisbury to act on housing, one of several campaigns in which the newspaperman demonstrated his belief that the 'Third Estate' could play a decisive role in social change.

In 1884 a royal commission was established to investigate why legislation in 1868 and 1875 (the Torrens and Cross Acts, respectively) had not succeeded in rectifying the problem of overcrowded slum housing.[29] Richard Cross's legislation, the Artisans Dwellings Act (1875) had given local authorities the power of compulsory purchase of 'insanitary' housing, to knock them down and build new homes for working families.[30] Like many examples of permissive legislation in the nineteenth century, the Cross Act wasn't applied systematically so housing reform was slow and piecemeal and would have to wait for later changes in the next century. What the royal commission discovered was that the poor had little choice but to share their rooms and beds with others because the cost of even the meanest accommodation represented a fifth to a half of their weekly income. Landlords were able to charge what they liked and local people were forced to live close by their places of work because of the cost of transport. The middle-class notion that the labouring poor would decamp to the healthier greener suburbs was a ridiculous pipe dream for most denizens of the East End. In reality, nearly a quarter of working-class families lived in one room and that room had to double as a bedroom and workspace for many. Even if some could afford the luxury of two rooms these were generally poorly furnished and heated, with little or no privacy for husbands and wives from their offspring. This must have been deeply shocking to the middle-class observer, obsessed as we have characterised them, with cleanliness, chastity and 'separate spheres'.

The 1881 census reveals that in Flower and Dean Street – which is now mostly demolished – nearly 1,000 people lived in just 20 lodging houses and that Number 5, on its own, was home to a staggering 222 souls. These lodging houses were even worse than the crowded rented homes that many Londoners lived in. One contemporary, speaking of George Yard and similar properties, wrote: 'They are about as unwholesome and unhealthy as well as dangerous to the community as can well be. There are places among them where the police dare not enter; and where the criminal hides all day long.'[31] Beds could be had there for a few pence a night but this rarely meant you had your own berth or anywhere to call 'home'. Several of the Whitechapel murder victims lived like this, forced to sell themselves to meet their rent for the night and to carry or wear all their possessions for want of anywhere to leave them. It must have been soul-destroying and so it is not at all surprising that many turned to drink as a source of solace or social anaesthetic.

Jack London, in 1902, and Howard Goldsmid before him, in 1886, went undercover to investigate the capital's' low lodging houses and both discovered that at the bottom end, housing in London was little more than a shelter from the outside world.[32] These places should not be seen as being totally devoid of humanity, however; friendship and conviviality could be found 'among the motely crowd in a "kip-house" kitchen'[33] just as warmth could be found in a shared family bed in a crowded tenement or model dwelling. Poverty has become the defining characteristic of 1880s Whitechapel and Spitalfields and this was reinforced by the press coverage of the murders in 1888. While there can be no dispute that poverty was endemic in the area this shouldn't mean we accept Mearns' depiction at face value. As with so many things about the Whitechapel murder cases, contemporary journalists were guilty of exaggeration – for both benign and less positive reasons. Charles Booth's social scientific study of poverty in London revealed that while high numbers of individuals and families could be described as 'poor' or 'very poor', by far the largest proportion were living on 'ordinary wages' or were 'comfortable'. If we look at his tables by district, then Whitechapel is not even the worst place in the East End. It had 39.2 per cent of people living in bands A–D, whereas Shoreditch, Bethnal Green and St George's all had higher percentages. Whitechapel and Spitalfields did, however, have the largest number of persons living at the bottom rung, 3.3 per cent, which was more than twice the average for the district as a whole, 1.2 per cent.[34] The popular author Walter Besant is probably as responsible as anyone for the representation of the East End that has persisted for more than a century. His early twentieth-century study is peppered with colourful characters but falls well short of being an accurate vision of the district. He may, like many others, have meant well but that doesn't mean he shunned the journalistic device of sensationalism.[35] In his fiction one critic remarked that he 'concentrates exclusively on creating an atmosphere of "meanness" and "monotony", so much so that the East End is finally seen as one huge cultureless void.'[36] Middle-class views dominate in all descriptions of the Victorian period, sadly, however, they are often the only narrative source we have since most working-class people had no time to record their own reflections on their experiences.

To modern sentiments then, the East End in 1888 would have stunk, literally and figuratively, but we should be wary of judging past societies by the standards of our own. This was a society without a welfare state, without unemployment benefits, childcare allowances, or a National Health Service; there were no social workers, and few effective controls on the behaviour of landlords.

The answer to almost every question concerning the poorest in society was the workhouse, which loomed large in the lives of working-class Londoners well into the twentieth century. Whitechapel in the 1880s was not a society devoid of community, however, and despite the 'progress' we have made there are still things we could learn from the ways in which working people in the East End supported each other and resisted the worst excesses of the rampant capitalist system they were exposed to.[37] Nor were the poor the only occupants of Whitechapel, as Booth was at pains to point out. William Fishman has shown that while many contemporary middle-class commentators were seemingly intent on painting the area as a bleak and degenerate wasteland, devoid of Christian values and hope, the reality was a little different. There were 'middle-class enclaves, well defined' but these were overlooked or ignored because they did not fit the discourse that writers wished to use to identify the East End.[38] Charles Booth's 1889 survey of London clearly shows us that while there were large pockets of poverty and slum housing – coloured blue and black on his maps – there were also areas of 'respectability' and relative comfort. As Fishman notes, 'the events of 1888 provided the opportunity' for the journalists and moral reformers to join arms in a crusade against the degeneracy of the entire district, and arguably this has established the reputation of the 'Ripper's' East End from then on.[39] This bothered some contemporaries as well, especially the owners and editors of the local press who were understandably piqued by the nationals' rush to condemn their area and its people as 'degraded' and 'unwashed'. At the height of the growing panic surrounding the 'Ripper' the *East End Observer* wrote:

It is [a] matter for supreme regret that the recent atrocious murders, following so closely upon one another, should have been the means of leading to the circulation of so much depreciation of our end of town. To quote a sample of the rubbish that is written. One paper says: 'One way or another, the East End is a plague spot on our civilisation.' The writer of these words cannot know the East of London, but the thoughtless use of them conveys to minds of those that read them an impression which is not easily effaced.[40]

The comment was prophetic because the image of a degraded and downtrodden corner of the empire has been very hard to shift.

But let us return to Gunthorpe Street and continue our journey into the heart of Whitechapel. Moving along and turning into Wentworth Street we would, in 1888, have been faced with a quite different vista. In the nineteenth century this was a street of crowded occupancy with a high immigrant population along its western length towards Middlesex Street, and Petticoat Lane market. At the corner of Goulston Street were the Wentworth Dwellings, almost entirely occupied by immigrant Jews from the Russian Pale of Settlement. It was outside the entrance to apartments 108–119 that PC Alfred Long made a discovery that has divided Ripperologists ever since: his finding of the so called 'Goulston Street graffito' and a piece of bloodied apron belonging to Catherine Eddowes. The dwellings have survived various attempts to have them demolished since the 1960s and remain a point of interest on 'Ripper' trails. Gustave Doré's 1872 engraving gives us some idea of what Wentworth Street once looked like – *see* plate section. The subjects are unmistakably members of the immigrant poor. The fact that they are sitting outside their homes is suggestive of the overcrowded nature of these properties and of the thriving street life that we associate with the nineteenth century. Doré has captured the despair of these people – represented by the young woman at the upstairs window – as well as the ramshackle nature of the buildings and overriding gloom. Booth also described the vibrant nature of 1880s Wentworth Street and its neighbour, Middlesex Street – or 'Petticoat Lane':

The neighbourhood of old Petticoat Lane on Sunday is one of the wonders of London, a medley of strange sights, strange sounds, and strange smells. Streets crowded as to be thoroughfares no longer, and lined with a double or treble row of hand-barrows, set fast with empty cases, so as to assume the guise of market stalls.[41]

Today the west end of Wentworth Street still boasts a thriving market, as it did in 1888, but the immigrant community has changed; where once there were Polish Jews there are now Bengalis, but the emphasis on the trade in cheap clothes is unchanged.

Wentworth Street extends to the west to Middlesex Street and runs east to Brick Lane. Today Brick Lane is a multi-coloured delight of sari shops, curry restaurants and Indian sweet shops; it is quite impossible to walk very far along it without being invited to sample the wares of one establishment or another. The street signs are printed in dual languages and it is quite easy to feel you are in foreign country. This must have been very like the Brick Lane that the 'Ripper's victims knew. Many of them would have worked for Jewish families around here – in the Rothschild or Wentworth Dwellings – or bought second-hand clothes, shawls or bonnets from Brick Lane, Wentworth Street or 'Petticoat Lane'. It is not easy to wander along Brick Lane's packed pavements now but the Victorian thoroughfare would have been even more clogged with stalls, people, carts and horses, all vying for space. Anyone unfamiliar with the area would have taken their life in their hands as they attempted to negotiate their way. If they happened to venture north along Brick Lane they were at a real risk of getting lost in the 'Jago', the semi-mythic creation of Arthur Morrison that was the real-life Old Nichol slum. As one writer has described it, the Old Nichol was a 'district of barely mapped alleyways, sunless cellars, tunnels and courts, cul-de-sacs, stables, barrows, and sheds' that was home to about 6,000 people in the 1880s.[42] In Morrison's 'slum novel' the area dominates the people that live in it, it is almost a living thing with a dread character all of its own. In the early twentieth century, this was where Arthur Harding, a 'pal of the Krays', grew up and where the twins themselves went to school in Brick Lane.[43] Back in the 1800s, the north of Brick

Lane was synonymous with crime and anyone who entered it unawares was likely to meet a sticky end or at the very least to lose the contents of his pockets. There was also a lively commercial side to this part of the East End, which is reflected in Booth's maps and in the number of businesses that operated here. Moving west from Brick Lane the modern tourist will also find themselves wandering around streets that reflect the nature of the area as it was in the seventeenth century. In the wake of the revocation of Edict of Nantes in 1685, which had followed the end of the French Wars of Religion in the previous century, thousands of French Protestants fled persecution and many of them settled in London. Here they brought their skills as silk weavers and the legacy of their occupation can still be seen in the elegant houses of Wilkes Street and Fournier Street. On the corner of Brick Lane and Fournier Street, which was once named Church Street, and in the shadow of Nicholas Hawksmoor's Christ Church, is the site of an old Huguenot chapel that is now an Islamic funeral centre, testimony to the way in which buildings of all sorts are recycled and put to new uses. This is an entrepreneurial, vital, and dynamic part of London and it owes that in no small part to its history of immigration, settlement, adaptation, and renewal. Every new set of migrants and settlers bring their own culture, language and customs and meld these with what they find here; no wonder it is among the most interesting districts of the capital.

Christ's Church Spitalfields was built between 1714 and 1729 as a part of an expansion of the Church of England into the East End to meet the needs of its supposedly neglected population. It is a magnificent church that looms over the nearby Ten Bells pub and Spitalfields Market on Commercial Street, and it must have been just as impressive in 1888. The Ten Bells, at 33 Church Street, is now a very trendy drinking hole, catering for City types and tourists alike. In the 1970s it briefly flirted with a name change, its landlord calling it The Jack the Ripper in desperate attempt to cash in on the renewed interest in the case. It boasts some interesting tiled images in the bar but has, rather disappointingly, recently cleaned up its graffiti encrusted toilets. Moving south from the pub and Christ's Church and crossing Commercial Street (the laying out of which effectively forced thousands of impoverished locals to seek new homes in the 1840s) a drab municipal car park until recently marked the site of the most notorious murder in the whole Whitechapel series – that of Mary Kelly. Formerly a home for many of the Huguenot weavers that had sought asylum here, by the 1840s Dorset Street had become a fearful slum of low lodging houses and later earned the sobriquet of the 'worst street in London'.[44] On the corner with Commercial Road stood the Britannia pub which, along with the Ten Bells and the Princess Alice situated a little further down Commercial Street towards Aldgate, was frequented by many of the victims and, almost undoubtedly, the killer himself. One of the notable features of this part of London is the rapidity at which it changes. Only the Ten Bells survives in anything like its nineteenth-century form; the Princess Alice has become an up-market gastro-pub and the Britannia has disappeared altogether.

Dorset Street had several lodging houses in 1888 and was nicknamed 'Dosset Street' as a result. Mary Kelly rented a room at Number 13 Miller's Court, which ran between Numbers 26 and 27 and was owned by John McCarthy. It was McCarthy's man who found Kelly's eviscerated body in November 1888. Beyond Dorset Street was the Providence Row night refuge, operated by the nuns of the Convent of the Sisters of Mercy. The shelter opened in 1868 and could accommodate 300 women and children, and 50 men. Legend has it that Mary Kelly was a beneficiary of the nuns' charity and that they helped find her employment in Cleveland Street, where she was to be drawn in to the so-called 'Royal Conspiracy' which Stephen Knight has argued explains the Whitechapel murders.[45] That may be fanciful but the presence of a night shelter (now occupied by students from the London School of Economics) reminds us of the underlying poverty of this part of London. The only rung below the doss house or charitable shelter was the workhouse and Whitechapel's was sited in what is now Vallance Road, just off the High Street.

Opposite Dorset Street and on the other side of Commercial Street were Flower and Dean Street, and Thrawl Street, both of which had close associations with the events of 1887–91. Polly Nichols, Catherine Eddowes and Elizabeth Stride all lived in lodgings in Flower and Dean Street at some point and Nichols and Frances Coles were also known to have lodged in Thrawl Street.[46] When Commercial Street was built in 1844 many of the local populace migrated to Flower and Dean Street and an 1877 report considered it to be 'perhaps the foulest and most dangerous street in the whole metropolis'.[47] In August 1888 Polly Nichols stayed at 56, Liz Stride lived at 32 for a time, and Eddowes at Number 55. Alice McKenzie, a much-disputed 'Ripper' victim, was seen there shortly before her death in 1891. In 1891 much of the street was torn down to make way for the new Nathanial Dwellings, which opened in 1892. Thrawl Street, equally grim in 1888, was described as a haven for 'thieves, loose women, and bad characters'. Polly Nichols lived in Wilmott's lodging house, at Number 18, and was seen there on the night she was murdered, famously having promised the deputy that she would soon be able to return with her doss money on account of her wearing such a 'jolly bonnet'.[48] Frances Coles also stayed at 18 and the man initially accused of killing her, James Sadler, was allegedly robbed here on the night she died.[49] Whitechapel and Spitalfields then was a mess of lodging houses, model dwellings and shelters, with a maze of interlinking alleyways and courts that continue to confound and confuse the modern visitor today. Here people lived day-by-day, hand-to-mouth. Booth recognised that poverty was relative and had multiple causes. 'It is to be remembered' he wrote, 'that the whole income of Class B [the 'very poor'] is absorbed by necessary expenditure. If exceptional hauls are made, they are matched by times of scarcity, when work fails. It is only by evading the payment of rent, or going short of food, that clothes or household things can be bought; and the same is very nearly true with Class D. How else can any unusual call be met, or any indulgence which costs money? The poor are very generous, but out of what fund, except the exchequer of the belly, is generosity to be indulged?'[50]

In Dorset Street and Thrawl Street, as in many parts of the 'abyss' wives sent their children out to buy just enough tea and sugar to make 'a brew' or enough food to make her family's dinner. The main diet avoided rich foods and most meat. Fish was a cheaper alternative; fish and fried potatoes a real treat. Across the district, Booth calculated that people were spending from about sixpence to just 2s per person, less probably, on meat. It was here, in this 'labyrinth' of imagined 'depravity', that 'Jack the Ripper' did his most awful work throughout his 'reign of terror'. His efforts weren't only confined to Whitechapel, however, we believe that a case can be made that 'Jack' was much busier than most studies have so far suggested and so, with the background of his main 'killing zone' established it is time to discover the awful extent of his crimes.

2

DREADFUL DISCOVERY
AT RAINHAM

On Friday 13 May 1887 the *Pall Mall Gazette* reported that:

> Portions of the body of a young woman have been washed
> ashore on the banks of the Thames at Rainham. Some of the
> limbs have been dismembered as if with a sharp instrument,
> and by one skilled in surgery.[51]

The *Gazette* offered a condensed version of news, gathered from
a variety of sources, and had a middle-class, if not particularly
conservative, audience. Its editor, William Stead, had acquired a
reputation as a firebrand, a campaigning journalist who believed in
the power of the press to bring about political and social change.
In a series of sensational articles in July 1885 he had exposed a
trade in young girls, bought and sold into prostitution to meet
the sexual demands of wealthy paedophiles.[52] That he did so by
arranging for the purchase of Eliza Armstrong, a girl of just 13,
for £5, was typical of Stead's methodology. As a firm believer
in the 'end justifies the means', Stead paid scant regard to the
feelings of the child or her mother as he pursued his objective.
The exposé, entitled the 'Maiden Tribute of Modern Babylon',
was very successful, with copies selling in unprecedented numbers,

and Parliament being forced to finally pass the Criminal Law Amendment Act (1885), which raised the age of consent for girls to 16. Stead and his accomplice, the procuress Rebecca Jarrett, may have subsequently been put on trial and sent to prison for the abduction and assault of Eliza, but the power of the press had been clearly demonstrated.[53] Stead continued in this vein for the rest of his career and became a thorn in the side of the Chief Commissioner of the Metropolitan Police, Sir Charles Warren, throughout the Whitechapel murder investigation.

In 1887 no one quite realised what horrors lay in wait for London when the body of a young woman washed up at Rainham, in Essex. According to the reports of the local press, the body had been discovered floating in the Thames by a bargeman named Edward Hughes, 'at Falls Point, near Mr. Hempleman's factory' at 11.30 in the morning as he steered his barge nearby. He fished the bag out of the water and opened it to find a human torso from which the head, arms and legs had been removed.[54] The hipbones had been prised from their sockets and the rest of the body 'more or less mutilated'. The victim was estimated to have been a young woman of '28 to 29' years of age and the police surgeon, not surprisingly, suggested she had been murdered.[55] It was estimated that the body had been in the water for about two weeks.

A further report in the local press gave more detail and speculated on the type of person that might have committed such a crime:

> The severing of the bones had been accomplished by means of a very fine instrument, and the flesh was cut as if by a person skilled in surgical operations. No other portions of the body were found, and there were no means of ascertaining when the body was dissected, but the opinion is that it must have been within a very recent period. [56]

If the report was accurate then the discovery of the torso in mid-May would mean that the woman had been murdered and dissected earlier in that month, or in late April. The spring of

1887 held a special significance for an individual whose personal life would become intimately connected to the fates of 13 murdered women during the next four years. But we run ahead of ourselves, let us concentrate on this murder victim first.

On the Saturday following the midweek discovery, a coroner's inquest was held in Rainham. This was widely reported, almost as a preamble to the Whitechapel murders the following year. The so-called 'Thames' or 'River' 'Mystery' drew interest from papers across Britain with reporters filing copy in (among others) Lancashire, the West Country and Aberdeen.[57] Medical opinion suggested the body had been sawn apart by someone who knew what they were doing and who wanted to hide the evidence of his crime. Dr Edward Galloway testified that there were no distinguishing marks on the corpse but estimated she had been 27 to 29 years of age, was 'well-nourished' and stated that he believed she had been cut up by 'an expert'. The chief investigating officer, Superintendent Dobson of the Essex County Constabulary, ruled out any notion the body had been stolen from a teaching hospital dissection table; this was the work of a killer, not a prankster or someone trying to circumvent the Anatomical Act.[58] He also stated that they had received no reports of a missing woman.[59] Given that the torso lacked the rest of the body parts (rendering identification impossible) the coroner, a Mr. C. C. Lewis, adjourned the inquest until 3 June. The police investigation now became a search for the rest of the poor woman since those who knew the river and its tides were 'tolerably sanguine' that these would turn up sooner or later.[60] In the meantime, the remaining torso was preserved in methylated spirits in the hope that 'when the other portions come to light they can be fitted together as in the case of Harriet Lane, the victim of the Wainwright murder.'[61]

However, in the three weeks following the gruesome discovery at Rainham nothing turned up, neither more body parts nor any clues as to a possible suspect. Even the identity of the deceased remained unclear although the police did receive a letter from a Mrs Cross, of Richmond, in Surrey, regarding a daughter who had disappeared.[62] Apparently, her daughter was a troubled youth of 'weak intellect' who would wander by the river and 'get upon any barge or boats which might happen to be moored alongside the towing path.'[63] The coroner's jury returned an open verdict on the death of the unknown woman but 'foul play' remained the most likely explanation. But as the lightermen and police had predicted, the Thames did eventually give up more of its secrets. On 5 June a human thigh, similarly wrapped to the Rainham torso, washed up by Temple pier close by the new Victoria Embankment and Waterloo Bridge. The thigh matched with the torso and the wrapping was of the same description as that found in Essex; it seemed that 'the Thames mystery' was about to get a new lease of life.[64] The City of London coroner decided not to open a fresh inquest but instead sent the newly discovered portion to the authorities in Rainham.[65] Meanwhile the press, with a new twist to explore, set off to interview Mrs Cross to find out more about her missing daughter.

Mrs Cross told them that her daughter had been missing since 7 a.m. on 20 January. She described her as aged 28, '5ft. 8in., complexion dark, eyes dark, pencilled eyebrows, short curly black hair, and exceedingly handsome face'. She also embroidered her story by adding that, some days before she had disappeared, a strange man, who had demanded money and threatened to cut her throat, had assaulted her daughter. The press report made it clear that the description of Miss Cross and the discovered remains could be one and the same person.[66] Of course, while it is not impossible that young Miss Cross was the victim of the Torso killer it is equally likely that she simply disappeared, drowned in the Thames, or that the grieving mother was making it all up for the sake of attracting press attention. It wasn't uncommon for people to end their own lives by throwing themselves in the Thames or one of London's canals in the late 1800s, and even a casual reading of reports from the Metropolitan Police Courts reveals that suicide or its attempt was endemic in the capital.[67] Another missing girl, 'Miss Carter of Vauxhall', was also believed to be a possible candidate for the victim and there must have been many other missing persons who could have met the unknown killer.[68] However, it is our belief that the torso probably belonged to the same class of women as those usually associated with the Whitechapel murders; in other words, she may have been one of London's many 'unfortunates' (a contemporary euphemism for street prostitutes) or, perhaps more accurately, those homeless women who were typically assumed to sell sex on the streets. Hopefully our reasons for this will become clear as we explore the wider 'Ripper' case and the circumstances that surround it.

On 8 June 8 the thorax of a young woman, including 'the lungs and most of the dorsal vertebrae', surfaced at Battersea in another package, similarly wrapped. [69] This was later matched with the trunk of the Rainham remains by Dr Galloway and detectives from C.I.D. Gradually then, an entire body (albeit minus the head) was emerging from the Thames. Later in the month a shoulder blade was discovered near Rainham pier, and there were reports in the local press that a head had now been found.[70] However, it is more likely that these were older bones, belonging to a victim of the *Princess Alice* disaster in 1878.[71] Then at the end of June, two boys fishing in the Regent's Canal, near St Pancras lock, found a leg, while another group of young lads discovered a second missing leg not far away, along another part of the canal tow path. On examination, the legs were found to be those of a young woman aged 25 to 30 and were 'small and well formed' – which eliminated Miss Cross whose feet were apparently 'abnormally large'.[72]

The C.I.D., on the medical advice of Dr Galloway, also misreported as 'Callaway', were now content that they were looking at the dismembered corpse of one murder victim but were unable to give her a name.[73] The Thames, and London's other waterways, had eventually disgorged its grim deposits, just as the Essex watermen had predicted. However, the police and press were no nearer discovering the identity of the victim or her killer than they were back in May. As we shall show, geography, means and opportunity all point to one particular individual being responsible for this and several other murders in a killing series that was to last almost four years.

While the police were investigating the discovery of another portion of female anatomy – this time a thigh that had seemingly nothing to do with the Rainham corpse (being from a much older woman) – the press covered the examination of Israel Lipski at Thames Police Court. Lipski, an immigrant Jew, had been brought up on a charge of murdering Miriam Angel, a young woman who was pregnant at the time. Lipski was accused of pouring nitric acid down the poor woman's throat and had been discovered hiding 'under the deceased's bed in an insensible condition, having evidently swallowed some of the same poison'. At the request of the police, Lipski was remanded in custody.[74] The scene of the murder was 16 Batty Street, which was the next street along Commercial Road from Berner Street, where one of the canonical five 'Ripper' victims, Elizabeth Stride, met her death in September 1888. It was also allegedly home to one of the many 'Ripper' suspects; the American 'quack' doctor, Francis Tumblety.[75] Lipski was convicted at the Old Bailey and despite considerable doubt over the evidence of his guilt, he was sentenced to death. The Home Secretary was considering a reprieve for Lipski when the prisoner apparently broke down and made a full confession to Simeon Singer, a local rabbi. Lipski was hanged on 21 August 1887 at Newgate.[76]

At the resumption of the Camden Town inquest into all the body parts associated with the Rainham torso, Dr Bond concluded that they belonged to a 'well-nourished stout woman' aged 25 to 35, with dark hair, 'who [...] was probably 5ft. 2in. to 5ft. 4in in height'. The body parts had entered the water about three months previously, he stated, and at the same time. The inquest jury concluded that 'there was not sufficient evidence to show as to how or by what means the said woman had come to her death'.[77]

Just over a month later the body of another young woman was pulled out of the Regent's Canal near the Muriel Street tunnel. The condition of her clothes, and the way in which she had secreted her small amount of coinage in her stocking, had persuaded the police constable that first responded to her discovery to decide she was a prostitute. The jury returned a verdict of 'found drowned'. Had she been pushed? Or had she simply fallen into the canal when drunk, or taken her own life, something that was not uncommon among London's sex workers? Perhaps instead, though, she had fled from a punter who had scared her, from someone that wanted to do to her what he had done to the mysterious victim whose body parts had been washed up in the summer of 1887.[78] The reality is we cannot know, but a killer was on the loose in the capital and the victims he chose were the vulnerable women he would find on London's dimly lit streets, towpaths, and alleys, so it is not unlikely that this victim had escaped an even worse fate.

The killer had needed a place where he could dismember the various pieces of the corpse that had been found in the river and canals, as well as transport to dispose of the body parts. Dr Galloway believed he had dumped all the portions in the river at the same time but it is possible that he stored some for a few days at least, since the doctor's testimony has to be taken with some qualification given the limited state of forensic science in the 1880s. The distance between the Regent's Canal at Camden and Rainham ferry is considerable but the river is tidal and washes out to the sea beyond Tilbury. Did the killer dump the smaller parts somewhere nearby his workplace and drop the larger torso in the Thames on one of his regular journeys to find work elsewhere? It is something worth considering, especially when a man engaged in one industry in particular could have found himself operating in and around various points on the river and its connecting waterways at this time. The industry in question was London's horsemeat trade and it is the subject of the next chapter.

3

THE LONDON HORSEMEAT TRADE AND THE RISE OF HARRISON, BARBER & CO.

It is quite hard for us to imagine London without motorised transport but the late nineteenth-century capital was almost entirely reliant on horse-drawn power rather than the internal combustion engine.[79] Horses were everywhere: William Gordon's wonderfully illustrated history of the horse trade in the capital reveals that in the late 1800s horses pulled trams, omnibuses, refuse carts, hansom cabs, post office coaches, delivery carts, brewers' carts, coal carts, as well as the Queen's coaches and those of the wealthy and better off.[80] Nowadays the 'white van man' has become ubiquitous but we forget that we have always needed to move goods and services around the city, well before Ford produced its first Transit van. The clip-clop of hooves on cobbles was an easily recognised and familiar sound of everyday life in the Victorian metropolis, and horses existed in much higher numbers than they do today. Nowadays Londoners are only likely to encounter horses being used by the police, in the barracks at Horse Guards or in some of the parks. For us, horses are a part of country life, not an essential component of urban living as they were for our ancestors.

The streets around Whitechapel must have been filled with horse-drawn vehicles that would have often presented the unwary pedestrian with obstacles to avoid if he did not want to tread in the manure they created. Horses attached to some vehicles, such as trams for example, were fitted with cloth bags (nappies if you prefer) to minimise mess, while companies and local vestries employed men to clear the roads of the horses' leavings. This was probably much better organised and enforced in wealthier parts of the capital than it might have been in the poorer districts. An area like Whitechapel would have streets that were strewn with dung while genteel St James might have appeared spotless by comparison. What happened to all these horses when they fell ill, died or simply became too old to work? The average working life of a horse was about 11 years and very few owners could afford to allow an old nag to simply enjoy its retirement in some idyllic pasture. Unfortunately for the horse old age, accident or infirmity meant the knackers' yard; there was little place for sentiment in the late 1800s. Only licensed horse slaughterers could legally despatch horses. In 1889 the *Pall Mall Gazette* reported the case of a hansom cab horse being crippled after a collision with a coach. 'A messenger was despatched to Messrs. Harrison, Barber & Co., the horse slaughters' it was reported, and the owner of the horse was called. But it took an age to get the horse away and a passing butcher offered to fetch his poleaxe but this 'was refused by a policeman.'[81] This situation must have been quite common. In 1893 a writer wrote of the 'dreadful object [...] of a suffering horse, sprawling in one of our main roads with the usual crowd around it. If someone asked: 'Why cannot he be killed at once? Why must he linger in agony?' – the answer was simple, if brutal: The horse was the property of the driver's employer, not the driver himself.

> The driver has no right to order the horse to be killed ... and before he can give the order the master has to be found, and the master does not, in many cases, care to lose his horse irrevocably, and appeals to his vet.; and so, while the driver is finding his master, and the master is finding his vet., the horse lies suffering in the street.[82]

When the decision to kill the horse was finally made a message had to be sent to the nearest horse slaughterer, and by the late 1880s that business was almost entirely in the hands of one company. In the 1889 edition of Kelly's *Trades Directory*, Harrison, Barber & Company are listed as having several different depots across the capital and only one other company, Hart Chase, with one listed premises, received a mention.[83] As far as horse slaughtering was concerned, Harrison, Barber had a virtual monopoly. At their yards in Queen Victoria Street, York Road, Garrett Lane, Winthrop Street, Westcott and Tabard Streets and others, the company kept its carts 'cleaned and in readiness like fire engines, ready to be turned out and on the way in less than five minutes from the receipt of the call.'[84]

Once the aged, sick or injured horses had been transported on these carts to one of these depots, they were quickly killed. The horses were slaughtered by 'knackers', who temporarily blinded them with a cloth before using a poleaxe to kill them. The horses' manes and then their hides were removed before the carcass was stripped and the meat cooked; nothing was wasted. In *The Horse World of London,* W. J. Gordon records his visit to Harrison, Barber's Wandsworth depot in Garrett lane, the largest in London. He wrote: 'In two seconds a horse is killed; in a little over half-an-hour his hide is in a heap of dozens, his feet are in another heap, his bones are boiling for oil; his flesh cooking for cat's meat.'. The meat was then sold on to horsemeat dealers (there were 28 of these listed in 1889) many of whom (19) operated from premises in the East End. From these dealers, cats' meat men could buy skewers of cooked horse and tripe that they could then sell as pet food. They sold the meat cheaply to the public, often at very little profit, and since many of their customers had the goods on credit, it was quite hard for the traders to make much of a living. By contrast, the owners of the slaughterhouses made large profits.[85] Charles Dickens visited one of the slaughterhouses and recorded what he saw, describing the fate of the horses in detail. He noted that in any given year 'an average of one hundred and seventy horses are killed every week here, [...] and that their flesh is boiled and sold for cats' meat.'[86] The scale of the operation is quite incredible until we remember that approximately 300,000 horses served London in the last decades of the 1800s. So great was the number of horses being slaughtered that supply sometimes outstripped demand. As a result, by the end of the 1880s, Harrison, Barber had established an innovation – a cold store at Wandsworth where 250 horse carcases could be kept until demand picked up again.[87] It may even have been in operation during the 'Ripper' murders, which could be significant, as we shall explain later.

The cats' meat man must have been a very familiar sight on the streets of Whitechapel; coming and going from the slaughterhouses and wholesale meat sellers, with a barrow piled with skewered meat on sacks, calling his wares and serving his regular customers. It was a poorly paid business, however, at the very bottom of London's meat trade, and it is quite likely that the men who sold horsemeat also worked as horse slaughterers or were in some other way connected to the trade. It is also entirely possible that some of the meat sold as pet food made its way onto the tables of the poorest families as well. Dickens certainly believed this and hinted that horseflesh was commonly eaten but the matter was rarely discussed or acknowledged. Being a cats' meat man was a precarious and somewhat shady occupation. Meat could be bought from dealers, or directly from slaughterhouses, especially if the cats' meat man also worked there or had good inside contacts. Some costermongers selling meat for human consumption may also, of course, have been willing to turn a blind eye to the provenance of the meat they purveyed from their handcarts. For our purposes the cat's meat and horse slaughtering trades offer an important way in which to understand what might have happened during the years that 'Jack the Ripper' and the 'Torso murderer' terrorised London. The success of Harrison, Barber in cornering the market in horseflesh meant that they had depots all across the capital.

Winthrop Street in Whitechapel is a stone's throw from Durward Street, and in 1888 the Harrison, Barber yard was close to the spot where Polly Nichols was murdered on what was then called Buck's Row.[88] But a closer look at the map in the plate section also reveals the geographical spread of the company's business; they owned property across the full breadth of the metropolis – east, west, south and central. With such a large business empire and such a demand for their services, the possibilities for weekend working or overtime during the evenings or at night must have been considerable. An employee of Harrison, Barber would also have had many opportunities to move around the capital – on foot, pushing a barrow, or riding on a cart – without attracting unwanted attention. He would be able to come and go, regardless of his possibly blood-stained appearance and no one is likely to have questioned him regarding the contents of his barrow, cart or sacks. In addition, he would have had quiet places where he could have worked undiscovered, at weekends and on holidays, where he could hide anything he didn't particularly want seen, such as a human corpse. In at least one of these sites, Garrett Lane, there may well have been a cold store should he have chosen to make use of it. It goes without saying that on top of the opportunities Harrison, Barber & Co.'s business empire would have offered such a man, he would also have become highly skilled with a sharp knife and familiar with (and inured to) the cutting up of dead animals. The doctor's report on the torso found at Rainham noted the skill used in cutting up the body from which it was separated: 'There was no jaggedness about any of the incisions,' Dr Galloway recorded, 'showing, as he thought, that they had been done by an expert.'[89] It is not impossible or improbable even, to imagine that the Whitechapel or Torso murderer could in some way have been connected to the horsemeat trade in 1888. In fact, we believe that such a person was *exactly* the type of individual the police should have been targeting in that late summer and autumn of 1888. It is not surprising to learn, therefore, that they did interview many of those working in and around the trade, including, presumably, many of those employed by Harrison, Barber & Co. Indeed, three of their employees were working in their Winthrop Street premises on the night Polly Nichols was murdered with one, Henry Tomkins, giving evidence at her inquest. Tomkins testified that he had been working at the yard from 'between eight and nine o'clock on Thursday evening till twenty minutes past four on Friday morning.'[90] No arrests were made, or at least no one was charged, but this does not mean that our killer was not a cat's meat man or an employee of the firm. We should remember that Peter Sutcliffe (better known as the 'Yorkshire Ripper') was questioned on more than one occasion by police, but released each time having satisfied detectives with his answers.[91]

If one examines the facts logically and without subscribing to conspiracy theories or attempting to reveal an individual on the basis of the unlikely survival of some obscure artefact, we need to ask questions about the sort of person that could have committed such a series of murders, undetected, in Victorian London. That individual needs to have been able to move around the streets of the city in the early hours of the day without attracting the suspicion of locals or of the increasingly large numbers of police on patrol. He had to have been able to kill and effect his escape, and be in possession of the skills and implements needed to butcher and sometimes dismember his victims. A cat's meat man or a horse slaughterer, or indeed someone who held multiple roles within the trade, fits that offender profile quite nicely. After all, a slaughterman or similar worked in an environment where blood was part and parcel of his trade, he worked at night and in the small hours, he was possessed of upper body strength and manual dexterity, and was familiar with knives. As we shall see, someone who fitted this profile very closely was living at the very heart of 'Jack's killing fields in 1888 – could he have been the murderer?

4

A KILLER AWAKES ON THE STREETS OF THE CAPITAL

On 31 March 1888 the messenger attached to the Whitechapel Union workhouse was briefly distracted from his conversation with one of the inmates. By the time he turned back to continue chatting, she had inexplicitly collapsed on the floor. When the doctor he summoned finally arrived, the woman was already dead, the cause being determined as a 'sudden effusion into the pericardium from the rupture of the left pulmonary artery through ulceration'.[92] The woman was an impoverished inhabitant of Spitalfields, probably usually living in one or more of the many cheap lodging houses that offered beds by the night. Her name was Annie Millwood and we know very little else about her.[93] She was 38, widowed, and probably earned money by prostituting herself when she couldn't find other paid work. In fact, her profile is reminiscent of most of the Whitechapel murder victims and while her death is rarely considered as part of the series, we believe it likely that she was attacked by the same man who was responsible for the other murders in the Whitechapel and Thames Torso series.

Annie Millwood was assaulted on a cold and windy Saturday in late February 1888.[94] At 5 o'clock on the 25th she was admitted to the Whitechapel Infirmary with multiple stab wounds. There is little detail of what actually happened because it appears that no newspapers reported the incident and there was no police investigation to speak of.[95] The only reason Millwood is known to us at all is that the press reported the inquest that followed her death in the workhouse. An unknown assailant had attacked Annie about the lower part of her body and legs with a clasp knife. Although badly injured, she survived the ordeal and had apparently recovered; only to die of seemingly unrelated causes a month later. No one was ever arrested because Annie was unable (or unwilling) to describe or name the person who had assaulted her.

Just over a month later, in the early hours of Wednesday 28 March, a man knocked on the door of a house at 19 Maidman Street, off Burdett Road in Bow, East London. When Ada Wilson answered the door, the man forced her backwards into the hallway and threatened her with a clasp knife, demanding money.[96] When she refused he stabbed her in the throat and ran off. This was the story that Ada told the police, but it might not be the entire truth. An upstairs neighbour of Wilson's testified that Ada would often entertain men in her rooms after dark, despite apparently being a married woman. Given that her husband had never been seen, this might suggest that Ada Wilson supported herself, at least in part, on her earnings as a prostitute. This makes even more sense when we learn from the same witness, Rose Bierman, that Ada was in a state of undress at the time of the attack. It was also suggested by the landlady's daughter that the man had been in the house for some time prior to the assault. The attacker could have been her lover, or perhaps even her long-lost husband, but it is far more likely that she had invented the attempted robbery story as a 'cover' to protect her private life from prying eyes. Whatever the truth, the man was seen to run off into the street but the police were unable to find him. This encounter has left us, however, with a tantalising description of a suspect who will reappear throughout this work. He was, according to Ada Wilson:

About 30 years old, 5' 6" with a fair moustache and 'sunburnt' face. Dressed in light trousers, a dark jacket and wideawake hat.[97]

Could this have been the same man who attacked Annie Millwood on 25 February? We know Annie had been discharged from the Baker's Row infirmary in Whitechapel on 21 March 1888 and that from there she was sent to the Whitechapel Union Workhouse, South Grove, where she died. Is it possible that Annie's attacker knew she had survived his assault and was keeping an eye on her recovery? It is of course possible that he was familiar with both Mile End and Whitechapel, as Burdett Road was an easy walk or a short tram ride away from Spitalfields – not a problem for someone used to covering a wide area in search of customers or work.

Ripperologists have so far been unconvinced that either of these women were early victims of 'Jack'. Can we really rule them out that easily, however? After all, as Paul Begg points out, serial killers develop their *modus operandi* (hereafter 'MO') over time and rarely emerge as fully formed killers at the start of their campaigns.[98] The focus of the attack on Millwood was on her abdomen and lower body, with Wilson's wounds being inflicted to the throat, both areas that were targeted by the killer in attacks on subsequent victims of the Whitechapel murderer. Is it such a leap of faith therefore to suggest that the same man could have perpetrated these attacks? At first glance at least, they would certainly seem more likely candidates to be 'Ripper' victims than that of the next high-profile attack in the district on 3 April 1888.

Emma Smith was assaulted and left for dead by a gang of men somewhere close to Whitechapel Church. According to her own account, two or three of them attacked her at about 1.30 a.m. as she tried to avoid them by crossing the road into Osborn Street, which merges to become Brick Lane. Emma was beaten, cut and a blunt instrument was thrust up inside her vagina.[99] Although she made it back to her lodgings at 19 George Street, near Flower and Dean Street, and was helped to the London Hospital, she died of her internal injuries. As recent work by Tom Westcott suggests, however, there is something rather fishy about the events surrounding Emma's murder.[100] Westcott presents a plausible case for a cover-up that involved Emma's fellow lodgers, several prominent lodging house owners and at least one member of H Division's detective force – Sgt Thick. This is not the place to re-examine Westcott's thesis, readers should explore that for themselves, suffice to say though, if he is right, Emma Smith may not have been randomly attacked by a gang of drunken yobs, or criminals demanding protection money.[101] One other witness testified to seeing Emma Smith on the night of her death, Margaret Hayes (or Hamer) stated that she had seen Emma talking to a man 'dressed in dark clothes and wearing a white scarf' at 12.15 a.m., just over an hour before she reported she had been attacked.[102] Westcott also makes a case for including another woman in the series of murders and attacks, another female resident of 19 George Street, Emily Horsnell, who was attacked on 5 November 1887 – again apparently by a gang of men. She also later died of peritonitis as a result of the injuries she received, as Smith was to in April of the following year.[103] The inquest returned an 'open' verdict instead of one of murder so there was no police investigation into her death. This may have been a convenience, as Howard Taylor has argued, the nineteenth-century police were reluctant to pursue cases which they would have had very little chance of solving.[104] If they had no leads, then, just as today, budgetary constraints would have meant that the death of an 'unfortunate' on the streets of one of the poorest parts of the city was unlikely to be investigated further. Nevertheless, Westcott prefers the notion of a cover-up once again, and there are certainly questions to be asked about why her death was not followed up. As the inquest was told, however, it may simply have been the case that the police had no clues to go on and did not expect any further information to be forthcoming. After all, in the closed world of East End lodging houses, talking to the police was not likely to win you many friends.[105]

The murder of Emily Horsnell in November was to be followed by what many have often regarded as a phantom killing – that of someone known simply as 'Fairy Fay'. She was supposedly found dead with a wooden stake through her abdomen in the vicinity of

Osborn Street and Wentworth Street some time between October and Boxing Day 1887 – depending on which contemporary account is consulted. Many researchers believe the incident to be an invention of the journalist Terence Robertson who published an account of it in *Reynolds Newspaper* in 1950, following its mention by Dr L. Forbes Winslow in his 1910 memoirs, *Recollections of Forty Years*.[106] It was stated that the murder was investigated by Inspector Edmund Reid (who would become a central figure in the investigation of subsequent killings) but that the enquiry was closed after a few weeks due to failure in identifying the victim and a general lack of progress.[107] Tom Cullen, resurrecting the story 15 years later, suggested that the victim was also mutilated,[108] although he may well have been influenced by an article in a November 1888 edition of the *New York Tribune*, which apparently described the same woman as having been 'frightfully lacerated'.[109] Although no actual contemporary reports relating to the event exist in the form of newspaper articles, police or death records, it does not necessarily mean that the attack did not occur or that an enquiry was not conducted.[110] After all, several near-contemporary press reports do relate it, and reference to the alleged incident was even made during parliamentary debate by an MP in November 1888.[111] Perhaps the semi-mythical 'Fairy Fay' was actually someone else, or an admixture of a variety of witnesses and/or possible victims. The murder apparently took place quite close to the other Whitechapel cases and it allegedly involved the targeting of the victim's abdomen, which had been the case with Millward and, indirectly, with Smith and Horsnell.

So, by the beginning of April 1888 it is possible that no fewer than six women had suffered at the hands of a serial-attacker, with only one, Ada Wilson, having lived to tell the tale. Indeed, the modern FBI report into the Whitechapel case maintains that the killer had probably attacked other women prior to the 'canonical five', with these incidents either going unreported or being considered by the police to be unconnected.[112] But while these killings might (with the exception of the Rainham torso) have been dismissed as little other than an illustration of 'the sort of casual violence that was common in the East End of London,'[113] the murder of a seventh woman, in early August 1888, shocked even the coldest of local inhabitants – and signalled an escalation of violence in the killer's MO.

On Tuesday 7 August 1888 the body of Martha Tabram (or Turner) was found at 4.50 a.m. on a landing at George Yard Buildings, Whitechapel, in what is now Gunthorpe Street. Martha's body was discovered by John Reeves, a local resident who was on his way to work.[114] Her post-mortem later revealed that she had been stabbed 39 times about the trunk and upper legs with perhaps two weapons – a small knife (as with Millwood and Wilson previously) and a larger one which had been responsible for one wound in particular. Two soldiers were believed by some to have been implicated in the crime but their identity was never satisfactorily established. The inquest jury returned a verdict of 'wilful murder by some person or persons unknown'. While Martha had not been 'ripped' – i.e. mutilated – in the manner that several of the subsequent Whitechapel murder victims were, the killer had certainly acted with extreme force and had assaulted her lower body in what seems to have been a frenzied attack. At her inquest the deputy coroner, George Collier, observed that 'the man must have been a perfect savage to have attacked the woman in that way.'[115]

Traditionally researchers have excluded Martha Tabram from the canon of victims (Nichols, Chapman, Stride, Eddowes and Kelly) chiefly on the grounds of the different killing 'signatures' exhibited in these examples. However, support for her inclusion has gained ground in recent years. An authoritative report published in 2005 by academics from Washington University, Seattle, and Sam Houston University, Texas, that made comparisons of the 'signatures' displayed in 3,359 Washington State murders between 1981 and 1995 with those in Whitechapel, concluded that Tabram had indeed been a 'Ripper' victim. Instrumental in their findings was the observation that such a killer's 'signatures' and MO changed over time in response to altered circumstances, either imposed or chosen.[116] This accords with our belief that Tabram was killed by the same hand as the other five victims and should also be afforded 'canonical' status.

Tabram, who had been living with a man named Turner, had not long before arrived in George Yard. Westcott has cast considerable doubt over what we know about the case and in particular with regards to the events leading up to her death in the early hours of 7 August. He argues that the story we have been presented with – that Tabram had spent the bank holiday drinking with another resident of George Street, Mary Ann Connolly, also known as 'Pearly Poll' – is possibly false. No one saw Tabram with anyone on the night of her murder and it may be, for reasons unknown to anyone but Pearly Poll that she invented the tale of the two off-duty soldiers. Inspector Reid may have shared this view as, after asking her to help identify the soldiers she and Martha picked up, her unreliability quickly became apparent; she wasn't asked to any subsequent parades.[117] Those who knew Tabram at the lodging house were not aware of her 'friendship' with Connolly, and the missing days when Connolly apparently went to ground, before acting strangely at an identity parade at the Tower, certainly undermines her testimony.[118] Regardless of the role of certain witnesses, or of Martha Tabram's movements on the night she died, another impoverished woman had met her death in mysterious circumstances on the streets of East London and the police were apparently baffled. Someone was attacking and, in most cases, killing women in a relatively small area of crowded streets and courts in the East End. These were not easy streets to navigate unless you were familiar with your surroundings. They were patrolled by the police (albeit if not into some of the most notorious areas of the Nichol slum at the top of Brick Lane) and an unwary killer might easily find himself arrested or pursued if he took a wrong turning.[119] Equally, anyone who looked as if he might be in the wrong place would arouse suspicion; so the idea that some top-hatted toff, or a doctor in a cape carrying a Gladstone bag, could have slipped away unnoticed seems unlikely.

The victims were all assumed to be prostitutes,[120] women who were less likely to be missed, all ideal targets for a serial murderer.[121] But as prostitutes they also carried something potentially important to the understanding of this case, something dangerous – sexually transmitted diseases. Throughout the nineteenth century, attitudes towards prostitutes fluctuated between those who saw them as the victims of male lust, as 'fallen' women who could be saved or reformed – or as moral and physical pollutants, as the destroyers of marriage, society and the empire. This was in part because they were held to be responsible for circulating a disease that made no distinction between guilt and innocence. That disease was the 'Great Pox', the 'French disease', or, to give it its proper name, syphilis.[122]

5

THE SCOURGE OF SYPHILIS

Victorian Britain was no stranger to disease; overcrowding in London and other cities encouraged the spread of infectious diseases such as measles, while damp conditions allowed tuberculosis to fester. There were outbreaks of Asiatic cholera in 1831–32 and 1848–49 that killed thousands of Londoners before John Snow published his ground-breaking thesis that linked the spread of the disease to contaminated water.[123] The 'Great Stink' of 1858 finally seems to have convinced the authorities that something needed to be done and London's sewer system underwent a major overhaul. Typhoid was another killer that made little distinction between rich and poor. It may well have caused the death of Prince Albert in 1861 and then afflicted the heir to the throne a decade later, causing Queen Victoria to fear that she would lose her eldest son to it as well. Life expectancy, especially among the very young, was low – with inhabitants of Liverpool lucky to make it past their 20s.[124] However, while cholera, tuberculosis, and typhoid (along with rickets, diphtheria, chicken pox, smallpox and polio) could all kill or otherwise undermine the lives of children and adults in Victorian London, the disease that came to dominate contemporary discourse was one that was intrinsically linked to wider debates about morality and sexuality. Syphilis, more than any other late nineteenth-century disease, seemed to embody everything the

Victorians feared. It was a hidden disease, something that could be contracted by one casual encounter with an 'unfortunate'. It was a dread sickness, supposedly spread by members of 'outcast' society, and so it represented the 'enemy within' and thus threatened to undermine society.

It is not always easy for us to understand just how frightening syphilis was to the Victorians; modern medicine has made such tremendous leaps in the past 100 years that we are now much better able to deal with bacterial infections – so now syphilis can be treated if it is caught early. But the necessary antibiotics were not available in the late 1800s. In fact, syphilis was not formally treatable until a breakthrough in 1905–6 allowed for the venereal syphilis treponema (the bacterial genus from which syphilis comes) to be isolated.[125] This led to the 'first successful aetiological drug ever developed against a bacterial disease' being available from 1909 onwards.[126] This should remind us of just how seriously society took the problem of syphilis in the early twentieth century.

Syphilis had ravaged European society in the 1490s and was then exported to the New World with Columbus and the waves of European conquistadors that followed in his wake. While the 'Great Pox' or the 'French disease' (as contemporaries in Renaissance Europe termed syphilis) had been present in human society much earlier in history, it remerged in the fifteenth century as a more virulent and destructive plague.[127] In 1530 Girolamo Fracastoro named the disease after the hero of his poem, a shepherd who was infected after he dared to upset the Sun God.[128] In early modern London, syphilis was rife but it is difficult to differentiate it from other forms of sexually transmitted diseases such as gonorrhoea; all came under the umbrella term of 'foul disease', 'venereal disease' or simply, 'the pox'.[129] By the middle of the nineteenth century, syphilis had become endemic in all industrial societies and there was seemingly no means to prevent its spread.

Victorian medical opinion was divided on whether syphilis was curable or not, it seems doctors and researchers mostly believed that the symptoms were treatable but not the disease itself. Throughout the nineteenth century, on both sides of the Channel, debates raged but a cure seemed to be a long way off.[130] Mercurial salivation (applying mercury to sweat out disease) was used in the early modern period and this continued into the nineteenth century, but it is hard to imagine that this did much good. In fact, it had serious side effects: it was painful and caused tremendous damage. This is because mercury poisoning can cause sensory impairment to the eyes and ears, hypertension and poor co-ordination. As well as sensory impairment users could expect gum disease, tooth loss and 'embarrassingly wretched bad breath'.[131] In desperation sufferers from syphilis looked to the market for folk remedies or the new medicines and panaceas advertised by 'quack' doctors, which (like 'Curtis' Manhood', or 'the Unfortunate's Friend') had names clearly intended to attract the unwary. None of them worked, of course. While treatment with mercury was not recommended by such experts as there were in the first-half of the nineteenth century, it enjoyed a revival of sorts in the 1860s, and it was added to other compounds that could be administered by injection as other remedies (quack or more scientific) demonstrably failed to do much good for sufferers.[132] So we can be fairly confident that those infected with 'the pox' in the 1880s were probably being treated (or were self-medicating) with mercury or a medicine compound which contained mercury.

Syphilis is a debilitating disease that attacks the body through three stages. Early sufferers exhibit indurated sores (inflamed hard spots on the skin) which is followed – at the second stage – by feelings of depression, lethargy, and a sensation of being chilled to the bone. In its third stage, which could take many years to develop, syphilis was believed to have adverse effects on several internal organs such as the liver, lungs, and brain. It was also thought to have exposed the sufferer to other ailments as a result of damage it did to the immune system. So like consumption (tuberculosis) the great killer of the Victorian and Edwardian period, it was believed that syphilis undermined the body's capacity to protect itself. Moreover, it was a disease that could be passed on, not only to those in contact with the diseased person, but by pregnant women to their children, causing stillbirth or very rapid infant death. The tragic consequence of hereditary infection is vividly illustrated by the following description of a baby born to syphilitic parents: 'it was a sickly creature of miniscule dimensions, a dirty yellow in colour, and so lifeless and emaciated that it hardly seemed worth taking care of it.'[133] Syphilis, then, was a silent killer, one that might lie dormant in the genes of Victorian families, before being passed on down the line to a succession of innocents, wreaking havoc as it did so. Not only was syphilis a debilitating physical disease, it also gnawed away at the sufferer's mind, and this had been officially recognised by the medical profession from at least 1822, although it had been mooted before then.[134] In 1809 John Haslam had written that the 'paralytic affections are a much more frequent cause of madness than is generally supposed.'[135] In 1884 the official French medical dictionary recognised that syphilis was linked to 'intellectual enfeeblement, disturbances of the personality and the moral sense, and [was] marked by an apoplectiforum ictus or a particularly violent fit of mania'.[136] Alfred Fournier was adamant that syphilis left its victims 'retarded, simple-minded, unbalanced, insane, imbecilic or idiotic'.[136]

William Acton (1813–1875) placed the problem of syphilis at the heart of his study of prostitution in the late 1850s.[137] He noted the high mortality rate of infected children (180 children below the age of five were reported to have died of syphilis in London in 1867) and described an infant victim as a 'small, wizened, atrophied, weakly, sickly creature', resembling a 'monkey or a little old man'. Others were described as apish, shrivelled, and prematurely aged – all 'living symbols of the devolutionary force of male vice'.[138] It is the virulence of the disease among those younger than five which matters here and contemporaries were well aware that the 'innocent victims of syphilis were more numerous than the guilty.'[139] Acton argued that the disease was unlikely to kill the women that caused it to spread – the prostitutes themselves – but instead it caused havoc among the wider population, claiming thousands of entirely innocent victims – the wives and children of the men who caught syphilis from street women.[140] We should be cautious, of course: Acton and others like him were quick to point the finger of blame at those who in his view undermined the moral fabric of society by selling sex or profiting from its sale.[141] The 1860s witnessed a moral panic about the state of the health of the nation's armed forces following the almost disastrous Crimean campaign when the vast majority of British casualties had been caused by disease rather than any engagement with the enemy. An increasing fear of the effects of syphilis on troops was therefore a causal factor in the passing of the Contagious Diseases Acts (hereafter CDAs) in the 1860s. The CDAs allowed for the forcible examination of women (usually, but not limited to, prostitutes) and their incarceration in lock hospitals if any evidence of disease was discovered. While the CDAs were largely restricted to garrison towns and naval ports (the intention being to protect the armed forces from disease) the wider effect of the legislation was to further demonise street prostitutes. The CDAs were fairly ineffectual because they did not impose any sanctions on the users of prostitutes, nor were they rolled out to cities such as London, where the problem was far greater. But it helped establish the myth that the problem was intimately related to the sex trade and to the corrupted body of the Victorian sex worker.[142]

Some of the rhetoric surrounding the 'Ripper' victims therefore needs to be seen in this context, with some observers apparently happy to see the killer's actions as a form of 'street cleaning'. For the late Victorians the prostitute was 'the agent of corruption and contamination, whose putrid body bred stench and disease.'[143] The horror of syphilis, and the role of the 'fallen' or 'unfortunate' woman (both popular euphemisms for prostitutes) made their way into Victorian popular culture and the arts. In several literary works, including Conan Doyle's *The Third Generation*, there are references to inherited syphilis, the so-called 'hereditary taint', which blighted the lives of young men and women whose parents had been careless in the past. In Robert Louis Stevenson's classic horror story, *Dr. Jekyll and Mr. Hyde*, the medical man's alter ego is 'represented as apelike, pale, and inexpressively deformed, echoing', as Elaine Showalter observed, 'the imagery of syphilitic afflictions in nineteenth-century medical texts'.[144] Contemporary descriptions of the disease were vivid; thus syphilis manifested a wide range of physical symptoms – skin disorders such as 'macules, papules, tubercules, pustules, blebs, tumours, lesions, scales, crusts, chancres, gummas, fissures, and scars' [...] 'to cardiovascular disturbances, locomotor ataxia, tabes, blindness, and dementia', all of which were used in attempts 'to control male sexuality' through deterrence.[145] Popular medical books[146] showed the effects of syphilis in graphic detail and in Blackpool a wax museum presented the symptoms in gruesome three dimentions as a warning to local sailors to avoid the prostitutes of the town.[147]

In the 1880s it was becoming clear that married men who used prostitutes were placing their wives and children at risk, a fact recognised by the civil courts, which began to accept that the 'matrimonial transmission of venereal disease' was 'cruelty and thus grounds for separation or divorce'.[148] Feminist campaigners were quick to condemn men for blaming this disease on the women they bought for sex, women from the lowest rungs of society. Josephine Butler[149] and her fellow campaigners for the repeal of the CDAs, while deploring the act of prostitution itself, refused to condemn the poor women that found themselves forced into the sordid trade. The CDAs were eventually repealed in 1886, just two years before the Whitechapel murder series commenced. The legacy of the CDAs and the discussions about sexually transmitted diseases that accompanied them remained very much in the public domain so it would be surprising if ordinary Londoners were not at least familiar with this, if not necessarily very well informed about the intricacies of medical knowledge of the issue.

Victorian medical science was far from squeamish about subjecting poor (or 'fallen') women to experiments aimed at discovering a cure for venereal diseases or attempts at its prevention. The CDAs were merely one manifestation of this. In a patriarchal society that placed working-class women at the bottom of the social ladder, the bodies of women who prostituted themselves were hardly worthy of any male sympathy. By choosing such a method of earning a living, women such as 'Pearly Poll' or Emma Smith had effectively placed themselves outside the protection of a male-dominated society. There was little emphasis placed on the transgressions of men who used prostitutes; to the Victorians it was the women who were at fault because they acted as the agents of corruption, while the men were simply indulging a very understandable and natural urge. This lack of regard for the bodies of women was not lost on the women who took the lessons they had learned from Josephine Butler's campaign against the CDAs into the struggle for the vote. As the twentieth century unfolded, the problem of syphilis and other forms of 'hidden' sexually transmitted diseases were used by the increasingly vocal women's suffrage movement as a counter to accusations of female violence against (male) property. In 1913 Christabel Pankhurst responded to criticism of militant actions by suffragettes by arguing that 'men have destroyed, and are destroying, the health and life of women in the pursuit of vice.'[151] She claimed that most men had contracted some form of venereal disease and while this may have been an exaggeration, it echoed claims from the late 1800s that at least 20 per cent of Englishmen were infected with syphilis. Reports differ, some suggest one in seven London males had the disease but, regardless of the actual levels of infection, it is clear that syphilis was endemic and occupied a position in contemporary fears that we might equate to the discovery of HIV/AIDS in late twentieth-century society. Syphilis, as 'the germ that dared not speak its name', was associated with sexual immorality and therefore bound up with feelings of guilt, anger and blame.[152]

The spectre of syphilis was to haunt the footsteps of the victims of the Whitechapel and Torso murderer in the years between 1887 and 1891 because the person we believe to have been responsible for the killings had almost certainly contracted the disease from a chance encounter with a woman. Having become a carrier, he had then gone on to infect his wife – who probably passed the disease onto their child, who died in infancy. Given the underlying discourse about venereal disease and the prevailing belief that prostitutes were the cause of its spread, and remembering that syphilis causes a gradual deterioration of the senses and affects a sufferer's brain, it is not too wild a leap to believe that a syphilitic killer was wreaking some kind of private, if misguided, war of vengeance on those who had infected him. Moreover, and more pertinently, the killer was also dosing himself with a compound of mercury and (most likely) potassium in the vain hope this would at least alleviate his symptoms. Proof that this sort of 'cure' was still prescribed long after the efficacy had been thrown into doubt comes from the letters of the French author Guy de Maupassant (1850–1893) who wrote to a friend in 1877 to tell him: 'I've got the pox!' and that he was living on a 'staple diet' of mercury and potassium iodide.[153]

If the mercury didn't impair the brain of the diseased individual, then the syphilis almost certainly would have. As we have heard, the physical effects of 'the pox' were matched by an even more frightening deterioration in the mental health and personality of the sufferer. As the French physician Alfred Fournier declared: 'the nervous system is the victim *par excellence* of tertiary syphilis,' and it would have eaten away at the mind of the Whitechapel murderer some time before it finally rendered his body incapable of continuing his private campaign of revenge.[154] Perhaps unsurprisingly, the FBI today believes it a distinct possibility that the killer might have derived his apparent hatred of women through his contraction of the disease from local prostitutes.[155] By August 1888 we think that circumstances had begun to coalesce to lead him to allow his violent urges full rein, with quite dreadful consequences for several of London's poorest inhabitants.

6

THE AUTUMN OF TERROR

The murder of Martha Tabram in George Yard was initially thought to be the work of a gang of 'roughs' from around the Old Nichol Street area of the East End, an area made infamous by Arthur Morrison as 'The Jago'. There were lots of gangs in London in the late nineteenth century, all sporting colourful names and exercising territorial rights over small areas of the capital. In 1888 the *Pall Mall Gazette* ran a feature on the 'gangs of London' listing the 'Monkey Parade gang', the 'Gang of Roughs', 'Jovial Thirty-Two', 'Marylebone gang', 'Fitzroy Place gang' and the 'New Cut gang'.[156] Historians have studied the phenomenon of nineteenth-century youth gangs in Liverpool, Salford and Manchester, as well as the capital, and have concluded that Victorian society was intermittently concerned about the actions of unruly working-class 'lads'.[157] However, the press was seemingly keen to present the existence of 'roughs' as evidence of deeper problems. The hooligan panic of the late 1890s preceded the outbreak of the South African (Boer) War and concerns over gangs can also be read as being indicative of wider fears over the state of the nation and the empire.

In May 1888 antipathy between two rival gangs in northwest London resulted in tragedy as a young man out for a stroll with his sweetheart was stabbed to death in Regent's Park. Joseph Rumbold had been mistaken as a member of a gang that had attacked another couple the previous evening and despite efforts to save him, he died in hospital from stab wounds to the neck. A crowded Old Bailey courtroom witnessed the trials of eight youths of whom one, George Galletly, was eventually convicted and sentenced to death.[158] Galletly was spared the rope on account of his age (he was barely 18) but the case was widely reported and added to the pervading disquiet about law and order, the criminal class and concerns about youth in particular. Consequently, then, the London press had a ready-made story to explain the death of Emma Smith in April, and the murder of Martha Tabram also seemed to fit this narrative. It was supposed that Martha had fallen victim to petty criminals who terrorised the area and demanded money from the 'working girls' in the streets.[159] This explanation began to unravel, however, when another prostitute was found dead at the end of August. Indeed, the circumstances surrounding this murder seemed to suggest that a very different sort of killer was operating in the East End.

The night of 30 August 1888 was stormy, and the thunder and lightning was quickly accompanied by the outbreak of a raging fire on the London docks. As hundreds of Londoners raced to watch firemen battle the flames, few of them would have suspected that both the storms and the conflagration were about to be eclipsed as front-page news by an event that was altogether more disturbing. At about 3.45 a.m., Charles Cross was making his way to work at Pickfords, the delivery firm. His route took him along Buck's Row and parallel to the Whitechapel High Street. Buck's Row is now called Durward Street and it has changed considerably, with recent work on the capital's Cross Rail project helping transform the area. In 1888, Buck's Row had a run of two-story 'shabby, dirty little houses', with several warehouses on the other side of the narrow road.[160] The pavements were minimal, the road was cobbled and, at the end of the run of houses, there was a board school that still stands today – however, the school building has now been converted into residential flats. Between the school and the houses was a stable yard belonging to one of the warehouses (Brown's) and as Charles Cross approached the gates, he noticed something lying against them. At first, he was not sure what it was because it was still quite dark: 'It looked to me like a tarpaulin sheet,' he later said.[161] It was only when he got closer to it that he realised that it was the body a woman. Moments later another man arrived at the scene. Robert Paul was a market porter and at first he tried to avoid Cross, wary that he might represent a threat in this dimly lit back street. But when Cross motioned him and said: 'Come and look at this woman,' he did so.[162] The two men examined her and found her hands were cold. Paul thought she might still be alive, if only just. Neither had heard anything in the street ahead; no disappearing footsteps that might suggest the killer had hurried off when he heard the two men approaching – nothing. Cross then disagreed with Paul's suggestion that they sit her up, and the two headed off in search of a policeman instead. Before they could find one the local beat bobby returned to Buck's Row and discovered the woman's body as they had left it. As PC Neil (97 J) shone his lamp at the figure on the ground, he noticed that the woman's throat had been cut. As he decided what to do, another officer (PC Thain, 96 H) passed the Brady Street entrance to Buck's Row, so Neil called to him to go and fetch a doctor. At 3.50 a.m., PC Thain returned with Dr Llewellyn (who lived conveniently close by at 152 Whitechapel Road) and he pronounced her dead.[163] In the meantime, Cross and Paul had found another policeman, Constable Mizen, at the intersection of Hanbury Street and Old Montague Street.[164] Having informed him of their grim discovery, they both hurried off so as not to be late for work.

So many things stand out today as examples of bad police practice but this is to view the case through modern eyes. No one thought to take proper statements from Cross and Paul and it is highly unlikely that either of them would have been allowed to continue on to work today without a more thorough interview. Nor would PC Thain have informed the workmen in the nearby slaughterhouse that a murder had just occurred, prompting them to rush out to have a look. A more astute policeman might have also ascertained exactly who was in and around Barber's yard (a part of the Harrison, Barber empire) that night, but PC Thain was more intent on picking up his cape and passing on a bit of spicy news than engaging in careful detective work. Finally, it is inconceivable that a modern detective would have allowed the dead body to have been unceremoniously lifted onto a handcart and taken to the nearby workhouse mortuary to be stripped by two pauper inmates while the murder scene was washed down before it could be properly inspected.[165] Of course, none of this should surprise us because contemporary understanding of forensic science was almost non-existent.

At least a police officer was present when the woman's body was stripped and it didn't take him long to realise that this was no ordinary killing, so he quickly sent for Dr Llewellyn to undertake a thorough post-mortem. The victim's throat had been cut and there was evidence that she may have been attacked from behind, with a hand or other item used to cover her mouth or otherwise choke or throttle her. Her carotid artery had been severed, from left to right; most of the blood from her wound had collected in her clothes and was not discovered until she was placed on the handcart to be transferred to the mortuary. Dr Llewelyn reported that the 'wounds must have been inflicted with a strong-bladed knife, moderately sharp, and used with great violence.'[166] The lack of blood on the front of the woman suggested either that her throat was slit when she was facing downwards and still alive (so that any arterial spray exuded away from her body) or that she was already dead when the killer cut across her neck. In either case it would help ensure that little or no blood stained the clothes of the perpetrator. If he had stood in front of her and slashed at her throat he would almost inevitably been showered in his victim's blood. In addition to the cuts to the throat and wounds on the cheek and jaw, there were also stab wounds and cuts to the abdomen. The abdomen had been opened from under her ribs to expose the stomach. There were additional stabs to the vagina and the doctor noted that he thought a left-handed man who possessed 'some rough anatomical knowledge' had made the attack.[167] Nothing was missing from the body – no organs had been removed – but this assault, even though it was believed to have lasted less than 5 minutes, constituted a further escalation from the attack on Martha Tabram. If they were the work of the same man, then he was growing bolder.

So, who was the victim? In terms of clues the police had little to go on. The woman was probably wearing most, if not all, of her possessions. These consisted of a variety of old clothes, a comb, hankie and a broken mirror. Her petticoats bore the mark of the Lambeth workhouse, suggesting she had been an inmate there at some point.[168] This was a useful lead and led to her identification a few days later. The other notable (and indeed now iconic) piece of property was a black straw bonnet trimmed with black velvet. The police investigation soon discovered that a woman named 'Polly' had been turned away from a lodging house in Thrawl Street on the evening of the murder for want of the 4d she needed for her doss. Polly seemed unperturbed by this minor inconvenience; 'I'll soon get my doss money,' she had told the warden, 'see what a jolly bonnet I've got now.'[169] That bonnet was found discarded close by her dead body on Buck's Row and it has remained a defining item in 'Ripper' mythology ever since.

The victim was finally named as Mary Ann Nichols, a 44-year-old woman who drank heavily but was known as a 'clean but poor woman', evidenced by the fact that she had been in and out of a variety of London workhouses. She had borne five children with her husband William Nichols but he had left her when her drinking became too much for him. This sorry tale of poverty and alcoholism was repeated in several of the women who were murdered in and around Whitechapel between 1887 and 1891 and it is unlikely that any of their deaths would have raised much more than a passing interest if it had not been for the brutal nature of the killings and the way in which they captured the imagination of the press.

'Polly' Nichols had almost escaped this hand-to-mouth existence but had blown the chance that someone, most probably the Lambeth workhouse board, had given her. Employed by a respectable family in Wandsworth, Mary had written to her father to tell him the good news. That was in April 1888 but by August she was back in digs in Thrawl Street, having run away from her new opportunity with some of her master's property. When a journalist from *The Star* viewed her body in the mortuary, however –another intrusion that would be forbidden in a modern investigation – he found a 'fairly plump' woman of about 5 foot 3 inches who appeared to him to be younger by about 10 years than she really was. Her 'features were small and delicate', her teeth discoloured and her hair, dark. A second journalist (this time from the local paper, the *East London Observer*) wrote that the 'expression on the face was a deeply painful one, and evidently a result of an agonising death.'[170]

Polly Nichols is generally considered to be the first of the 'Ripper's 'canonical five' victims. But this was a quite efficient killing and it is very unlikely that it was the murderer's first strike. The method suggests that he knew this area well and that Polly either knew him personally or was at least familiar with him as a local character. If Polly Nichols was a prostitute – or was someone who occasionally sold sex – then this might explain her encounter with her murderer. In this case then, she probably turned her back on her assailant, expecting sex, leaving herself vulnerable to his attack. However, it is also possible that her killer found her – drunk and almost insensible – staggering along Buck's Row and took full advantage. Polly had drunk her lodging fee several times over that night but with her 'jolly bonnet' and relatively youthful looks, she possibly felt that a local punter would part with the few pennies she needed to secure her night's kip. She may have wandered up from the Whitechapel High Street knowing that she was likely to find such a man near the warehouses and yards surrounding Whitechapel railway station, or simply used it as a route back to her digs in Thrawl Street. Nichols was reportedly very tipsy and almost unable to stand at 2.30 a.m., and her senses would hardly have improved dramatically by 3.30 when we might have expected her to have met with her assassin. She would have presented a very easy target and we suspect that our killer thrived on exactly these sorts of situations. Canon Barnet, the 'slum priest' who founded Toynbee Hall, recognised that the inebriated condition many of the streetwalkers of Whitechapel were in made things easy for the killer. Writing to *The Times* in late July 1889 Barnett commented:

> There is no lack of victims ready to his hand, for scores of these unfortunate women may be seen any night muddled with drink in the streets or alleys, perfectly reckless as to their safety and only anxious to meet with anyone who will help them in plying their miserable trade.[171]

Being routinely equipped with the necessary implements to both kill and mutilate, and familiar enough with his surroundings to know exactly what he could, and could not, get away with, a drunken woman in a dimly lit street (on a night when many locals had already drunk themselves to sleep after the excitement of the dock fire) was too good an opportunity for the killer to pass up. Having quickly carried out the murder he would have found it quite easy to slip away into the shadows at the sound of Cross and Paul's approaching footsteps, especially if he lived and worked nearby.

In Winthrop Street, which runs behind Buck's Row, there was a yard owned by Harrison, Barber & Co., the horse slaughterers. The yard would have provided an ideal cover for someone whose hands or clothes must have been stained with blood. Unlike today, Winthrop Street in 1888 allowed an escape by going back down to Brady Street or up into Spitalfields and Brick Lane. From there the killer could have expected to reach safety within minutes and then sit back and revel in his ability to do what he liked, when he liked, without anyone – including the Met's finest – being able to stop him.

On 8 September the *East London Advertiser* made a grim prediction. Likening the murderer of Polly Nichols to a character on the London stage, it augured that 'the mysterious lunatic, who issues forth at night like another Hyde to prey upon the defenceless "unfortunate class"' would strike again.[172] The notion that the killer was a lone assassin, deranged and quite unlike any other murderer, was now gaining ground as the press (and police) moved away from the 'gang' theory. Newspapers did (and do) tend to follow each other's leads to create a composite story – an angle – and this is very evident in the Whitechapel murders. The *Northern Echo,* a Darlington-based newspaper, reported the link that all the papers had made between the deaths of Smith, Tabram and Nichols with Richard Mansfield's performance of *Dr. Jekyll and Mr. Hyde* at the Lyceum theatre. The *Echo* was prepared to believe the killer was a madman, as the killings were 'absolutely destitute of any of the ordinary motives which impel to the commission of murder'. In fact, it thought it would be worse if the murderer was sane, or if they were not the work of a sole killer.[173] Mansfield eventually brought this production of Stevenson's horror story to an end with a separate benefit show for the people of the East End; the 'Ripper' had made this sort of 'horror' entertainment unpalatable by bringing real terror to the streets.

Meanwhile, another seemingly random attack on a woman leaving a music hall on Cambridge Heath Road was interpreted as a potential 'Ripper' attack by some sections of the London press. An apparently well-dressed man approached her and inveigled her down a quiet street (not far, the paper stated, from Buck's Row) where she was attacked by a 'gang of women and bullies' and robbed. When she attempted to cry out one of the group put a knife to her throat and darkly warned her that 'we will serve you as we did the others.'[174] This refuelled the 'gang' theory and allowed both notions to remain in the public consciousness. However, it was the idea that this was a solitary killer, in some way insane or otherwise inhuman, which eventually became the dominant narrative as far as the press were concerned. What was clear, to the press at least, was that the killings were connected and that meant, as the *East London Advertiser* had already opined, that the killer would strike again, and soon. That prediction was to be realised within just over a week of the Nichols murder.

This time the scene was 29 Hanbury Street, close to the junction with Brick Lane in the very heart of Spitalfields. In 1881, 15 people were listed as living at that address with 20 lodging next door, at 27, and a further seven living at Number 31. This then was a crowded set of dwellings with back yards that could be accessed from the street. Local prostitutes were known to use the yards for their business.[175] One family in particular, the Hardimans, stand out here; mostly dealers in horsemeat, they lived at 27 or 29 between 1881 and 1891. Another family resident at No. 29 were the Richardsons. In 1881 Thomas and Amelia Richardson were in their late 50s and living with their five-year-old grandson, also named Thomas. Amelia was still listed there with a grandson in 1891 although apparently she went by the name of Ann and was without her husband, who had died some time prior to the murder.[176] Amelia was also the landlady at No. 29.[177]

At 4.45 a.m. on 8 September 1888, Amelia's son John, who lived elsewhere, stopped off at No. 29 on his way to work to check on things, as he often did. Sitting down on the steps in the back yard he set about making some minor repairs to his boots. It was dark (dawn broke at 4.51 that day but the sun wasn't due to rise for almost another hour)[178] but he saw nothing unusual. Half-an-hour or so later, at 5.20 a.m., another resident, Albert Cadosch, went out into the yard behind 27, probably to relieve himself. He heard voices coming from No. 29 but all he recalled hearing was the word 'No'. Later, about 4 minutes afterwards, he reported hearing something fall against the fence, but did not investigate.[179] This is one of those moments in any police investigation when the actions of a potential witness must seem so frustrating. If Cadosch's curiosity had got the better of him, he would surely have seen the murderer in action; it may not have resulted in an arrest, but we will never know. By 5.32, Cadosch was on his way to work and passed the clock at Christ's Church, opposite Spitalfields Market. Some time between 5.15 and 5.20, a local woman, Elizabeth Long, who was very sure of the time because the nearby Truman Brewery clock had just struck as she turned into Hanbury Street, saw a woman talking to a man in front of Number 29. Unfortunately, she could not see the man's face but described him as being about 5 foot 5 inches tall, wearing dark clothes with a 'shabby genteel appearance'.[180] She also said he looked foreign, by which she probably meant he looked Jewish but given that she did not see his face and only got a fleeting glance as she passed by, we should not place too much store by that. After all, the local area was heavily populated by immigrant Jews and Mrs Long may well have resented their presence, as many East Enders did in the 1880s. Anti-alienism (what we would term racism) was endemic in late-Victorian Britain and anti-Semitism was an especial problem in East London.[181] Soon after the events of 8 September, the idea that the killer was a local Jew began to gain ground and Mrs Long's evidence no doubt helped to fuel that speculation. However, Elizabeth Long did hear the man ask the woman a question, 'Will you?' and the woman's reply, 'Yes'. Elizabeth Long later identified the woman she'd seen as the murder victim found in the back yard of 29 Hanbury Street.

At 6 a.m. John Davis entered the yard and found a horrific sight. A woman lay on her back with her legs and skirts drawn up, as if she had been placed on an operating table. Davis went for help and at 6.30 the police surgeon – Dr George Bagster Phillips – examined the body. At first it appeared that the woman had not only been murdered, she had been ritually laid out. The victim seemed to have been strangled before having her throat cut. The protrusion of the tongue suggested throttling had taken place and it is likely that the killer grabbed her by the chin and then lowered her to the ground when she was dead – or at least unconscious. He cut her throat, from left to right, as she lay by the fence. Cutting her throat was unnecessary in terms of killing but it would have enabled him to drain the body of blood and make his next actions easier. Cutting open her abdomen, the murderer was then able to reach his intended target – the uterus. Lifting the small intestines out of the way, he placed these over her right shoulder and left some of the stomach membranes above her left one.[182] To some, this has suggested a ritualistic element but of course it could have been merely expedient.[183] It was just about light and he had some time to work, as this killer knew his surroundings intimately and probably the movements of all the occupants as well.

He took away her rings, which were of little value but may have been symbolic to him – given that rings are associated with relationships and marriage – as well as removing her uterus along with some portions of her vagina and bladder. That he managed to escape into the dawn, with bloodied hands (he did not bother to use the tap in the yard to clean himself) and a knife on his person, suggests this was either someone who was either extremely reckless or confident in their ability to fade into the background. Just along from 29 Hanbury Street was a yard belonging to the same firm of horse slaughterers that operated from Winthrop Street, near Buck's Row. As before, there would have been plenty of private space to hide, clean up and perhaps secrete a knife. Coincidence perhaps, but again this was a bold and opportunistic murder carried out by someone who was very familiar with his environment. But who was his victim and why was she in Hanbury Street?

Elizabeth Long was able to identify the person she saw talking to a 'shabby genteel' man at half-past five on the morning of 8 September; she had not known her, but nevertheless recognised her when she was taken to view the body in the mortuary. The dead woman's name was Annie Chapman, although she was often known as Annie Sivvey (or 'Siffey') having taken the name of her former partner, John or 'Jack' Sivvey.[184] By 1888 Jack and Annie had separated and she was living at Crossingham's lodging house on Dorset Street.[185] In 1888 Annie was 47, and she was ill. In all probability she had TB and may well have had syphilis; she liked a glass or two of rum but is not normally referred to as an alcoholic as were some of the other victims. This notwithstanding, it was drink that was cited as the reason for the breakdown of her marriage to a coachman (John Chapman) some time in 1884–5. John died of cirrhosis of the liver at Christmas in 1886 and the money that he had been sending Annie stopped. It was at this point that she may have started to resort to prostitution and by 1888, this seems to have undermined her latest relationship with a bricklayer's mate named Edward Stanley.[186] In early September Chapman quarrelled with another local woman, Eliza Cooper, in the Britannia pub at the corner of Dorset Street. The dispute apparently concerned Stanley, but it might have been caused by Annie accusing Eliza of stealing a florin from one of their party, or have arisen over something as trivial as soap. The truth is probably not that important; Annie ended up with a black eye and a bruised chest and seems to have stayed away from the lodging house in the week before she died.

On the night she was killed there were several sightings of her prior to her being seen by Mrs Long. Around midnight she had returned to Dorset Street and she stayed long enough to drink a pint of beer with a fellow lodger. He noted she was already tipsy. According to Chapman, she had been to Vauxhall to visit her sister who may have given her the money to drink. She might also have been to the casual ward at the workhouse to get some medication for her illness. At 1.35 a.m. she was back at the lodging house but did not have enough money for her bed. She told the warden he should keep her bed for her, as she would return with the money later.[187] No one knows what happened to her between then and being killed but, since she had headed off in the general direction of Spitalfields Market, we might imagine that she was hoping to solicit some trade or beg for some favours along Commercial Street. There were no further reports of Annie that night but it seems likely that she wandered the streets in vain looking for a customer who would secure her bed for the night. Instead of a punter, however, she picked up her killer.

In the aftermath of Annie Chapman's murder, the press whipped up a panic and the idea that the killer had to be a foreigner gathered momentum. Mrs Long's testimony helped but she may have already been drawing on a popular belief that a mysterious character named 'Leather Apron' was to blame for the murders. Leather Apron was soon associated with a Jewish tradesman, John Pizer, who had been, it was claimed, 'in the habit of ill-using prostitutes'. *The Star* ran a feature on 'Leather Apron' on 5 September. On the 10th, Sergeant Thick of H division arrested Pizer and took him back to Leman Street Police Station, where he was questioned. He was held for two days and then released without charge; he had alibis for all the previous murders and the police had no reason to hold him.[188] His subsequent appearance at Chapman's inquest has been the source of considerable speculation among researchers but there seems to be no clear evidence at all that Pizer was the 'Ripper'.[189]

On the day the inquest opened, a group of local businessmen raised a sum of money for a reward and formed a vigilance committee, headed by George Lusk, builder and decorator, churchwarden, and a Freemason. The government had refused to issue an official reward –the practice, once usual, having fallen out of favour. This emphasised the reality that the Whitechapel murders were now front-page news, and not just in the capital. One of the many consequences of this was that every snippet of information was poured over and analysed by contemporaries and a host of suggestions as to the killer's identity and motive were debated and dismissed within the pages of the Victorian newspapers. If the murderer was not a local Jew, then perhaps he was a Portuguese sailor? Or a 'Red Indian' from Buffalo Bill's travelling Wild West Show? Maybe he was a 'toff' – a 'Champagne Charley' acting without care or consideration for the lowest class in society?

But the coroner, Wynne Baxter, has to take the blame for one of the most enduring theories concerning the murderer. In summing up at 'Dark' Annie's inquest, he concluded that the mutilations she had suffered had 'been made by someone who had considerable anatomical skill and knowledge.'[190] The intention of the killer, he believed, was to kill in order to remove her vital organs and the police, so it followed, should be looking for a medical man and not simply a butcher or horse slaughterer.[191] His conclusion had largely been based on the opinion of the doctor who had attended Annie at the scene and subsequently carried out her post-mortem, George Bagster Phillips. He believed that the knife used had been a very sharp one, about 6–8 inches long, and likely of the type used for post-mortem purposes – but also, of course, for slaughtering and cutting up horses. The way in which the pelvic organs had been so deftly secured however, inclined him to believe that the work was that of an expert rather than a mere slaughterman – someone with 'great anatomical knowledge' and 'experience of anatomical and pathological examinations'[192] – especially given the speed with which he had worked.

Inspector Abberline and the rest of H Division's detective force must have been at their wits' end. In the space of a few months three women (Tabram, Nichols and Chapman) had been brutally murdered and all their leads had gone cold. Who were they to look for – a Jew, a mad doctor or a decadent aristocrat?[193] They should have ignored the hype and the pressures that were increasingly being placed upon them by the press, the Home Office and the residents of the East End, and looked somewhat closer to home instead.

7

LONDON'S TRANSPORT NETWORK, AND THE WHITEHALL MYSTERY

On Friday 14 September, just less than a week after the discovery of Annie Chapman's mutilated body in Hanbury Street, the caretaker of the Tower Subway had an unsettling encounter that was widely reported in the press. At around ten o'clock in the evening a man crossing from the 'Middlesex to the Surrey side' (from north to south) stopped and asked the caretaker there a question: 'Have they caught any of the Whitechapel murderers yet?'

He then produced a knife, about a foot in length, with a curved blade, and remarked, 'This will do for them.'

The man was chased by several bystanders but managed to get away. The caretaker described him as being about 30 years of age, 5 foot 5 inches tall, with 'moustaches and false whiskers, which he pulled off while running away.'[194] This all sounds a little fanciful and so, as with much of the 'Ripper' and 'Torso' reportage, it needs to be treated with a healthy dose of caution.[195] It may have been that the caretaker's imagination was running away with him, or he might have been seeking some of the attention that the press were so happy to provide and so he embroidered his evidence – just as PC Spicer may have done all those years later. On the other hand, the description which he gave does have some things in common with those people who believed they might have seen 'the Ripper'.

Of course given the furore surrounding the murders, the police and papers were being bombarded with sightings of potential suspects and this made it hard for those working the case at the time, and for legions of amateur sleuths ever since, to pick the truth from the fiction and false rumour.

For example, at the same time that a strange man was spotted in the Tower subway, the papers reported the release of 'Leather Apron' and sightings of other possible suspects in the case. One of these was Charles Ludwig Wetzel ('a decently dressed German') who appeared at the Thames Police court accused of being drunk and of threatening a man with a knife. Wetzel had apparently attacked or threatened several people in the past few weeks, including at least one 'unfortunate' woman on the streets of Whitechapel.[196] Was he 'the Ripper' – or even the man in the subway perhaps? *See* the plate section for map from 1895, showing its position in relation to the Tower of London and Tower Bridge, which was completed in 1894.

Again, we need to work with what is likely and with what is plausible, rather than purely speculating or relying overmuch on contemporary hearsay. However, it remains the case that whoever the killer was, he needed to have been able to move about the city with a certain degree of freedom and ease. If, as we suspect, he was associated in some way with a number of premises owned by Harrison, Barber & Co., then he must have been familiar with London's extensive transport network as well as knowing the quickest routes north and south of the river. In 1888 the Tower Subway was a dank, dimly lit pedestrian-only tunnel, used mainly by the working classes, which ran under the river between the Tower of London and Bermondsey. It was open from 5.30 a.m. to midnight, seven days a week, and cost a mere ha'penny to cross. It had opened in 1870, equipped with a wooden trolley that was pulled on a cable system so that passengers could be ferried underneath the river, but this proved prohibitively expensive. Nevertheless, the subway represented an amazing feat of Victorian engineering, and was only the second such tunnel to be built under a river in Europe – the nearby Thames Tunnel, constructed by Brunel in 1843, being the first. The tunnel was also the first 'tube' under the Thames and is a real case of 'what might have been'. Then, in 1894, Tower Bridge opened and effectively killed off the tunnel as a commercially viable venture. Tower Bridge was free to use, and above ground, so no one was likely to want to pay to experience the stygian gloom of the subway when they could promenade along the grand lines of the new crossing. As a result, the Tower Subway was sold off to the London Hydraulic Power Company, who used it to lay hydraulic tubes and water mains.[197] A contemporary drawing of the inside of of the Tower Subway is in the plate section.

Whether the man seen running away while clutching a knife was a phantom of the caretaker's imagination or not, the reality is that the Tower Subway offered a perfect route for any would-be assassin to use as a means of escape. Dark and threatening as it was at night, he could be pretty confident that he would encounter few other travellers late at night or early in the morning. Most, if not all, would have hurried on without taking the least notice of anyone else using the subterranean passageway. Irrespective of whether the caretaker had encountered 'Jack' that night or not, the episode is instructive in reminding us of the importance of transit routes across the Victorian metropolis, a subject warranting greater scrutiny than has previously been afforded by books on the Whitechapel or Thames Torso murders.[198]

By 1887 Londoners could utilise a variety of forms of transport to navigate their city.[199] There were hansom cabs and private coaches for the well-to-do, trains and omnibuses for the middling and clerical classes, and early running trams for the workers. By the late 1830s horse-drawn omnibuses (the forerunners of today's red London buses) were taking paying customers from as far as Croydon, Teddington and Bromley in the south, through the heart of the city to the expanding suburbs of Enfield, Pinner and Hampstead in the north. This means of travel was necessarily slow and there were plenty of complaints about drivers who waited until their 'buses were nearly full' before starting off again. There were no fixed stopping places and there was fierce competition between rival companies, and these early omnibuses were condemned as 'lumbering, clumsy conveyances in which the public were packed like coal sacks and jolted through the streets'.[200] Not surprisingly then, the omnibus companies soon faced a new challenge, as the railway offered passengers a faster (if not necessarily more comfortable) way to get around. London's streets were becoming increasingly congested with horse-drawn vehicles and an obvious solution was to build railways into and out of the city, or later, underneath it.

In the late 1850s and early '60s the London General Omnibus Company (hereafter LGOC) was carrying on average 40,000,000 passengers annually, but there were 100 smaller companies that were operating in the capital, so its profits were constantly being reduced. By the 1880s, and the time of the Whitechapel and Torso murders, the LGOC was facing severe completion from the London Road Car Company and the two larger firms effectively carved up trade between themselves.[201] Moreover, in 1863, the Metropolitan Railway opened the very first underground railway in the world, from Paddington to Farringdon Street, which was extended to Moorgate by the end of 1865. Londoners now had real alternatives to taking the 'bus.[202]

The issue of cost was crucial and the train operators quickly recognised this. The Metropolitan was 'the first company [...] to operate workmen's trains in the London area'. These ran from 5.30 a.m. – many working people had to be at work very early in the 1800s – at 10-minute intervals. They cost just 'thruppence' return.[203] These were steam trains, of course, and apart from expanding the networks within the confines of the densely populated central area, the most pressing engineering problem was in inventing a means of travelling underground without a reliance on coal and steam. The breakthrough was not to come until after the Whitechapel and Torso murder series had almost ended, in November 1890, when the City & South London

Railway entered service. But even before this latest innovation London's railway network, like its omnibuses, carried passengers far and wide. Overground trains had been running for much longer than 'the tube'. Londoners could easily traverse the city via a number of routes run by independent companies such as the Great Eastern or South Eastern Railways. From 1876, for example, the Great Eastern Railways utilised Brunel's Thames Tunnel to ferry commuters from Wapping to Rotherhithe, and quite cheaply – a working man could now travel from Enfield to Liverpool Street and back for just 2d return.[204] By 1887, trains interconnected north and south of the river with lines reaching out to Erith in the east and Hounslow and Southall in the west. There were stations at Liverpool Street, and the Underground served Aldgate in Whitechapel throughout the 'Ripper' period, as well as extending west in the opposite direction along the Embankment and past Sloane Square in Chelsea via the Circle Line.

The novelty of the underground railway must have been somewhat countered by the noise and dirt it produced, and this was certainly the fear of some contemporaries. If you are familiar with the problems of travelling on crowded, hot and uncomfortable 'tube' trains today, imagine what it must have been like when the carriages were served by steam engines belching soot into the tunnel networks. Some commentators (perhaps with little to compare it with, and awed by the technology) suggested it wasn't too bad. In 1863 the *Daily News* was pleasantly surprised by the short journey its correspondent took – it was disappointingly slow but while it was not as pleasant as a journey in the open air, there 'was no inconvenience from vapour'.[205]

The underground may have offered an alternative means of getting around the city but it also offered opportunities to those who harboured desires to not only disrupt travel but also to bring terror to the population for political reasons. On 2 January 1885, as the 8.57 a.m. underground train bound for Hammersmith (which was 4 minutes late, some things never change) passed the signal before Gower Street, a loud explosion was heard. PC Crawford, who was on his beat above ground, heard the bang and reported seeing 'a flash and a cloud of dust'.[206] Hurrying to see what had happened, he 'calmed a screaming woman who had sustained a nosebleed'. Below the ground on the network, several commuters had been thrown about in their carriages and the gas lamps that illuminated them had been extinguished, leaving everyone in darkness. Apart from the fear and panic this might have been expected to cause, there does not appear to have been anything more than minor injuries.[207] The explosion had been caused by a bomb, placed in the tunnel by Fenian (Irish Republican) terrorists who had made several attacks on London in the 1880s.[208] The bomb did little physical damage to the railway, merely blowing a small hole in the tunnel wall, but it was a forerunner of what was to come in the twentieth century and a reminder that the underground was a potentially dangerous place.

Londoners who preferred not to travel under the streets of the city could, by the 1870s at least, use the widening network of trams. These were, like the omnibuses, powered by horses but were far more efficient. As the trams ran on metal rails it took only two horses to pull a tram, as opposed to four to draw a 'bus. Trams were also supposed to be safer than omnibuses, as they were fitted with brakes, and were certainly faster. Tramlines extended across the capital from the early 1870s and while they were largely excluded from the central shopping areas, such as Regent's Street and Piccadilly, they did serve working-class commuters en route to the docks beyond Poplar, to Stratford in the east, Greenwich and Brixton south of the river, and to Archway and Finsbury Park in the north. Perhaps just as importantly, the trams were cheap; initial workmen's trams ran from 4.45 a.m. with fares of no more than a ha'penny a mile. By '1872, 69 per cent of the London Tramways' fares were 2*d*. ones', so this was a relatively fast and cheap way for people to get around.[209] In 1883, the Cheap Trains Act recognised the importance of affordable transport for the working man. Part of the desire for interlinking and efficient transport was to enable London to grow and for this expansion to allow for the redevelopment of the slum areas of the city. Attempts at improving living conditions in London had often floundered because working people needed to remain close to their places of work – for those in the East End, this meant the docks.[210] So, if the authorities wished to see Londoners move out to the less densely populated suburbs, towards Tottenham, Finchley and Enfield, affordable transport links had to be established. By the middle of the 1880s the omnibus, trains, underground railway and trams were beginning to allow this to happen. The fact that London was now crisscrossed by all manner of affordable and relatively fast transport also meant that at least one individual could use it to escape the net thrown out by a police force desperate to catch the most elusive serial killer the world had known to date. To see how this may have specifically helped him, we need to look at the routes the various London transport providers used – and how they interconnect with the sites of murders, the discoveries of body parts, the London meat trade, and a number of possible sightings of the killer. Let us start on the banks of the Thames, where another disturbing discovery was made in the autumn of 1888.

Three days after the death of Annie Chapman, on Tuesday 11 September, a severed arm belonging to a woman was found on the foreshore along Chelsea Reach – not far from where one of the 'Rainham' body parts had been discovered the previous year.[211] The police doctors who examined it (Neville, Bond and Hebbert), thought that it had been skilfully removed post-mortem by someone with anatomical knowledge. What would, in any other year at least, have been a sensational crime story was overshadowed by the discovery of Annie Chapman's mutilated body in Hanbury Street.

Three weeks later, on Monday 1 October 1888, as Whitechapel began to digest the horror that two women (Elizabeth Stride and Catherine Eddowes) had met premature and brutal ends in one night, Frederick Windborn returned to collect the tools he had secreted behind some boards deep in the bowels of a building site on the Victoria Embankment, which was destined to become the new headquarters of the Metropolitan Police. It was 6 a.m. and it was only just getting light. Windborn noticed that there was something lying there and lit a match to see what it was. He found a parcel wrapped in paper but 'thought no more about it' and went off to start his daily shift as a carpenter.[212] On the following day the package was still there and so, at lunchtime, he reported it to his supervisor who decided they should open it. To what must have been their horror and disgust, they discovered that inside the wrapping was the torso of a woman in an advanced state of decomposition.

How had the body got there, seemingly without anyone noticing? One theory was that the killer, under cover of darkness, had climbed an 8-foot fence or hoarding protecting the site on Cannon Row. He had then found the darkest place on the building site (the basement) to bury his trophy. The practicalities don't make this very likely and the idea was quickly dismissed. There were other more obvious ways into the site but it was also thought unlikely that the killer would have taken such brazen risks with so many eyes upon him. In the end, it was concluded that he had probably driven or pulled a cart onto the site and blended in with the workmen. Now, if this was the case, he would also have had to be familiar with the people and operations there so as not to arouse suspicion, and considerable practical difficulties would have remained.[213] The answer, in fact, probably hinges on *when* exactly the torso was placed there and it is far from clear whether Windborn and his colleagues had been accurate in their recollections. Another worker, Ernest Hodge, was adamant that the parcel had not been present on the previous Saturday (29 September) although, as author M. J. Trow notes, the possibility exists that 'he may have missed it'.[214]

An inquest was told that the torso belonged to a young woman whose lungs were generally healthy, as were her heart and other internal organs.[215] Most important of all for the eyes of the watching press and public, was the crucial fact that the torso and the arm belonged to the same victim. As there was no head to identify her, the police were unable to give this mysterious woman a name. Doctors Bond and Hebbert were inclined to believe that she had met her death around mid-August 1888 (and therefore quite close to the killing of Martha Tabram) as the wrapping for the torso included pages from the *Echo* newspaper of 24 August.

The fact that the torso was found in the new Scotland Yard building then under construction could, of course, have been a coincidence – but what if it was not? What if a serial killer was poking fun at the inability of the capital's finest detectives to capture him? It is a question worth asking and one that becomes more credible when we consider the city's geography and its associated transport connections.

A little later, an enterprising journalist achieved what the searching police had failed to do. Using a terrier dog, he unearthed a more-or-less complete human leg and arm at the site where the torso had been found. At a time when the police were under pressure to catch the Whitechapel murderer, it was a public relations disaster that an enthusiastic amateur had managed to succeed where the cream of the Metropolitan Police had failed, let alone the dawning reality that a murderer may deliberately have chosen the site of the new police headquarters to dispose of his latest victim. It seemed that the missing limbs had been buried before the appearance of the torso. Had this audacious killer rubbed the noses of the police in it, on more than one occasion, and got away without anyone noticing? In examining the left leg (the right was never discovered) medical opinion inclined towards a time of death in late August or early September but burial could, of course, have slowed decomposition somewhat, skewing their judgement; forensic science was in its infancy in the 1880s and there is plenty of room for doubt in all contemporary calculations of the time of death of murder victims.

During the investigation (and before the leg and arm were found on the Whitehall site) a small boy found another body part – this time a decomposing arm – similarly wrapped, in the gardens of the Indigent Blind School on Lambeth Road.[216] The arm had been coated in lime that was widely, and erroneously, believed to quicken decomposition. The location of the find is interesting because on 5 October 1888, *The Star* newspaper published a report of a tram passenger, travelling between Vauxhall station and London Bridge, who had been acting strangely a little more than three weeks previously. A witness, Edward Deuchar, stated that when he embarked at Vauxhall he noticed another passenger holding what appeared to be a heavy and bad-smelling brown-paper parcel. His description of the man is as follows:

> Powerfully built of Rough appearance and Shabbily dressed with a Goatee beard.[217]

The man apparently got off just after the obelisk at St George's Circus and Deuchar was sufficiently concerned to alight himself shortly afterwards to inform a policeman. Despite a search, however, the man could not be found.

The Indigent Blind School on Lambeth Road was close to St George's Circus.[218] The tram in question was likely to have been the No. 12, which ran from Tooting Junction to London Bridge, via Garrett Lane, Battersea Park and Vauxhall. It thus served two locations of interest in our investigation: Garret Lane, the site of a Harrison, Barber slaughterhouse,[219] and Battersea Park – where another gruesome discovery would later be made. The terminus of the No. 12 was London Bridge – conveniently close to the southern entry/exit of the Tower Subway, which, as we have shown, afforded easy access to both the City and the East End. Interestingly, several other routes intersected with this one at Lambeth Bridge, giving access to Charing Cross via Lambeth Palace Road, Westminster Bridge and the Victoria Embankment.

The press had dismissed the 'Lambeth arm' as the work of a hoaxer, being quick to conclude that the woman whose body parts had previously been found along Chelsea Reach and the building site on the embankment was of a different social class to victims of 'the Ripper'. Indeed, the inquest held at Westminster concluded that the torso, arms and leg belonged to 'a very fine' and 'well nourished' woman and probably not to a Whitechapel street walker.[220] The body had been partly wrapped in what seems to have been black petticoats, with the assumption being that these had belonged to the victim. Of course, this clothing proves nothing and she could have been a member of the 'unfortunate' class, perhaps just one with access to some better second-hand clothes. However, for much of the time it seems the police and press had been relatively clueless and (as is almost everyone who has attempted to 'solve' the case ever since) limited to informed speculation. Without doubt, though, the body parts found at Whitehall had been an acute embarrassment to the police and the Home Office – something the press were very quick to jump upon. Some elements of the press, at least those who had no love for the police, quickly moved to link the torso found near Whitehall with the 'Ripper' murders in the East End. *Freeman's Journal,* a Dublin paper, noted that the 'place selected for the concealment of the body was in the building which is to be the new headquarters of the detective department. It appears that almost literally the most audacious crimes can be committed under the very nose of that body.'[221] Perhaps understandably then, senior police officers attempted to separate the two crimes and dismiss the Lambeth discovery as the work of a crank or publicity seeker; akin perhaps to the writers of the numerous 'Ripper' letters. But what if the man seen on the tram was making use of London's widening transport network to dispose of the smaller body parts? Can we really dismiss only those contemporary press reports we deem to be fanciful and believe only those the police took seriously? This is one of the problems anyone trying to 'solve' the mystery has, and we are quite transparent about this in our own analysis. The only option open to anyone studying the Whitechapel and Torso murder series is to look at what is possible, plausible and probable and to reconstruct 'history' from the sources that seem credible, if not perfect.

One report the police had taken seriously, however, was that of a respectably dressed man of about 35 years of age who was seen climbing over the building site hoarding into Cannon Row at around 5.20 p.m. on the Saturday afternoon. He had then apparently quickly made off. According to the newspaper, his description was promptly circulated at the time to all stations.[222] Could this man have been the killer then and, if the press had been right in linking the two sets, could he also have been responsible for the deaths of Liz Stride and Catherine Eddowes later that night? We believe the answer to both questions is yes, quite conceivably he could. For reasons already given, however, and the fact that he didn't seem to be using any public transport at the time, it is unlikely he had taken the remains to the site on this occasion. Indeed, Dr Bond believed that the torso had been *in situ* there for about three days or so. If we are right and this was the man, he was a very long way from his usual East End hunting ground. Is it also possible then that he had an alternative operating base away from Whitechapel – a base that allowed, or even impelled him, to vary both the location of his crimes *and* his MO?

The two obvious possibilities in this context are his place of work and his residence. Regarding the former, it is worth noting that Harrison, Barber & Co. had premises in Queen Victoria Street in the City – not far from where one of the Rainham river parts was found, off Temple Pier. This was also just a stone's throw from where two body parts relating to the subsequent 'Horsleydown Torso' would be discovered in June the following year. Moreover, the newspaper used to wrap the Whitehall torso had been stained with blood that the police believed could have been of animal origin although they were unable to speculate on which type of animal it might have been, given the limits of forensic science in the late 1800s.

But what of a possible residence? Did the killer make use of accommodation in this area also? For reasons that will become clear later, we are now convinced that he did – regularly living at an address that was just a few hundred metres along the Victoria Embankment at Charing Cross. For the moment though, let us concentrate on the Whitehall Torso victim. Is it possible in this instance that the deceased woman was already hidden on the site with the killer merely re-visiting the scene at this time in order to expose the torso to view? Indeed, the buried leg found there was only unearthed by the superior senses of a dog. If the torso had also been similarly hidden it could have lain there *in situ* for some considerable time without anyone being alerted by the smell of decomposing flesh. Furthermore, given the difficulty and dangers involved in transporting a corpse or body parts to the site, is it not far more likely that the victim was actually killed and dismembered there on some quiet occasion when the site was shut?

In this context, we should also bear in mind the availability of victims right on the doorstep, as homeless men and women were known to sleep rough at night on the Victoria Embankment. This was also the case on the Chelsea Embankment, which could be a significant factor in the killing of another 'Torso' victim the following year, a woman who has subsequently been named as Elizabeth Jackson. If this was the case, the original estimated time of death would take us back to the weekend of the 4th and 5th of August. This weekend was especially significant since it was followed by a Bank Holiday. The site would have been closed, leaving the killer free to act with impunity. Indeed, the whole of that weekend, probably from late Saturday onwards, would have been ideal for his purposes. Newspaper reports tell us that this particular bank holiday was dull and rainy, with people eschewing normal outdoor pursuits in favour of visits to indoor attractions such as museums and galleries. As a refuge from the elements then, it may well have been easier than usual to encourage an unsuspecting companion into the building site.[223] We should certainly not overlook the fact either that the tools suitable for such a task, such as saws and pliers, would have been readily available. Frederick Windborn we should remember, the man that made the awful discovery of the woman's torso, was looking for his carpentry tools when he did so. In addition, subsequent weekends – either until 24 August (when the remains appear to have been partially wrapped in newspaper) or up until Tuesday

11 September (when the arm was discovered at Pimlico) – would have afforded numerous opportunities for both dismemberment and distribution.

As we have said, though, this was also the time (at around 2.30 on the Tuesday morning) that Martha Tabram had met her killer in Whitechapel. Had the murderer, while living in the Charing Cross area over the holiday weekend, killed his Whitehall victim before heading back east and striking again with Tabram – the first 'double event' of his series of killings? Likewise, Chapman was killed in the early hours of the Saturday preceding the Pimlico find. Had he then spent Friday night in Whitechapel lining up his victim before heading back to the scene of his crime in Whitehall for the weekend – the previous scenario in reverse? Indeed, the arm had been found in the river on the Tuesday and it was around this time also that the man with the parcel was spotted on the tram headed for London Bridge and the Thames Subway. Then, three weekends later, on Saturday 29 September, there was the sighting of the man on the Whitehall hoarding. Had he concluded unfinished business there again over the weekend, before returning once more to kill Elizabeth Stride in Whitechapel at the beginning of that other 'double event'? The 'respectably' dressed appearance of the suspect on this occasion certainly chimes with witness testimony in several of the subsequent attacks – not least those relating to Elizabeth Stride.

Although we can only speculate as to the killer's precise movements over the two-month period between the August bank holiday weekend and the discovery of the torso, we can perhaps see an emerging pattern here of this particular individual operating in the Whitehall area at weekends (probably for the purposes of dismemberment and body part distribution) while continuing his campaign in Whitechapel. Tabram, Chapman, Stride and Eddowes could all have been attacked either immediately prior to him leaving the area, or just as he returned. If it was a deliberate strategy designed to confuse the police then it certainly succeeded. But what had attracted him to the West End in the first place? There was no shortage of victims at home, after all. Hopefully in later chapters, we will be able to shed some light on this question, along with his apparent preference for remaining in Whitechapel during the week.

The discovery of body parts belonging to the unnamed victim at Whitehall has gone down in history as the 'Pimlico mystery', another unsolved crime in the year that a far more widely reported series of murders were taking place. The inquest jury were unable to do more than record an 'open verdict' on the remains and hope that subsequent evidence might allow a more accurate finding in the future.[224] It had now been more than three weeks since the killer had struck in Whitechapel and while the press and public continued to speculate, and the police forces of the City and the wider capital continued to look in vain for the murderer (or murderers if one chooses to believe that two serial killers were operating in London that year) the perpetrator was apparently lying low and avoiding his pursuers. His next move was perhaps his most visibly dramatic to date, however, and was to take place just hours after the sighting of the man on the Whitehall hoarding.

8

THE 'DOUBLE EVENT'

The murders of Mary Ann 'Polly' Nichols and Annie Chapman were out of the 'ordinary' in contemporary murder terms, as indeed had been that of Martha Tabram. There were many more homicides in London in 1888, some of which found their way to the Old Bailey and a trial. A number of these, and many more from across the country, made the pages of the newspapers because the Victorian reading public loved a good murder story.[225] The conspiracy of Maria and Frederick Manning had dominated the newsstands in 1849, while the Road House Murder had a similar impact in 1860. Indeed, in other years the discovery of a series of headless torsos and body parts floating around various watercourses would have dominated the news, but not in 1888. In that 'autumn of terror' even someone who chopped off the heads of his victims and threw their bodies in the Thames was not as a newsworthy as 'Jack the Ripper'. But what if they were one and the same person? What if the killer was not some semi-mythical demonic figure but an ordinary man with a deep-rooted, if misguided, hatred of street prostitutes and a compulsion to kill? If that person was able to vary his location using the various transport options available and use temporary accommodation to suit, should we not seriously consider the possibility that there was just one serial killer operating in the capital at that time rather than two? We will return to the 'Whitehall' or 'Pimlico Mystery' again, but for the moment we must concentrate on events in Whitechapel in September 1888.

Some years later, in July 1900, an unknown photographer, possibly accompanying an early 'Ripper' tour around the murder sites, took a posed photograph of Dutfield's Yard in Berner Street – modern day Henriques Street, off the Commercial Road. Among the carefully arranged subjects one stands out – a Jewish tradesman in cap and apron smiles at the camera as he stands in front of an iron gate.[226] It was there, at 1 a.m. on 30 September 1888, that Louis Diemschutz found the body of Elizabeth Stride.

Stride's throat had been cut (from left to right) but apart from evidence of some historical minor injuries there were no other signs that her body had been abused or mutilated. The carotid artery was not completely severed, and the first doctor on the scene – Dr Blackwell – judged that she would have bled out quite slowly and painfully.[227] At the post-mortem, Dr George Bagster Phillips, who had also attended at the scene, attributed death to the severing of the carotid artery and added that the murderer had probably forced her to the ground to carry out the killing. This was based entirely on the presence of bruising on her shoulders, so, and on balance, we think this unlikely. Dr Blackwell's alternative hypothesis was that the murderer had used the woman's neckerchief to pull her head back so that he could then cut her throat from the rear. This would imply that Stride had turned her back on her assailant (to facilitate quick sexual intercourse) and that the killer had taken advantage of the situation as he appears to have done previously. We believe though that she was probably 'garrotted' from behind from a standing position prior to having her throat cut when she was on the ground.

The fact that Stride's body was not mutilated has led some theorists to speculate that she was not a part of the Whitechapel murder series at all. Indeed, the Berner Street murder has provided some of the most contentious and, at the same time, fascinating discussions of the 'Ripper' series. During the 131 years since 1888, the small amount of contemporary 'evidence' has been eroded and what might be considered *official* and *unofficial* evidence has become interwoven to the extent that it is quite difficult to separate the two. This has allowed theories to develop that have very little basis in reality, such as the notion (repeated in at least two 'Ripper' films)[228] that Stride and some of the other victims were drugged, or poisoned, with grapes.

In Stride's case, one witness has assumed considerable prominence and fuelled speculation that the killer was not operating on his own. A local man named Israel Schwartz reportedly saw a man throw a woman to the ground in Berner Street at about 12.45 a.m., while a second man, seen smoking a pipe, looked on. The man rough-handling the woman seemed to shout something rather unintelligible towards Schwartz (a Jewish Hungarian immigrant with little or no English) and all he could apparently understand was the word 'Lipski!' Israel Lipski, as we mentioned earlier, was a convicted murderer who had poisoned a young pregnant Jewish woman called Miriam Angel with prussic acid two years before. This had taken place in Batty Street, which runs parallel to Berner Street. It is not exactly clear who shouted 'Lipski', however, or, indeed, who it was specifically aimed at, but Schwartz did not stick around long enough to investigate – clearly frightened, he hurried off; later giving a description of the men to the police following Stride's murder.[229] Schwartz was able to identify the woman he'd seen attacked in the street when he viewed her corpse in the mortuary.

Paul Begg suggests that while Schwartz's evidence is problematic (or at least the reporting of it is contradictory since Schwartz gave an interview to the *Star* that contains a slightly different and more sensational account) it is significant. Given that the incident Schwartz described occurred just 15 minutes before Stride's dead body was discovered, it must mean that either the man who threw the woman to the ground was the killer, or else the mysterious pipe-smoking man was.[230] But there was another witness who also claimed to have seen Stride at 12.45. James Brown, a dock labourer, reportedly saw someone he was certain was Stride talking to a man at the junction of Fairclough Street and Berner Street, while her back was turned to the Board School wall. At the inquest, he stated that this person was a 'stoutish' man, about 5 foot 7 inches tall, who was wearing a long coat that almost reached his heels.[231] Begg dismisses Brown's evidence, suggesting he probably saw a courting couple. In his book *By Ears and Eyes*, Karyo Magellan is less sure we should believe Schwartz, however. Such is the nature of Ripperology! Quite simply, whom do we believe and what evidence is credible?

Schwartz described the man he saw as being about 30 years old, 5 foot 5 inches tall, with a small brown moustache, dark hair and a fair complexion. He also noted that he was 'broad-shouldered', wearing a dark jacket and trousers, along with a 'peaked' black cap. Berner Street was, according to Louis Diemschutz's evidence, very dark at that time. This is quite likely; there was little or no moon that night as it was waning with only 29–39 per cent of its crescent revealed. It was 1 o'clock in the morning and there was little in the way of street lighting to illuminate matters.[232] Another witness, William Marshall, also saw a strange man that night with Stride. This was about an hour earlier, opposite his house at 64 Berner Street, which was between Christian Street and Boyd Street. The man kissed Stride and said (in a mild, English accent) 'You would say anything but your prayers,' before they moved off together in the direction of Ellen Street. At Stride's inquest, Marshall described the man as being about 5 foot 6 inches tall, and said he was wearing a small black coat, dark trousers and a cap. He also said the man was of stout build and 'decently dressed'. Again, identification was difficult due to the darkness of the street at the time but he said the man had 'the appearance of a clerk'.[233]

PC Smith (252 H) also testified that he had noticed a woman, whom he later identified as Stride. She was seen talking to a man at 12.35 in the street directly opposite Dutfield's Yard. Smith described him as 28 years of age, 5 foot 7 inches, wearing dark clothing and a similarly dark deerstalker hat. The cop thought the man was clean-shaven and recollected that Stride wore a red flower in her jacket and that the man had a parcel, 18 inches by 6–8 inches, wrapped in newspaper, in his hand.[234] So either PC Smith had little trouble making a more accurate description, despite the dimly lit environment, or he was following procedure that required him to take more account of suspicious people he saw in the street, or he was embroidering his evidence. [235]

While all of the descriptions appear to give the potential attacker a similar height (between 5 foot 5 inches and 5 foot 7 inches), enough discrepancies exist for us to question whether the person being described was, in fact, the same man. A simple experiment we conduct with undergraduates demonstrates the problem with witness statements. Asking one individual to stand up, we then get the others to give his height and any other distinguishing features. Even in a well-lit room and with someone familiar, they invariably offer differing descriptions and make mistakes in key facts, such as height, weight and age. Modern criminology has also suggested that witnesses can be influenced by the nature of questions asked of them and how they are phrased.[236] This suggests that we need to treat contemporary fleeting glances in darkly lit streets with some caution.

Even so, it is striking in this case how many general similarities there seem to be. In addition to the similar heights, three of the witnesses stated that the person they saw was of stout build. Furthermore, all of them seem to indicate that he wore dark, respectable clothing, which afforded him something of a 'clerkly' appearance. They also credit him with wearing a dark hat of some description, although this seemed to resemble anything from a billycock type through to a deerstalker or peaked cap.

Two labourers, who had earlier observed Stride with a man, close-up and in pretty good light, gave similar descriptions. According to the testimony given to a newspaper, they had been going in to the Bricklayer's Arms in nearby Settle Street at around 11 p.m., when they encountered the pair as they were just leaving. Apparently the labourers were quite taken aback by the way the man was 'going on' at a known prostitute, given his respectable dress, and some 'banter' had evidently ensued as the couple sheltered momentarily from the rain. They noted the flower pinned to Stride's dress that Constable Smith also noticed later, and they described the man as being 5 foot 5 inches tall with a black moustache and sandy-coloured eyelashes, wearing a morning suit and billycock hat. According to them, he was 'definitely English'. Had the man's dress been out of kilter with his true social class? Indeed, we should not forget that the person seen jumping over the building site hoarding in the case of the Whitehall Torso a few hours earlier had similarly been 'respectfully dressed' – as was, interestingly, the 'good doctor' PC Spicer had encountered in Heneage Street at the start of our story. The pair had then wandered off in the direction of Commercial Road and the subsequent crime scene in Berner Street. We should note that Settle Street lies in between Berner Street and Heneage Street in the very heart of Jack's 'hot zone'.

Israel Schwartz has remained centre stage in discussions of the case, even though he did not give evidence at the inquest into Stride's murder. Chief Inspector Donald Swanson's memoirs suggested that Schwartz may have held the key to the mystery, having supposedly identified a local Jew, Aaron Kosminski, as the suspect alluded to in his memoirs by his friend and superior Robert Anderson.[237] Kosminski was also among the list of suspects of another officer, Sir Melville Mcnaghten, who wrote a report on the murders in the 1890s. According to Inspector Swanson, it had been Schwartz's refusal to testify against a supposed fellow Jew that had prevented Kosminski from being put before a jury. But, if Schwartz's evidence *was* unreliable in certain areas, which it appears it may have been, then the case against Kosminski is seriously undermined.[238] Indeed, there is also some conjecture as to whether or not it was actually Schwartz who made the identification as opposed to Joseph Lawende, the witness in the Eddowes case.[239] Is it possible then that the killer might just have been a gentile Englishman after all? As with so much of the

'Ripper' case and the search for its solution, the more one delves into it, the more complicated and obfuscated it can become.

The death of Elizabeth ('Long Liz') Stride was met with horror, as those gathered at the Berner Street International Working Men's Educational Club began to take in the awful reality of what had happened on their doorstep. At first, when his pony had shied at something resting by the gates of the yard, Louis Diemschutz, the steward of the club, could not see what had disturbed it, so he got down from his cart to investigate. It was only when he struck a match that he could see for sure that a woman was lying there. He thought it was just a drunken woman, maybe even his wife. He rushed into the club to find his wife and fetch help. As he and another club member returned with more light they could now see blood and when Mrs Diemschutz saw the woman's face, which 'looked ghastly', she screamed. That resulted in many more of the assembled members hurrying out into the yard.[240]

Morris Eagle went to fetch a policeman, and PC Lamb and two others followed him back to Berner Street. The murder scene rapidly became crowded with police, witnesses and onlookers, and the constables did their best to hold them back while a doctor and detectives were sent for from Leman Street. While the doctors (Blackwell and Johnson, his assistant) were examining the body, PC Lamb made a 'cursory investigation of the club premises' and the nearby houses in Berner Street. In his book, *The Complete History of Jack the Ripper,* Philip Sugden credits Lamb for acting properly but suggests that most of this was simply either perfunctory or carried out to reassure the locals.[241] Nothing was found that might indicate who had carried out the killing and yet again it seemed as if the murderer had slipped away without anyone noticing him.

Many seem to believe that the Berner Street killing holds the key to solving the 'Ripper' murders perhaps because of the seemingly detailed sightings of Stride with the same man, or perhaps, different men, in the hours before she died. The problem is though that the more one reads the evidence the more contradictory and confusing it can appear. Schwartz and Brown cannot both have been correct in seeing a man and a woman at 12.45 and there was a further witness, Mrs Fanny Mortimer, who told a news reporter that she had heard a policeman pass along Berner Street at that time. She also saw someone else, a young man who was later eliminated from the inquiry.[242] Neither she nor the man (Leon Goldstein) saw or heard anything else until Mrs Mortimer first heard the rumble of Diemschutz's cart and the furore caused by the discovery of Stride's dead body. It seems unusual that she (or the police constable) would have failed to hear the altercation between Schwartz, the mysterious man (or men) and Stride, so either Schwartz had invented it, or his timings were out. Regardless, it throws serious doubt on the thesis that the killer was a Jew such as Aaron Kosminski if the main reason for believing it is the evidence provided by Schwartz. Whatever the case, we cannot ignore the fact that the physical description of the assailant provided by Schwartz correlates closely in many respects with credible witness testimony regarding the suspect in a previous assault – that on Ada Wilson. And what if Schwartz's timing *was* out and James Brown's had been correct? If it was a minute or two later that Schwartz turned into Berner Street and followed the man down towards Dutfield's Yard, perhaps things could be explained a little differently. Could it have been the case that when Marshall first saw the pair, they were heading to the dark and secluded arches of Pinchin Street for sex? It was after all a spot that was notorious for soliciting at the time. On their arrival however, had the killer tried to persuade Stride to do something she didn't want to do – or go somewhere she didn't want to go? If we imagine for the moment that Stride had refused to comply with such a request – were Smith and Brown witnesses to the killer's attempt to make her reconsider when they saw them further back up the road?

If reconciliation had proved impossible they could have parted company and crossed over the road, leaving Stride waiting outside the club (perhaps perceiving it to be safer if she had aroused his wrath) and him heading up towards Commercial Road. Had his anger at being rebuffed got the better of him, though? Determined not to have his intentions frustrated, perhaps, had he then turned around and headed back towards Stride – at the very moment Schwartz turned the corner into Berner Street? Indeed, Schwartz seems to imply that a fairly instantaneous, unprovoked attack then took place, without any argument between them. Was this because everything had already been said previously, the killer now merely returning to carry out his original intention of killing and mutilating his victim irrespective of the circumstances? The location was, after all, a very poor choice for a murder site and a certain degree of impulsiveness may well have influenced his decision to attack there. Indeed, apart from one aspect perhaps, it very much appears to have been something of a 'Plan B' and not a course of action he would originally have contemplated – a notion that we will return to later. Having cut her throat, however, he would be frustrated yet again by the arrival of Diemschutz and his vehicle. The killer was, therefore, subsequently forced to search elsewhere in order to accomplish the original objective of his night's work – the torture and murder of a woman and the harvesting of her organs.

At half past twelve on the following night (Monday 1 October 1888) a knife was discovered on the steps of a laundry at 253 Whitechapel Road. It had been found by a passer-by, Thomas Coram, a few metres east of Court Street, close by the London Hospital. The knife was heavily blood stained and flat-topped, with a 12 inch blade and a 6 inch handle, and was wrapped in a handkerchief which, not surprisingly, was also stained with blood. Constable Smith had, of course, mentioned a parcel of similar dimensions in the suspect's hand when he had seen them opposite the club the previous evening. Doctors at the post-mortem believed this type of knife could well have been used during Stride's murder. The timing and location of the discovery could also be significant.

Court Street is a cut-through that runs between Whitechapel Road and Winthrop Street – a thoroughfare that would have been well known to the killer, given its proximity to the site of Polly Nichols' murder in Bucks Row. Furthermore, the streets around the London Hospital opposite were also where further evidence would be discovered in a subsequent killing. A year later a note prophesying a resumption of the murders was found there, just a week before the discovery of a torso in Pinchin Street. The killer, it seems, knew this area well. For the moment though, let us consider what we know so far.

It is generally believed that most murder victims know their killers and this is usually what leads the police to make arrests. With serial killers, however, the situation is quite different. Men like Stephen Wright (the 'Suffolk Ripper') and Peter Sutcliffe (the 'Yorkshire Ripper') picked on strangers, making it hard for the police to find connections between them. Both acted on opportunity and both usually chose prostitutes (or women they thought were prostitutes) because they would be likely to be on the streets at night, less wary of the intentions of a single man and could be easily directed into a vulnerable position. We might add that they were also less likely to be missed but this perhaps presents an inaccurate and stereotypical view of sex workers; Tabram, Nichols, and Chapman all had friends and some family, and their deaths touched a wider community than perhaps even they would have suspected.

Liz Stride was no different. She was nearly 45 when she died and had already had an eventful and traumatic life. Liz was an immigrant to London, arriving from Sweden in 1866 to work as a servant. Before that, the records show she had been a prostitute and had at some point been treated for a sexually transmitted disease. Was this syphilis? If so, it was something contemporary medicine could not cure, only the symptoms of it could be treated. One possible connection between all the women murdered from 1887 to 1891 was that, at some points in their lives, they reportedly sold sex and so potentially carried a debilitating disease; a disease that a husband might inadvertently pass on to his wife and subsequently to any of their children.

Liz had married a carpenter named John Thomas Stride in 1869, and two years later the couple were living in Poplar, where they had established a coffee house. Over the next decade or so, it all seems to have gone wrong for Liz. She drank too much, as far as her husband and his family were concerned, and this soured their relationship. Stride appears to have been something of a fantasist, inventing numerous children and even at one time claiming her husband, who was very much alive, had died in the *Princess Alice* disaster on the Thames in 1878.[243] In 1881 she was admitted to the Whitechapel workhouse infirmary, suffering with bronchitis. In July 1884, her husband John died of a heart condition. In the intervening years it seems that Liz had several brushes with the law, appearing at Thames Magistrates Court on a number of occasions for drunkenness and soliciting. Her behaviour irritated Michael Kidney, the man she had taken up with following her husband's death, and this led him to assault her on a number of occasions, seriously enough in one instance for her to lay charges against him. By the time of her death, Liz was lodging in Flower and Dean Street, at Number 32, and her usual 'beat' was Commercial Road, so she would have been familiar with Berner Street and Dutfield's Yard.[244]

On the night she was killed she probably spoke to several men, soliciting business and perhaps turning some down. It would make sense if, during the heightened tension of the murders, some of the street girls were at least a little discerning or careful about whom they took down a dark alley or into a quiet corner. Alcohol might well have limited their ability to react, or have impaired their judgment, but it is plausible to suggest that the man who killed Liz Stride did not seem threatening, at least to her. He was not an immigrant Jew or a top-hatted gent, or indeed a doctor with a Gladstone bag. Instead he was someone she had possibly met before, or knew from the local area – perhaps even done 'business' with. He would have been on the lookout for victims who would not make a fuss and be pliant, but he was particularly looking for those he suspected of giving the dread disease he carried so they had to be women he had already slept with or at least women he could be reasonably sure were, like himself, syphilitic.

The fact that Liz Stride was not mutilated has led some to argue that she was not a 'Ripper' victim at all, but that is to misunderstand the killer and the particular circumstances surrounding her murder. This killer's MO was adaptable to whatever the situation was in which he found himself. Given the chance, he enjoyed the time to cut up his victims; the act of killing itself was in some respects simply a means to an end. When he had killed, he then wanted to open up the corpse and attack those parts he associated with womanhood. However, in the case of Stride, the location was poorly chosen and the arrival of Diemschutz's pony and cart necessitated a quick getaway. The killer, however, as on a previous occasion, had unfinished business and that is why he now made his way west to see what new opportunities might present themselves. This was a calculating killer who was confident in his ability to evade the police. While the area around the Commercial Road was in uproar and policeman rushed in and out of Leman Street Police Station, he would, we believe, have calmly walked away and gone down in the direction of the Pinchin Street arches. His most likely route from Berner Street to the night's second atrocity would be highly significant for two future events, so let us consider his possible movements for a moment. One way would have taken him south, down Phillip Street, before turning right into Pinchin Street (where another headless female torso would be discovered just less than a year later) and eventually coming out at the lower end of Backchurch Lane. At this point, however, rather than heading fairly conspicuously west along Cable Street, the killer could have made use of a tunnel, which still partly exists. It was situated close to the premises of a local cart and barrow manufacturer named Arthur Dutfield, after whom the yard in nearby Berner Street had been named. This passageway ran parallel with Cable Street, underneath the main railway lines. In 1888, the tunnel ran all the way through to the Brown Bear public house at the southern end of Leman Street. If, as seems likely, he had then continued to the City via Chamber Street, this route would have taken him past yet another future murder site at Swallow Gardens – the location of Frances Coles' killing in February 1891. What's more, the pub itself would have offered a strategic view both of potential victims and the murder site approaches, including the movements of beat officers from Leman Street Police Station further up the road. Alternatively, he could have followed Back Church Lane all the way down to Hooper Street, where he may have been able to cross the railway tracks and continue his journey via Leman Street, Great Prescott Street and The Minories. Great Prescott Street was home to a local synagogue – as well as to the Whitechapel County Courts, an establishment the killer may well have been familiar with. The Minories was where Frances Coles had once worked. Hooper Street itself is also significant, being the location where possible evidence relating to the Pinchin Street Torso case was subsequently found in 1889. Whichever route he chose to take that night, it would seem to be yet more evidence of the killer's familiarity with a number of sites of significance related to future killings.

Meanwhile, on the night of the 'double event', Catherine Eddowes had been sleeping off the consequences of an evening of heavy drinking in a cell at Bishopsgate Police Station in the City. By some accounts she had crossed the river to Lambeth to try to borrow money from her daughter. At 8.30 p.m. she had been arrested for being drunk and incapable by a City policeman. In 1888, as today, the City of London had its own, separate, police force, with its own, jealously guarded jurisdictions. Up until 30 September 1888, the City of London police had not been actively involved with the Whitechapel murders – but that was about to change. Eddowes should have been kept in overnight and presented to the magistrate at either the Guildhall or Mansion House Police Courts in the morning for him to determine whether or not to fine or admonish her for her drunken behaviour the night before. In reality, of course, that all involved quite a bit of police time and paperwork and to what end? The 'beak' would likely tell her off, or issue a fine she would struggle to pay. The desk sergeant, James Byfield, probably thought he was doing himself, her, and society, a favour by letting her go with a ticking off at 12.55. She hurried into Bishopsgate Street with a 'Good night, old cock' and turned left – and not therefore in the direction of her lodgings at Flower and Dean Street.[245]

By all accounts Eddowes had had an unusual few days. She had been away picking hops in Kent, something many East Enders did, both as a way to earn money and to enjoy a bit of a holiday from the crowded capital. However, she and her partner John Kelly had returned on 27 September with no money and so had to sleep in the casual ward of Shoe Lane workhouse in the City of London. In fact Kelly later told the inquest into Eddowes' murder that his partner had been to see her daughter in Bermondsey 'so that I shouldn't see her walk about the streets at night'. Asked to clarify what he meant – and clearly this was meant to infer that Eddowes was a 'street walker' (i.e. a prostitute) – Kelly did so. He explained that if they had no money to pay for a bed at night, 'we would have to walk about all night.'[246] So she'd been to see her daughter to get money, if she could. The next day Kelly had earned some money and told Eddowes to secure herself a room but she had apparently told him to get himself a bed instead while she headed for the Mile End casual ward.[247]

Following her arrival, a rather curious conversation was reported. Apparently, Eddowes told the ward superintendent that she had come back from Kent because she knew whom the Whitechapel murderer was, and that she was intent on claiming a reward. It is hard to verify this statement and even harder to know what Eddowes could have meant by it. She and Kelly were definitely hard-up, though, as the very next day she took his boots to pawn them. The couple were living hand-to-mouth, which makes a mockery of recent suggestions that Eddowes was in possession of an exquisite silk shawl that was later found on her murdered body. Such an item would have generated the pair sufficient funds for several nights at a lodging house and plenty to eat and drink.[248] Had she really known who the killer was, though, or did she suspect someone in particular? Given that she lived in and around Spitalfields and Whitechapel, and occasionally prostituted herself when the money ran out, it is very likely that she would have met her killer at some stage. However, it could all merely have been bravado, with Eddowes believing she was just as capable as any other local in figuring out the killer's identity.

Whatever the case, she gave Sergeant Byfield a false name on her discharge from Bishopsgate station in the early hours of the morning and thus threw future researchers another curve ball. The name she gave – Mary Ann Kelly – has fascinated conspiracy theorists ever since. It is of course, very close to the name of the youngest and most brutally murdered women in the Whitechapel series. But, then again, why not give the police a false name? By giving the surname of her current partner, John Kelly, she had used a plausible lie. It is likely that Eddowes was simply trying to avoid any repercussions from her night in the cells in the form of future fines or worse if she came before the magistracy. Most of those arrested and produced before London's Police Court magistrates tried to bluff their way out and conceal their real identity. Previous convictions could blight an individual's life, leading as they did, to increased punishments and longer (and longer) spells in prison. Most gave a false name to the police or magistrate and tried not to get 'nicked' in the same police court area too frequently.

Why did Eddowes not go 'home' or try to find Kelly? The most obvious answer perhaps is that he would probably have been angry to hear that she had been arrested and may well have been worried about her absence. She was flat broke too, so returning to their lodgings without any money and smelling of drink might well have 'earned' her the beating she told Sergeant Byfield she expected. Perhaps Eddowes chose to clear her head, then keep an eye out for one or two punters, which would mean she could at least head home with some money in her pockets. In any event, about a half-hour after her release, Eddowes was seen talking with a man by the entrance to Church Passage, a narrow pathway that leads into Mitre Square; seemingly she had her hand on his chest.[249] The men who saw her did not take that much notice, probably because they disapproved of what they thought they saw – a negotiation between a prostitute and her client for sex. One of the trio, Joseph Lawende, later identified the woman he saw as Eddowes by the clothes she was wearing and described the man with her as aged 30, 5 foot 7 inches tall, with fair skin and a moustache[250] – again, a description not dissimilar to many other accounts. Lawende added, however, that he would be unlikely to recognise the man again (which may simply have indicated that he did not wish to get drawn into the inquiry) while the other men, Joseph Hyam Levy and Harry Harries, claimed not to have seen enough to be of use to the police. By now locals were probably dividing into those who welcomed a chance to get their names in the papers as witnesses and those that avoided all opportunities for the sort of fame that probably meant a dozen journalists would be door-stopping you at every moment of the day.

After the three men left Church Passage a City of London policeman, PC Harvey, passed the top of Mitre Square but saw or heard nothing out of the ordinary.[251] Five minutes later PC Watkins' beat took him into the square, where he soon found Eddowes' dead body lying at the southern corner near to the Mitre Street entrance. Given the timing, it is almost certain that the man Lawende had seen talking to Catherine was her killer. Regardless of whether this was the case, however, PC Watkins was about to witness one of the most disturbing things of his entire police career.

Today Mitre Square is no longer an atmospheric cobbled space and the walled flowerbed and wooden bench that used to serve as a marker to where Eddowes' body was found has gone. A massive new development has been constructed that has altered the geography of the square forever. It might be appropriate for the City authorities, or the new owners, to take this opportunity to erect some small monument to Eddowes and the other victims of the Whitechapel murderer but, sadly, this is unlikely to happen. There seems to be little appetite to commemorate the victims; outside what was Dorset Street there is a Spitalfields heritage way-finder blade, which fails to mention the murders at all.

In 1888, Mitre Square was very different; four large warehouses, including one owned by Kearley & Tonge (a grocery firm), dominated it.[252] They had employed an ex-policeman, George Morris, as a night watchman and when PC Watkins made his discovery in front of Heydermann & Co.'s yard, he had rushed across to ask for Morris' help. When Morris asked him what the problem was, Watkins replied: 'Oh dear, there's been another woman cut up to pieces!' There were three lamps in the square (at the entrance from Mitre Street, outside the Kearley & Tonge warehouse, and at the square end of Church Passage) but Eddowes was laid out in the only unlit corner.[253]

It was the ideal spot for a sexual encounter and a murder. Not all the buildings were commercial and even within those that were, there were people living or working that night. With George Morris there was George Clapp, who worked as a caretaker for Heydermann's, and a City policeman (not on duty that night) PC Pearce. No one heard or saw anything unusual. Given the sightings recorded, and the pattern of PC Watkins' beat, it becomes evident that Eddowes' killer struck sometime between 1.35 and 1.45 a.m. – and the damage he caused to her body in that short time was considerable. If he had been unable to complete his work in Berner Street then he more than made up for it in Mitre Square.

While Morris guarded the body, PC Watkins went for help. In line with contemporary police procedure, the first medical man to arrive was Dr Sequira who lived on Jewry Street, just south of Aldgate High Street, and therefore the nearest to the scene of crime.[254] However, the first police examination was carried out by the divisional police surgeon, Dr Frederick Brown, who was attached to the City police. Eddowes lay on her back with her arms by her side, palms upwards. Her left leg was straight but her right was angled at the knee. After an initial examination had been made, Eddowes' corpse was transferred to the Golden Lane mortuary in the City of London for a more detailed post-mortem. Yet again, her throat had suffered a deep cut, from left to right, and her carotid artery had been severed, ensuring death. On this occasion, there were no apparent signs of suffocation and the surgeon believed that the killing blow had been dealt when she was on the ground.[255] There was no sign of any struggle either, so the attack must have been delivered with some speed.

The mortuary photographs of Catherine Eddowes after her post-mortem show the line of the cuts made to her abdomen and the extent of the other mutilations to her face – which represented a further escalation of violence – even after her body had been stitched back together.[256] In fictionalised interpretations of the 'Royal Conspiracy' theory, this is explained by the killer believing he had finally caught up with Mary Kelly, the intended target of the Crown and State's fury.

Stephen Knight proposed the idea of a 'Royal Conspiracy' in his 1976 book, *Jack the Ripper: The Final Solution* (London, Grafton Books, 1976). According to Knight (and a related BBC TV drama) Prince Albert Victor Christian Edward, or plain 'Eddy' to his friends, Queen Victoria's grandson and heir to the throne, began a relationship with a working class girl named Annie Crook. The couple had been introduced by Walter Sickert (himself later to be tagged as a 'Ripper' suspect) and Annie was probably a prostitute. Allegedly, Annie fell pregnant by Eddy and the pair married in secret. This posed a serious problem for the Queen and the government as Annie was both commoner and a Catholic, both of which effectively debarred her and the prince from the throne. Lord Salisbury, as Prime Minister, ordered Annie and her child to be taken away and be committed to an asylum out of sight but the couple got wind of this and the child, Alice Margaret, was spirited away by Sickert who arranged for a nanny to care for her. This nanny was Mary Kelly. Kelly struggled to live with the knowledge she carried, however, and eventually she gave in to alcoholism and ended up on the streets of Whitechapel as a common prostitute. Very soon she was telling anyone that would listen about her awful secret. This is when the conspiracy really gains legs as Mary had three friends on the street – Polly Nichols, Elizabeth Stride and Annie Chapman – and they realised how valuable this information might be and set out to blackmail the government. Salisbury acted fast and employed Sir William Gull, the Queen's personal physician, and a cab driver, Netley, to track down the women and remove the problem they posed. The murder of Kate Eddowes (who gave the name Kelly when she was arrested) was a mistake, but the other killings were a deliberate government plot to wipe out all knowledge of Eddy's indiscretion. Finally, since Gull, Salisbury and the head of the Met, Sir Charles Warren, were all high-ranking Freemasons it was a simple thing to cover the whole sordid business up and place the crime at the door of an innocent but convenient stooge, Montague Druitt, whose dead body was dragged from the Thames some weeks after Kelly was murdered in Dorset Street.

But what if there is another more plausible explanation? Eddowes had suggested she knew who the killer was and perhaps she had piqued his anger in particular? He cut off the tip of her nose, cut deeply into the face and sliced through her right ear. Significantly, he cut symmetrically and almost identically into both eyelids – a reference that he knew she had 'seen' him perhaps – or otherwise knew his identity? This could also perhaps be indicative of another type of behaviour the killer was wont to indulge in when he had more time and privacy. We will return to this aspect a little later.

Nevertheless, this killer knew the location well and understood exactly how much time he had to play with on this occasion – possibly less than 10 minutes. Eddowes 'was ripped up like a pig in the market,' PC Watkins told a *Star* reporter, 'a more dreadful sight I never saw; it quite knocked me over.'[257] As well as attacking the face the killer cut open her abdomen from the 'breast bones to the pubes'. Working upwards he then lifted out her intestines and draped them over her right shoulder, just as he had with Chapman's; one small section was placed between her left arm and her body, 'apparently by design', according to Dr Brown. The killer had stabbed and cut at the liver and had removed the left kidney entirely. He had also taken the uterus and Brown, as with

Dr Philips in Chapman's case, surmised that the killer must have possessed 'a good deal of [medical] knowledge'. However, he also agreed that the killer could have been someone who was 'in the habit of cutting up animals'.[258]

If the killing had taken place in the twenty-first century, then the killer made one potentially fatal mistake – in cutting off a small piece of Catherine's apron with which, it has been suggested, he wiped his hands, he would have given the police several clues to his identity. In 1888 though, he had been lucky, the only 'clue' the police were able to garner was the apparent direction of his escape from Mitre Square, as they had no understanding of forensics that equates to anything in existence today. But that one apparent slip by the killer, if indeed it was a slip, is significant because the piece of apron, which was later found in Goulston Street (alongside another clue – the 'writing on the wall') has divided researchers ever since. The murderer, having gorged himself on the borders of the City of London, now headed back into the 'abyss' and more familiar territory.

In killing on the Metropolitan Police's patch and then again within the City of London's jurisdiction, the murderer had demonstrated both arrogance and cunning. There were now two rival forces hunting for him, separate organisations jealously guarding their own 'turf', with communication between them sluggish at best. By adopting this strategy, he could be sure that any pursuers would be reluctant to follow a lead over the 'border', while also being confident that news of Berner Street would take time to reach the City. Although the killer was taking a calculated risk, at the same time he was increasing the thrill factor – he now had most of the capital's finest detectives completely baffled as they hunted a killer who had disappeared from under their very noses and made good his escape into the night.

His precise movements subsequently, however, are perhaps harder to determine than the location of the 'evidence' would at first seem to suggest. At 2.55 a.m. PC Long noticed something lying near the entrance to 108–119 Wentworth Dwellings as he followed his beat along Goulston Street. He was sure it had not been there earlier when he had made his rounds at 2.20.[259] Nor was it seen by Detective Constable Halse, who was part of the squad of men hunting for the killer of Catherine Eddowes and who had also passed by around the same time. What PC Long found was a segment of bloodied cloth and, above it in the doorway, some crude writing in chalk. When it was established that the cloth matched the apron worn by Catherine Eddowes, this appeared to offer a very real clue as to the killer's subsequent movements. He must, it seems, have left Mitre Square and made his way back east, discarding the cloth in Goulston Street on the way. This would certainly make sense if the murderer was a local man familiar with the geography of Whitechapel and its interlinking series of courts, alleys and streets. What about the chalked writing on the wall though? This is a question that has bemused and fascinated researchers for more than 100 years and there is no real consensus as to what it meant, or who could have penned it. The words said either:

The Juwes are The men That Will not be Blamed for nothing.

Or:

The Juwes are not The men that Will be Blamed for nothing.

Juwes may be a misspelling of 'Jews' (or Jewes, which some mistakenly believed to be the Yiddish spelling) or it could be a French rendering of Jews ('Juives') that the constable wrote down incorrectly.[260] Alternatively 'Juwes' was used deliberately to indicate a sinister connection to Freemasonry. It can never categorically be established what the writing said because while two policemen wrote it down, it was washed off the wall without being photographed, another example of how contemporary police practice failed to preserve evidence. It was erased on the direct orders of the Metropolitan Police Commissioner,

Sir Charles Warren, who was understandably worried about local reaction to the discovery of the graffito. Warren was backing up his man on the ground, Superintendent Arnold, who had the sponge ready when Warren arrived.[261] The City Police objected to the destruction of evidence but Goulston Street was not in their territory so it wasn't their decision to make.[262] Wentworth Dwellings was almost entirely occupied by Jewish immigrants and it might well have inflamed an already volatile situation if evidence had pointed the finger of blame for the killings at the Jewish community. After all, the uproar surrounding 'Leather Apron' had already caused enough trouble for the police. But Warren could have secured the street and had the offending writing photographed before rubbing it off, and discussion of the graffito soon reached the press anyway, so Warren's attempt to calm the situation merely led to later suggestions that this was all part of a Masonic cover-up.[263]

If it is unclear what exactly the writing said, then there is just as much speculation as to who wrote it. The assumption was, at first at least, that the killer had stopped to leave a message to his pursuers. The fact that a definite piece of evidence (the segment of apron) was found next to the graffito certainly suggests a connection between the two. If the writing is to be interpreted as a denial that the Jewish community was involved (as Paul Begg suggests it might be read)[264] then does that indicate that the killer was (or indeed was not) Jewish? When this is placed alongside Israel Schwartz's evidence of the men he saw in Berner Street and the use of the word 'Lipski' this adds momentum to an argument that points the blame at someone like Aaron Kosminski. However, just as we should be cautious of giving too much weight to Schwartz's testimony over Brown's, especially with regard to his timings, we should be equally wary of reading too much into the Goulston Street graffito. What if, as Sugden argues, the police believed the writing was actually meant to indicate that the Jews *were* responsible and that it had been written to throw the police off the scent of the real killer?[265]

If the killer was a gentile, as Gary Rowlands has argued,[266] then as a member of the indigenous British population of Whitechapel, perhaps it would have been in his interests to perpetuate the myth that the murderer was a crazed Jew such as John Pizer. Many of the local people, especially the women (and several of the victims) worked for Jewish families from time to time. Jews needed gentiles to light their fires on the evening of the Sabbath and during their religious holidays, and many women took in washing or cleaned for Jews in their dwellings or local businesses. Nor were Jewish men averse to using local women for sex and it is easy to see how a prejudiced mind might associate his own sufferings with the influx of strangers with different traditions. The Goulston Street graffito could be the biggest 'red herring' of the whole 'Ripper' case – but at the same time it could well help in ruling out the hand of Kosminski or any other local Jewish suspect.

Of course, there is also the possibility that the killer did not write anything on the wall in Goulston Street. As Walter Dew (who was part of the detective team chasing the killer in 1888) later noted, why would the murderer risk capture penning a few lines on a darkened doorway?[267] Then again, if the words were intended to be anti-Semitic and had been there *before* the apron was left, why had they not been wiped off by one of the many Jewish residents? Perhaps the most interesting question of all, however, is this: if the killer did write these words some time between 20 minutes to 2 a.m. (when both DC Halse and PC Long reported seeing nothing at the doorway) and just before 3 (when Long found both the writing and the bloodied cloth) – where had he been between roughly 1.40 and 2.55 – a possible gap of 1 hour and 15 minutes? Can we, in fact, be sure that he had written the words and deposited the cloth immediately after his departure from the square while heading into the heart of Spitalfields?

It is about a 3-minute walk from Mitre Square to Goulston Street today, and one that involves crossing two busy roads and negotiating the crowded pavements. In the early hours of the morning of 30 September 1888, the killer could conceivably have made it in not much more than 2 minutes – especially if he was running part of the way, which would seem likely. He would have been aware that the police were looking for him and that H Division had been reinforced with extra men from across the capital.[268] He may have secreted himself around Mitre Square or in Wentworth Dwellings – or perhaps he had holed up in one of the characteristic alleyways or dosshouses nearby before leaving his mark? Or perhaps he ventured further afield before deciding to double back?

Intriguingly, the acting Commissioner of the City police, Major Henry Smith, claimed to have been close on the trail of the killer shortly after he'd killed Kate Eddowes. He believed he was only 5 minutes behind him when he happened upon a bloodied water trough, in a close off Dorset Street, in which he presumed the killer must have washed his hands.[269] Dorset Street would be the scene of Mary Kelly's demise just over a month later and it was also the logical route between Mitre Square/Goulston Street and Heneage Court, which was the location of PC Spicer's 'strange encounter' with the 'good doctor' at around 1.45 that morning.

Given that it is possible to jog between Mitre Square and Heneage Court in approximately 5 minutes, is it possible that Eddowes' killer and the 'good doctor' could have been the same person? If the killer had departed Mitre Square in full flight around 1.40, then certainly it would just be possible. If, however, one accepts a degree of latitude for the chronology of events, which Morley's later timing of 3 o'clock suggests, then the proposition becomes even more feasible.

Indeed, if Acting Commissioner Smith's suspicions regarding the water trough were correct, such ablutions could well have accounted for the bloodstained shirt cuffs noted by PC Spicer on the suspect he arrested. Furthermore, the Heneage Court encounter offers up another possibility for consideration: If Eddowes' killer had utilised the piece of apron to wrap the victim's kidney and uterus in for transportation purposes rather than merely to wipe his hands, as has been suggested, is it possible these could have been in the 'good doctor's' bag all along?[270] The constable, after all, was most indignant that it had not been searched at the station – perhaps rightly so. On release from police custody at Commercial Street, 'the doctor' could have gone home, discarded the kidney and changed, only to return to Goulston Street with his alibi secure. By implicating the Jews with the inscription and the planted evidence, he could deflect any lingering suspicion from his detention that night. Such behaviour would also be consistent with the killer's apparent penchant for 'game-playing', which had already been in evidence with his torment of the police over the Whitehall Torso and which would come to the fore again at Pinchin Street. The timeframe of events would seem to allow for such a scenario and such a hypothesis would certainly help explain the gap between the murder and the later appearance of the evidence. Again, we should not overlook here the prior association with murder sites that this possible sequence of events would represent in respect of the next murder in the series, that of Mary Kelly who would be found horrifically mutilated very close to the bloodied water trough in Dorset Street a little over a month later.

Before leaving Goulston Street, however, we should reflect on the appearance of the graffito there a little longer as it may be indicative of a wider agenda on the part of the killer. On other occasions he had carefully chosen quiet locations for his purposes, yet in Stride's case he had attacked right next to a busy club with people coming and going in the street outside – an unlikely choice for a murder. Were there other factors at play here? Indeed, had the fact that it was a Jewish club figured in the killer's thinking that night? Could it be that having realised the inferences that could be drawn from the location of Stride's demise, he sought to perpetuate the theme with his subsequent actions? Certainly, the choice of Mitre Square would be consistent with such a strategy, flanked as it was by the Great Synagogue, with another, Bevis Marks, located just next door. Another large Jewish club, The Imperial (from which the witness Lawende and his friends had departed) also stood just over the road. This area, in fact, was at the heart of London's Jewish community with the very first synagogue in England having opened in adjacent Creechurch Lane in 1657, following the Jews' readmission under Oliver Cromwell in the 1650s. Taken together with the anti-Semitic nuance of the Goulston Street evidence, could it be that, on this night at least, the killer's actions had been carefully calculated to throw suspicion on the local immigrant community as well as being a possible expression of his own anti-alien (and in modern terms, anti-Semitic) beliefs?[271]

Buoyed by his success in evading not one, but two, police forces, it seems that the killer nevertheless had become careless in allowing himself to be arrested chatting to yet another local prostitute. Not for the first time, though, fortune had apparently smiled on him, allowing him the freedom to continue his deadly crusade.

Perhaps this had been part of his plan all along. By quickly distancing himself from the murder, inventing an *alter ego* and securing an alibi, he could convincingly protest his innocence. It seems to have worked for him on this occasion at least. In the meantime, the inquiry into the murders took a new and disturbing turn as the police were presented with another set of confusing evidence. On the day after the murders, the Central News agency received a postcard that gave the killings of Stride and Eddowes the collective name that has been used ever since, the 'double event'. It was not the first letter the agency had been sent and it was not to be the last.

9

THE 'RIPPER' LETTERS AND PUBLIC ENGAGEMENT WITH THE MURDERS

One of the most enigmatic elements of the Whitechapel murder series are the hundreds of letters and postcards that were sent to the news agencies and police throughout the investigation. Some of them offered advice about catching the killer, suggesting that the police should dress as 'women of the same class as the victims', for example,[272] others posited theories on the murderer's identity (a foreign sailor, or a 'red Indian' from a travelling show) but the most interesting ones are those that purport to be from the killer himself. Is it possible that among the letters from well-meaning amateur sleuths, worried citizens and cranks, there is one or more from the murderer himself? Did the killer try to communicate with the police and public, or were all of those many hundreds of missives simply an unwelcome distraction for the two police forces that were scouring London to find him?[273]

In attempting to reach any useful conclusion here, we have to consider the role of the contemporary press in the daily life and culture of Londoners. More particularly, it is necessary to remind ourselves that some elements of the press, notably the popular and more radical newspapers, held the police, or at least the Metropolitan Police Commissioner, in some contempt by the autumn of 1888. Sir Charles Warren had taken up the reins of the Met following a debacle in Trafalgar Square in February 1886. Then a section of a protesting crowd had veered off towards Pall Mall and, as a result of miscommunication and poor organisation, the police were unable to prevent them from damaging property, resulting in the 'West End Riots'. Warren resolved that no such reoccurrence should happen on his watch and so when the socialist Social Democratic Foundation (SDF) and advocates of Irish Home Rule planned separate demonstrations in the square the following year, he promptly banned all assemblies. This ignited the indignation of protestors, who challenged his authority, and the resulting strong-arm tactics, which precipitated hundreds of injuries and at least one death, led to the event going down in history as 'Bloody Sunday'.[274] Radicals including William Morris, Annie Besant and George Bernard Shaw combined with editors such as William Stead to condemn police brutality. Stead, in fact, was already on Warren's case following the trial and execution of Israel Lipski, whom Stead believed to be innocent.[275]

The 1880s had seen the full flowering of Victorian newspapers, which had benefitted from improvements in technology and distribution, as well as a reduction in the taxes imposed on them earlier in the century.[276] Newspapers were now more profitable and so could be made available at a cheaper price and, as literacy rates rose, more and more people of all classes were exposed to the output of the Third Estate. Stead had already demonstrated the power and influence of the press with his 1885 campaign to raise the age of consent. The series of articles, 'The Maiden Tribute of Modern Babylon', might have shocked middle-class readers with its sordid tale of child prostitution but the editions of the newspaper that carried it outsold anything previously published and it forced the government to enact legislation that had become a quagmire of parliamentary procedure and factional opposition.[277] Likewise, Josephine Butler used her paper, *The Shield*, as an effective campaigning tool against the Contagious Diseases Acts. Stead and Annie Besant later united to highlight the awful conditions experienced by workers in 'sweated' trades, and the plight of the

Bryant & May 'match girls' in particular.[278] The so-called 'New Journalism' had flexed its muscles in the 1880s and the government soon realised that it needed to sit up and take notice.

In tandem with the rise of campaigning newspapers, the popular press was also aware that a growing readership was ready to part with money if it was offered sensational stories in easily digestible 'titbits'. It is no coincidence that the longevity of the Whitechapel murders (and the persona of 'Jack the Ripper') interconnected with the rise of popular journalism. Arguably if 'Jack' had started his campaign of terror a half-century or more earlier, we might not still be as fascinated by him as we are today. One of the papers that was able to profit most of all from the events of that long summer and autumn was *The Star*, a brand-new organ founded in 1888. The creation of T. P. O'Connor, *The Star's* market was the working class of London and the 'Ripper' murders were a godsend to it. Another popular paper was Edward Dicey's *Daily Telegraph*, which already had a well-established readership due, in large part, to its coverage of crime and order issues. So, when the Central News Agency received the most significant of many 'Ripper' letters, it was the *Telegraph*, much to the chagrin of its rivals, which splashed the first public 'Ripper' letter across its front page.

This was the 'Dear Boss' letter, such an iconic item that it recently made its way into a British Library exhibition on Gothic literature, art and culture.[279] Written in red ink (the author apologised that the blood he saved was too clotted to use) it mocked the police, hinted at the killer's motives and offered up a 'trade name' to history. From this moment onwards, 'Jack the Ripper' was born. Letters had been received before the 'Dear Boss' missive but it was this one (and, of course, its publication) that 'inspired almost all of the others'.[280] The letter writer is now widely believed to have been a journalist, possibly Tom Bulling of the Central News Agency, or his manager John Moore.[281] Of course it is conceivable that all the letters were hoaxes, and none were written by the killer; leaving explanations that have relied heavily on the letters as evidence in danger of unravelling quite quickly.[282] However, the 'Dear Boss' letter, dated 25 September, and a postcard in the same handwriting that was received a few days later, did appear to contain information about the murders of Stride and Eddowes. 'Grand work the last job was. I gave the lady no time to squeal,' it gloated. The author was presumably referring to the murder of Annie Chapman in the yard at 29 Hanbury Street. The writer went on to promise more killings and wrote that he would 'clip the lady's ears off and send to the police officers just for jolly'.[283]

The letter is a piece of pure Victorian sensation and deserved its place in the *Gothic Imagination* exhibition. It drew on contemporary popular culture, on 'penny dreadfuls' and melodrama, and invoked the spirit of Spring-Heeled Jack and Sweeney Todd. The 'saucy Jack' postcard referenced the 'double event' and this led the police to publish both pieces of correspondence in an attempt to trace the writer. Did the author have information only available to the killer? He apologised that 'number one squealed a bit couldn't finish straight off. Had not time to get ears for police.' This might suggest a close involvement with the details of the case, but could also easily be the work of a journalist with a good source in the police. Moreover, unlike today, the newspapers of 1888 carried considerable detail of the murders and, depending on when the 'Saucy Jack' postcard was posted, the author may simply have been able to read the latest details about the case in the press. Regardless of when the postcard was written or sent, the reality remains that there is nothing in either communication that suggests inside knowledge. The consensus seems to be that the 'Dear Boss' and 'Saucy Jack' correspondence is a massive red herring.

It has so far proved much harder, however, to reach consensus on the other important 'Ripper' communication, the so-called 'From Hell' letter. This arrived at the home of George Lusk, the chairman of the Whitechapel Vigilance Committee, on 16 October. The letter was far more crudely written than the 'Dear Boss' missive and is worth setting out in full:

From Hell
Mr. Lusk
Sor,
I send you half the kidne I took from one woman prasarved it for you, tother piece I fried and ate; it was very nise. I may send you the bloody knif that took it out if only you wate a while longer.
[signed] 'catch me when you can
Mishter Lusk'.[284]

The letter was packaged with a small box, which Lusk was horrified to discover contained what appeared to be a portion of the kidney mentioned in the text. While he was initially minded to treat the whole thing as a joke in very poor taste, the fact that he had received a similar message a few days earlier in similar handwriting (the 'box of toys' postcard) ensured that he showed it to his fellow committee members.[285] The kidney was examined by Dr Thomas Openshaw at the London Hospital and he declared it to be human and possibly from the body of Eddowes. Over in the City, however, the police were far from convinced – with Dr Brown opining that 'the probability is slight of its being a portion of the murdered woman of Mitre Square.'[286] The kidney no longer exists and an examination of the original medical examination notes in 1989 was inconclusive; the contemporary examination seemed to have established that the kidney was human but whether it belonged to a murder victim, or had been extracted from a diseased corpse in a hospital or workhouse, could not be determined.[287] More recently, however, Senior Coroner and Forensic Medical Examiner Peter Dean has concluded that taken together, the presence of Bright's disease and the remaining corresponding lengths of renal artery suggest that the kidney may well have come from Eddowes – a finding which, if correct, means this letter (and the postcard) could be genuine.[288]

The letter continues to divide researchers, partly because it is not signed 'Jack the Ripper' and so it isn't such an obvious hoax. The now missing communication (or facsimiles of it) has been subject to scrutiny from myriad graphologists, psychologists and criminologists over the years. One of the more eminent among these has been the forensic document examiner Thomas Mann who concluded in 1975 that this letter very likely *was* genuine and had probably been written by a semi-literate person who was unused to writing. Forensic linguist Dr Frances Rock of Cardiff University has also stated her belief, in a recent documentary, that the letter is by the hand of a poorly educated person.[289] If we proceed on the basis that the 'From Hell' letter *was* or *could be* genuine then, what does it reveal – and what sort of author are we looking at?

For a start, it would seem to suggest someone who was semi-literate and had been learning to read and write fairly recently – indeed, the letter looks like an attempt at a formal note by someone who is not at all used to writing that way. This could be someone intent on bettering themselves – consistent, perhaps, with a person who dressed in clothes that were more respectable than his humble, and indeed brutal and bloody, background might suggest. While it does not offer any motive for the killings, it does, nevertheless, reveal a glimpse into the mind of the murderer. In the letter the writer claims to have eaten the other half of the kidney, which is not an entirely uncommon tendency among serial killers. Had the trophy been consumed as a 'treat' perhaps – 'praserved' (*sic*) as it says in wine for some specific 'special' occasion? Again, this tendency for rewarding oneself with prized body parts at such times is not unknown among serial killers and, indeed, the individual we have identified as a plausible 'Ripper' had just celebrated his 29th birthday a week previously – on 8 October. It has been suggested that rather than the apparently misspelled 'preserved', the author had probably penned 'marined' in a vain attempt to write 'marinaded'; either way, in the absence of refrigeration, it would have served the purpose until the desired moment. Equally so, this element could merely have been invented to further enhance (if it needed enhancing) the shock value of the package.

The implied cannibalism might simply have been a sick joke but what if this *was* what the killer was doing with the organs he removed? The Canadian graphologist C. M. MacLeod concluded in 1968 that the writer of the letter was probably a cunning, misogynistic sadist; a gregarious, working-class man between the ages of 20 and 45 who was prone to drink but capable of disguising his true character and holding down a day job in order to mask his crimes.[290] It has also been suggested that the misspellings could indicate a writer of cockney origins, rather than the Irish antecedents often presumed. Again, these traits certainly fit the profile of the person we will identify shortly.

Moreover, the marriage certificate of this particular individual's sister-in-law could suggest that he, like his wife, had been unable to write five years earlier (they made their marks as witnesses)[291] in contrast to his sister-in-law and younger sister, who evidently could – although this is not certain as literate people sometimes also used this device. Whatever the case, it is certainly possible that he may have been having writing lessons in the years leading up to his dreadful crimes either through his relatives, or even at the nearby philanthropic mission Toynbee Hall, which opened its doors in 1884.[292] Literacy lessons were just one of the things the institution offered to the district's poor. If this had been the case, it could well explain the seemingly uneducated schoolboy handwriting in the letter. Forensic psychologist Professor Laurence Alison of Liverpool University has stated his belief that, of all the letters received, this particular one displays an authenticity of style that is generally absent from the others.[293]

Between these two murders and the receipt of the kidney by Mr Lusk, however, the newspapers carried muted reports of a woman's torso found wrapped in cloth in the basement of the nascent police headquarters on the Victoria Embankment. It would have been hardly noticed during all the furore surrounding the 'double event' and the escalation of public interest in 'Jack the Ripper', and it was entirely eclipsed by the horrific murder of the youngest Whitechapel victim, in Miller's Court in early November.

IO

MILLER'S COURT

It has become fairly commonplace to conclude the Whitechapel murder series with the slaughter of the next victim, Marie Jane Kelly, on the eve of the Lord Mayor's Show. The murder was horrendous, even within a set of particularly gruesome deaths, and continues to rank as one of the worst homicides in British history. Nevertheless, however awful the murder of Kelly was, it did not mark the end of the attacks on women in London in 1888. It suits some accounts (for example the so-called 'royal conspiracy') to end with Kelly because they rely on a thesis that argues she was the main target of the killer all along.[294] Montague Druitt's supposed suicide (*see* below) also fits neatly with Kelly's murder as the apogee of the assassin's killing spree. It would seem, however, that the murder in Miller's Court was actually another example of the killer's ability to modify his MO to suit his situation.

In 1888 Miller's Court was little more than a 'stone flagged passage between two houses' between Nos. 26 and 27 Dorset Street.[295] Dorset Street was described as the 'worst street in London' and unsurprisingly it had connections to several of the Whitechapel victims. Mary Kelly had taken a room at 13 Miller's Court where she lived, off and on it seems, with her boyfriend Joseph Barnett, himself a 'Ripper' suspect. Kelly's personal history is perhaps the most documented and yet the hardest to verify of the five canonical victims.[296] She *may* have lived in Wales,[297] she *could* have been trafficked (or went voluntarily) to the Continent to work in a brothel,[298] and it is suggested that she was terrified of 'Jack the Ripper'.[299] We can be sure that she was, at 'about 25',[300] the youngest of the killer's 'Whitechapel' victims who have been identified and that she was, like many of her contemporaries, someone who prostituted herself in the local area when she had to.[301] It would appear that after August 1888 she did have to, as Barnett had lost his job and the couple were forced to rely on what Mary could bring in. The desperation that drove some women to prostitution is evident in the statement made by Mary's friend, Lizzie Albrook, after her death. Albrook told the press that Kelly had often warned her of the perils of the trade and wished she could leave it behind her and go back to Ireland but the realities of life got in the way: 'I don't believe she would have gone out as she did if she had not been obliged to do so to keep herself from starvation.'[302] That Mary managed to maintain a room (even a room in Dorset Street) at 4s 6d a week suggests she was able to command a slightly higher fee for her services than some of the other murdered women, or was able to bring in money in other ways. Younger, stronger and feistier, she would have represented an altogether different proposition for the killer and this is evident in the manner of her death.

Kelly's body was discovered on the morning of 9 November when Thomas Bowyer, on instructions from his boss John McCarthy, who was Kelly's landlord, tried to collect some of Kelly's rent arrears. Getting no answer to his knock, Bowyer peered in through the broken window of the room and saw 'a body on the bed and blood on the floor'. He rushed off to find his boss and to (quietly) tell him the awful news.[303] Having reported what he had seen, Bowyer was despatched to fetch the police. He rushed off to Commercial Street Police Station where he found Inspector Beck and Detective Constable Walter Dew and breathlessly told them: 'Another one. Jack the Ripper. Awful. Jack McCarthy sent me.'[304]

It *was* awful. Kelly had been eviscerated and the bed on which the remains of her body were lying was soaked in blood. There was blood on the floor and on the walls. Her face had been obliterated, with Barnett only being able to identify his lover by her remaining 'eyes and ears'.[305] As with Eddowes, the killer had inflicted disfigurements on his victim's face although on this occasion it was far more extreme and seemingly uncontrolled, suggesting an element of rage. Her breasts had been cut off; one was placed under her head and the other by her right foot. Her heart was removed from the body and (although there is considerable doubt about this) does not appear to have been in the room, or at least it was not identified as being there in Dr Bond's report. The possible absence of the heart is intriguing. As with the removal of Eddowes' kidney (and the suggestion in the Lusk letter) had the killer again satisfied his macabre need to dominate, control and humiliate his victims by eating parts of them? The killer had not left the rest of the body untouched either, the abdomen had been opened up and all the internal organs (uterus, kidneys, liver, spleen, intestines) had been taken out and distributed about the room. The police photographs of the murder scene, perhaps among the very first such images in history, still make hard viewing today.

The brutality of this murder has led some (particularly those who favour an explanation in which Barnett himself is the killer) to suggest that Kelly was not killed by 'Jack the Ripper' at all.[306] Instead, we are asked to view this as one-off murder (a *crime passionnel)* and one that was disguised to look like a 'Ripper' crime. This seems unlikely, to say the least. Joe Barnett could have murdered Mary Kelly if he had wanted to and got away with it easily enough without going to such lengths; there were plenty of unsolved or unprosecuted domestic assaults in later nineteenth-century London, one more would not have garnered that much attention. But this was worse than the others and there are clear reasons for this, which have nothing to do with Kelly's personally and everything to do with the circumstances and the location. As was noted earlier, Mary was younger and fitter than the other identified victims and, by all accounts, pretty combative too. When she awoke in the early hours of the morning to find that her client was about to kill her, she had both the strength and attitude to fight for her life. It must have given the killer one of the biggest shocks of his murderous life so far.

In most, if not all, the 'street' attacks the killer had only a few minutes with his victim, the most likely scenario being that having agreed a price, the woman presented herself for sex from behind in a standing position. It is unlikely that without a room to go to, any woman would be keen to lie down on a cold, hard, wet or dirty pavement or yard. Moreover, this approach allowed the woman some element of control, as she was not underneath her client, and probably ensured the transaction didn't last very long. It may also have served the women better in that their often drunk and unsuspecting clients may not have been able to distinguish between the inner flesh of the vagina and the outer flesh of the thighs, meaning there was less chance of impregnation or of catching a sexually transmitted disease.

So, with her skirts pulled up and her client behind her, the Victorian sex worker was literally and metaphorically exposed – and this would have played very conveniently into the killer's hands. Using some cord or a piece of cloth held in both hands, a scarf or handkerchief wound tightly perhaps, he would have been able to move quickly to choke his victim before she had an opportunity to react. Although there is some evidence to suggest that at least one victim (Tabram) could have been manually strangled from the front, we believe, for reasons explained later, that this would not have been the killer's preferred approach and that he would alter this according to circumstance. Moreover, the garrotte was a pretty common form of attack, which had been popularised by street robbers in the second-half of the 1800s. Its use, in fact, had caused a panic in 1862 that had occasioned a pretty heavy-handed response from the police, courts and legislators.[307] Indeed, tales of garrotting periodically dominated the news agenda in the 1850s and '60s and permeated popular depictions of the so-called 'criminal class'.[308] Our killer, then, would undoubtedly have been familiar with the practice – and especially so if he had served time in one the capital's prisons.

Garrotting can do more than simply disable a victim; applied effectively, it can kill silently within seconds by depriving the brain of blood-borne oxygen via the carotid artery. The next move of the killer was to cut the throat, a deep cut that completely severed the carotid. But why do this if the victim was probably already dead? Because, we believe, it allowed for a draining of the body, without arterial spray, and prevented the killer from becoming covered in his victim's blood. His aim, we believe, was not just to kill, but also to eviscerate. This would probably come more easily to someone who was familiar with slaughtering animals. He could then turn over the body and perform his 'autopsy', cutting into the flesh and removing organs as he so wished. The removal of internal body parts may have offered him a bonus, trophies he might later reflect on, or as has been suggested, eat.

The amount of mutilation or dissection that he committed seems to have been determined by the amount of time he had available, as well as the security of the location. Thus we see differences between, at one extreme, Liz Stride, and at the other, Mary Kelly and the Torso victims. This was an opportunistic killer, someone who could vary his pattern depending on the circumstances, but, crucially, he was also someone who could get close to his victims by engendering their trust in the first place. The fact that in Kelly's case there was an obvious place for sex to which they would naturally gravitate – the bed – means that the killer would have been denied his usual opportunity of effecting unconsciousness or death from behind. Instead, he may have bided his time and waited for her to fall asleep post-coitus before attempting to smother and restrain her by tying and gagging. He would then be free to indulge himself in private and at leisure, as perhaps was his preference – a disturbing avenue that we will explore later.

Dr Bond believed Mary had been asleep up until the point at which the attack on her took place, so this is further evidence that 'she was comfortable with and unafraid of the man in bed with her.'[309] The idea that a crazed foreigner, a doctor with a surgical bag, or an aristocrat with a coach 'parked' nearby could have garnered such trust stretches the bounds of plausibility somewhat too far. Instead, we should be looking for someone ordinary, local and familiar. In the case of Kelly's murder, that someone had managed to get inside her home and had presumably negotiated for something more than a 'quick one'; he intended to stay the night. Indeed, the murderer may have seized an opportunity to engage in behaviour in the heart of his killing zone, which he normally reserved for more remote locations where his security and leisure was guaranteed. His near undoing here, however, shows that he became seriously detached from his 'comfort zone' on this occasion – the ferocity of the killing being entirely down to his fear of being discovered.

Whether or not the couple did have sex is now impossible to determine but at some point it seems likely that the killer realised Mary was asleep and decided to attack her. Sitting either astride or beside Kelly, he had probably taken hold of a pillow with the intention of smothering her. Opening her eyes at that very moment however, and realising immediately that she was fighting for her life, Kelly must have resisted fiercely and managed to frustrate the attack. At the start she got out the cry 'Oh murder!' which was heard by Elizabeth Prater and Sarah Lewis, two independent witnesses who testified at the subsequent inquest.[310] Realising the futility of continuing with this approach, the killer then resorted to his knife in a desperate attempt to finish the job quickly.

At this juncture, it seems two possible scenarios for the future course of events probably exist. One imagines the killer countering Mary's resistance by pulling the bed sheet tightly up over her head with one hand while stabbing and slashing through the sheet with the knife in the other, as Dr Bond's subsequent comparative report into the canonical murders suggested.[311] Alternatively, Kelly may have pulled the sheet up over herself in an instinctive yet futile attempt at protecting herself from the assailant's blows.

Either way, this would account for the defensive wounds on the forearms and hands identified in the post-mortem and explain the frenzied nature of the assault – the killer's overriding consideration being to silence his victim quickly. On previous occasions the killer had been in complete control of both his victim and surroundings. In the novel circumstances of Miller's Court, however, it seems he lost control of both the situation *and* himself – and came very close to being discovered in the process.

The police found evidence that some of the woman's clothes (and perhaps those of a friend) had been consumed by a fire in the room and this suggested to Inspector Abberline at the time that the killer had required additional light to carry out his grisly work.[312] This is entirely plausible, of course, but it is not as if his 'work' was particularly tidy or thorough in a medical sense. Instead, it may have been the case that he needed to destroy incriminating evidence that he did not want to take with him from the scene. If we bear in mind that he was probably wearing underwear consisting of long johns and a vest, which would invariably have been covered in blood, it is a good bet that these would have ended up in the fire with the killer leaving the scene in just his outer garments. The risk of being discovered wearing them during his escape would have been just too great. Being saturated in blood and thus difficult to ignite, it is possible that the missing women's clothing (which was dry) was used to encourage combustion and ensure complete incineration of the evidence. This would be particularly important if there were any identifying marks on the garments and goes some way in explaining the evident size and ferocity of the fire.

As with the other Whitechapel victims, Mary Kelly had been seen at various points in the lead up to her murder. The degree to which any of these sightings offer clues as to the identity of her killer is far less easy to determine. We should not forget that Miller's Court was located close by the water trough mentioned by Henry Smith in his pursuit of Kate Eddowes' killer, just before PC Spicer's encounter with an unnamed man in Heneage Court.[313] It seems the killer may well have been familiar with the area. On the night in question, however, unconfirmed reports suggest that Kelly was drinking in the Britannia pub around 11 p.m. on 8 November, possibly with a young man who looked 'respectable'. She had also apparently been seen at the Ten Bells earlier in the evening and may well have been fairly drunk by this stage. On returning home at 11.45, Mary Ann Cox, a local resident, reported seeing Kelly talking to a 'stout man' whom she described as aged 35–36, 5 foot 5 inches tall, 'shabbily dressed' with a long coat and 'billycock hat'. His face was blotchy and he had a carroty moustache, suggesting he was an alcoholic or a regular drinker and that he was ginger haired. Given the timing, it is unlikely he was Mary's killer, but he was quite possibly one of her clients because she seems to have had more than one visitor that evening. Cox later heard Mary singing a popular music hall tune, *A Violet from Mother's Grave*, which she was again heard to sing at half-past midnight, when it disturbed her neighbours Mr and Mrs Pickett, and possibly again at 1 a.m. when Cox went back out.[314]

The next sighting of Kelly was at 2 a.m. and seems to be one of the more problematic witness statements of the whole case. George Hutchinson was strolling along Commercial Street and, as he passed Thrawl Street, he passed by a man 'but paid him scant attention'.[315] The next person he met was Mary Kelly, presumably having dispensed with her 'carroty' punter. She was after money and asked Hutchinson for sixpence, which he said he did not have as he had just visited 'Romford' – perhaps he meant the beer shop in Heneage Street, later known as the Romford Arms, and now as The Pride of Spitalfields.[316] By now she may have sobered up a bit as Hutchinson did not describe her as drunk, just a 'little bit spreeish', meaning unsteady on her feet. He watched as she then approached the man he had just encountered. This time, it seems, Mary had more luck as the man laughed and Hutchinson heard Kelly say 'All right' and the man reply 'You will be all right for what I have told you.'[317] The couple walked back towards Kelly's lodgings and Hutchinson leaned against a lamppost and watched them. His description of the man was quite precise by comparison to other witness statements and perhaps a bit too precise for some researchers.[318] We have two descriptions – one given to the police, and a second given to the press, which then led to an elaborate illustration in the *Illustrated Police News*. The man was aged 34 to 35, 5 foot 6 inches tall, and 'looked Jewish'. His eyes were dark, his skin pale, with a curly moustache, and he was 'very surly looking'. He was wearing a long dark coat, trimmed with astrakhan fur, waistcoat, dark trousers, and sported 'a massive gold chain', a watch chain with a 'big seal, [...] a red stone hanging from it'. Importantly he carried a parcel, about 8 inches long, and a pair of kid gloves. Hutchinson thought he was local and that he had seen him before around Petticoat Lane.[319] Abberline believed Hutchinson and sent two officers with him to see if they could spot the mysterious foreigner.

Hutchinson probably knew Mary Kelly better than he was letting on and his behaviour that night is suggestive of this. Having seen Kelly talk to the man, he followed them back to Miller's Court and waited around for nearly an hour to see if they emerged from her room, but they did not. He left at 3 a.m. to wander the streets on his own. Hutchinson's suspect was in the right place, at the right sort of time, but only if he was ever there at all. Sarah Lewis reported seeing a man outside Miller's Court at 2.30 a.m. and this could, of course, have been Hutchinson, although, evidently, he did not see her. Mary had apparently sobered up according to Hutchinson – but had she? She had been very drunk only a couple of hours earlier. On balance, Hutchinson's evidence is a bit too neat and unlikely.[320] Regardless of his evidence, Hutchinson had, by his own admission, left at 3 a.m. and Mary Ann Cox returned home at that time. She saw no light in Mary's room, nor heard any sound.

At 4 a.m. Elizabeth Prater was awakened by her kitten.[321] She and Sarah Lewis reported hearing a faint cry of 'Oh murder!' but ignored it, as it was not uncommon in that area of London. The man Hutchinson said he saw may have slipped away unnoticed by him, or simply left after 3 a.m.; there is nothing that ties him to Mary's murder. Indeed, it is possible that the killer could have arrived while Kelly was asleep, which might explain the cry of 'murder' as she awoke to find him atop her. If Hutchinson's story is mere fabrication, however, then what of the previous punter with the carroty moustache seen by Mary Cox – had he actually left the premises? The description of him is very similar to several other sightings of a possible killer – the 'blotchy face' especially striking a chord with the testimony of PC Spicer in Heneage Street at the start of our story and Ada Wilson's in relation to her 'assailant'.[322]

Who was Mary Kelly though, and can anything about her offer an explanation for her murder? As was noted earlier, Kelly's history is perhaps the most mythologised of all the canonical victims and negotiating a path between fact and fiction is extremely tricky. She was born in about 1863 and so, at 25, was still a young woman at the time of her death.[323] She was attractive and seemingly well liked in the area. Originally from Ireland, Mary Kelly apparently moved to Wales, and was married at 16 to a man named Davies, who died in a colliery accident. Sometime in 1884, Kelly arrived in London and worked in a high-class brothel and possibly lodged at other times in the Providence Row night shelter close by Dorset Street. By 1886 she was lodging in Thrawl Street (like several of the other victims) and in 1887 she started her relationship with Joseph Barnett, a porter at Billingsgate fish market. The couple had separated at the time of her murder because Barnett was unhappy about her returning to prostitution and her habit of allowing other prostitutes to lodge at Miller's Court. Mary certainly appears to have been a likable character, the sort of young woman who was kind and friendly to everyone except when she had drunk too much, which was when her fiery Celtic temper came to the surface. There is no indication that she was carrying a disease but it is not impossible and – regardless of whether she was exhibiting any symptoms of syphilis or not – her murderer may well have simply classed her as one of many possible carriers. Her murder shocked the small community of Dorset Street and the police officers, like Walter Dew, who viewed the remains of her body *in situ*.

In the aftermath, despite the careful description given by George Hutchinson, the police still seemed to have no real clue as to the identity of the killer and as the news of Kelly's inquest died away in the papers, so came the announcement that Sir Charles Warren had resigned as head of the Met.[324] This was perhaps a victory for the media, despite it apparently being unconnected to the case, but did little to help catch the 'Ripper'.[325] As Paul Begg explains, Warren did not resign because of the failure to catch 'Jack' but for procedural and political reasons. He had, however, had a difficult relationship with some sections of the press ever since 'Bloody Sunday' and in the wake of Kelly's murder, it seemed appropriate that the titular head of the police had stepped aside to allow someone else to have a go at catching the capital's most notorious killer.[326]

Kelly's inquest, held at Shoreditch Town Hall, was exceptionally brief and only established the cause of death ('wilful murder') and not the extent of her injuries. As a result, Hutchinson was not examined under oath and the whole case was hushed up. It is hard to resist the conclusion that the government was keen to see an end to the public criticism of the police and Home Office over the murders. Of course, the best way to do that was to catch the killer, or at the very least thwart any further attempts he might have for committing future murders. Failing that, it was essential that the news story surrounding the 'autumn of terror' should die down and fade away. This would seem to have been the main point of curtailing the coroner's inquest into the Miller's Court murder. If the police hoped it would put an end to the press criticism then they were to be disappointed. *Reynold's Newspaper,* generally a paper that challenged the establishment throughout the second half of the 1800s, continued to try to hold the Met to account. On 25 November it reported an attack on a woman inside a lodging house and asked the question, 'Where were the police?' While the assault was non-fatal, the paper was at pains to point out that while the police guarded Dorset Street, Berner Street and Mitre Square, it was hardly likely that the killer would return to any of these sites to repeat his crimes. 'Must he oblige the police by committing the murder under their noses before they arrest him?' it enquired. Warren had resigned, the head of the C.I.D. was an unknown quantity and the Home Secretary was 'incompetent'; it was a ghastly state of affairs and 'all is discord, all confusion and imbecility,' the paper concluded.[327] The attack that the paper referred to had taken place on the previous Tuesday, 20 November, in George Street (where Martha Tabram had lodged) and while it is rarely seen as a 'Ripper' attack, we feel it certainly bears consideration for several reasons. Annie Farmer, a 41-year-old prostitute who was also known as 'Laughing Liz' and 'Flossie', had picked up a man in the early morning of Tuesday 20 November 1888 and, following drinks at a local pub, they had gone to a common lodging house where they took a bed. By Annie's account the man had attempted to cut her throat later that morning and had only been thwarted by her struggling and screams. He had fled the house at 9.30, leaving Annie with a cut to her throat that needed dressing. Several people saw the man exit the building and make good his escape, with some of them giving chase. He was seemingly headed in the direction of Heneage Street when he was lost. By most accounts (and these did vary considerably)[328] the man was described as:

> About 30 years old, 5'4" – 5'6/7", thick-set with a fair complexion and moustache. He was wearing a black diagonal overcoat, speckled grey trousers and a hard, round black felt hat.

Two witnesses, Ellen Marks and Philip Harris, reported that he was wearing a white handkerchief around his neck, which might have been an attempt to cover a scar or abscess that they said was visible on the left side of his neck. As he ran away another onlooker, Sarah Turner, said that he held a handkerchief to his mouth 'as if he were suffering'. Suffering with a respiratory disease such as tuberculosis perhaps? This man was apparently known as a member of the community and so was dismissed as having any relationship with the notorious 'Ripper' – but why? Farmer also confided to the police that she had met the man some 12 months previously in her 'working' capacity, which seemed to have further inclined them, rather strangely, to the belief that he could not be 'Jack'. In fact, this arouses our suspicion all the more. Here was someone local, who used prostitutes, and who apparently had some cause to dislike them. What is more, he had shown his dislike by cutting the throat of one of them.

Whatever the case, given the location and nature of the offence, it is certainly a mystery why this incident was apparently not further investigated. Perhaps it was, but with no definite outcome.[329] It seems that we shall never know whether a man was interviewed about this incident, as police files detailing persons arrested in relation to the murders have been missing for many years. The FBI profile considers it likely that at some stage the killer did come under police questioning, perhaps even on several occasions, although, unlike today, they had no means then of correlating the information.[330] If this was another missed opportunity following on from PC Spicer's encounter in Heneage Court, however, it seems that it would not be long before he would again come to the notice of the police. For the time being, the similarity of the assailant's description with those of previous attacks cannot be ignored.

With the media storm subsiding after the closure of the inquest held on Mary Kelly's body, it would be easy to conclude that the series of murders associated with the 'Whitechapel fiend' had come to an end. That is what many commentators have decided, and most explanations as to the identity of the murder start with this premise. However, the killer was far from finished, and why would he be? After all, it is a reasonably well-established truism that serial killers usually do not stop killing unless something makes them: either they get caught, kill themselves or otherwise die, or in some way become institutionalised or incapacitated. In the case of the Whitechapel and Thames Torso murderer, the slaying of Mary Kelly did not represent the last of his exertions – there were to be at least four more victims attributable to his knife. Nevertheless, there would appear to have been a gap in his killing, unless, that is, we are prepared to accept that he was responsible for one more final murder in 1888 – that of Rose Mylett.

Mylett (also known as Lizzie Davis)[331] was found dead on the morning of 20 December 1888, near Poplar High Street in East London. The police rejected the idea that she was another 'Ripper' victim because she had not been mutilated and Assistant Commissioner Robert Anderson and Dr Bond even doubted whether she was a homicide victim at all.[332] At first glance, Poplar's relative remoteness from the other murders in Whitechapel would seem to make it an unlikely location for the next murder in the series. The inquest jury at the time, however, remained unconvinced by the police line and so Mylett's death would also seem to warrant some serious consideration. In particular, Dr Brownfield was sure Mylett had been 'foully murdered' and said so.[333] With no cuts to her throat, abdominal mutilations or any other signs of significant trauma, the evidence nonetheless suggested that Mylett had been 'garrotted' from behind. This was the conclusion of five doctors who examined the body although one of them, Dr Thomas Bond, subsequently recanted and ruled out foul play – seemingly succumbing to police pressure to do so. Compared to smothering from the rear – another possible approach with all the victims – garrotting offers very little chance of effective defence, enabling the victim to be silenced both quickly *and* quietly – far more quickly than by smothering, which can take longer than 1 minute and sometimes more than 2 minutes. As garrotting constricts the carotid artery and prevents it from feeding oxygenated blood to the brain, in addition to stopping the windpipe feeding oxygen to the lungs, it not only renders the victim unconscious in 1–15 seconds due to oxygen starvation of the brain, it also makes it impossible for the victim to cry out. By using this method, the killer would also avoid the violent response of 'air hunger' syndrome, which is triggered in a victim as they fight desperately for air during smothering. It goes without saying, therefore, that garrotting would be by far the most preferable form of attack from the killer's point of view. The same effect can be achieved by a standing chokehold administered from the side or rear, although the person using it would need to be strong enough to ensure sufficient constriction of both arteries and windpipe to cause the rapid unconsciousness and silence required. This method would have been a useful alternative for the killer though, if no ligature happened to be available. Attacks from the rear would be easier for him than any from the front, as mentioned earlier in relation to Chapman, because a frontal attack would invariably have resulted in noise and left him open to retaliation from the victim, especially from potentially incapacitating strikes to the eyes or groin.

The Whitechapel and Thames Torso killer may well have deployed this tactic on other occasions and indeed he may have learned it from a brief spell of imprisonment or simply have been aware of the practice from popular culture and 'folk' knowledge in the wake of the London garrottings, previously mentioned. Stories of such horrors would no doubt have been recounted to impressionable youngsters for a good number of years afterwards. There are indications that it could have been a 'signature' in the Chapman case although the subsequent throat cutting would have obliterated any evidence in this regard. It is, of course, possible that this approach was adopted with several of the victims and was the actual cause of their death, rather than the subsequent lacerations to the throat. Simply applying the ligature for a few seconds longer could have achieved death. Only in the case of Mylett had the absence of any subsequent throat cutting not covered this up. It was noted by Dr Philips that as well as the swelling of Chapman's lips and fingers and the protruding tongue of Mylett, both of their hearts and lungs, as well as Chapman's brain, were engorged with black (de-oxygenated) blood – a sure sign of asphyxiation.

In any event, when Mylett's body was found by PC Robert Goulding it was still warm and he believed he had stumbled upon another example of Jack's work.[334] Why were the police and the coroner, Wynne Baxter, so at odds here though? It is interesting to note that the police had been keen to see that Baxter was not in charge of Kelly's inquest either. With Warren gone, there was no longer any obvious scapegoat to represent press antipathy towards the police and Anderson may simply have been trying to return to a situation where the occasional death of a street prostitute failed to garner the attention of the newspapers.[335] *The Star* made an attempt to link the murder to the Indian Thuggee cult and also raised the possibility that instead of being unconnected to the previous murders, Mylett's killing was instead 'a new revelation of his old methods' – a very astute (if overlooked) observation, which very much accords with our own conclusions.[336] The lack of mutilation on this occasion may simply have been a result of the killer being disturbed, as he was in Berner Street. But why had he struck so far from Spitalfields? One possible answer could be that the area around Brick Lane had become too hot for the killer to operate in and yet his desire to continue to attack local woman was still strong, compelling him to range a little further afield – as we know that his namesake did in the 1970s in Yorkshire. We suspect, though, that other factors were at play that influenced the location of the killings.

Rose Mylett may have been the victim of some other unpleasant killer, of course, perhaps one of the two men seen with her earlier that night, but we certainly shouldn't rule out the possibility that she was killed by the same hand that had already murdered up to eight other women across the capital. Indeed, we should bear in mind that this assault took place only a few minutes' walk from the site of the attack on Ada Wilson and from the Harrison, Barber slaughterhouse on Tredegar Terrace, off Burdett Road. Furthermore, Poplar, like Burdett Road in Bow, was served by the London and Blackwall Railway (LBR), which ran from Fenchurch Street in the City to Blackwall docks, with stops at Leman Street and Cannon Street in Whitechapel, among others. The lines of this railway also ran along the top of the arches at Pinchin Street, which also had its own station – a location that will be of interest later. A new tram service operated by the North

Metropolitan Tramways Company had also opened the previous month. This line now connected Bloomsbury and Poplar via Commercial Street in Spitalfields and allowed passengers to travel for just thruppence one way.[337]

Furthermore, there also appears to have been a connection between one of the Whitechapel victims, Elizabeth Stride, and Rose Mylett. Stride had run a coffee shop with her husband in Chrisp Street, Poplar – perhaps until the time of his death in 1884. Chrisp Street was just north of the High Street where Rose Mylett was murdered. Poplar station was on the LBR line that ran west to Pinchin Street, affording access to Burdett Road (where Ada Wilson was attacked) via the Bow spur, and it also served as the southern terminus of the Northern Railway, which headed up into the very heartlands of John Harrison's business empire around Sugar House Lane in Stratford. Moreover, just off this line at Bromley-by-Bow was the Poplar and Stepney Sick Asylum, where Mylett had been admitted on several occasions during the 1880s suffering from a persistent, unspecified ailment. The last time she stayed there was apparently between 20 January and 14 March 1888 – 10 months or so before her death.[338] Had the killer previously come across Mylett here, perhaps on the train or at the nearby station? It is probably no coincidence either that upon her relocation to the Spitalfields area, Stride resided at various establishments in Dorset, Fashion, and Flower and Dean Streets – right in the heart of 'Jack's killing fields – and very close to the killer's home. It would seem therefore that the killer would very likely have been acquainted with Stride for some considerable time prior to her murder – not necessarily just in Whitechapel.

The LBR also had an offshoot known as the Millwall Extension Railway, which ran south through the Isle of Dogs and served the Greenwich Peninsular via a ferry. Once across the river, it was only a short tram ride away from yet another Harrison, Barber slaughterhouse located by the riverbank on what is now John Harrison Way. This was just upstream and on the opposite side of the river from where the Rainham Torso body part had been discovered at Templeman's Wharf during the previous year. Another LBR location – Fenchurch Street Station – was virtually adjacent to the Middlesex side entry/exit point of the next crossing on the river in a westerly direction, the Tower Subway, which, as has already been noted, provided access to several key locations of interest south of the river. In conjunction with the subway, therefore, dual transport systems (the trams and the LBR) provided an east/west axis for the two extremes of the killer's likely sphere of operations – from Garret Lane, Wandsworth, in the west, to Poplar and the Greenwich Peninsular, in the east. A tram serving the Victoria Embankment and Charing Cross also integrated with this network via Westminster Bridge, with Sloane Square station in Chelsea being served by the Circle Line of the London Underground. The same line also ran north from Aldgate on the border of Whitechapel to King's Cross station and the Brandon Road slaughterhouse at Camden. Whitechapel itself was home to two stations – Leman Street and Pinchin Street.

So far we have provided a number of clues and hinted at the identity of the individual we think might have been responsible for these killings, and in the next chapter we will name him. Before we do, however, we should note that Rose Mylett had also once lived in the very heart of 'Jack's 'killing fields' – at Pelham Street. Pelham (now Woodseer) Street is just across the other side of Brick Lane from Hanbury Street – the location of Annie Chapman's murder three months earlier. The man we believe to be a plausible candidate for both the Whitechapel and Thames Torso murders had lived both at Hanbury Street and in nearby Heneage Street and it is high time we looked at him and his life in some detail.

II

THE LIFE AND TIMES OF JAMES HARDIMAN

On 13 November 1859, Edward and Harriet Hardiman took their son James and his elder sister, Sarah, to be baptised at St Matthew's Church, Bethnal Green. This was not far from their home in High Street, Mile End New Town (now Greatorex Street) in London's East End. Depending on which record is believed, the church register or his birth certificate, James had been born on either 8 or 12 October 1859. This made him the second of seven children in a fairly large family, which must have severely stretched the domestic budget of the slipper-maker and his wife.[339] The baptism must have been one of the last in 1859 because on what was described as a freezing cold night, a fire destroyed the interior of George Dance's eighteenth-century building. Disputes between the architect (Knightly) and the local committee, plus a series of strikes by workmen, meant that the church was not fully restored until 1861. In the twentieth century, it saw the funerals of the notorious Kray twins, Ronnie and Reggie, as well as their brother Charlie, reminding us (if we needed reminding) of the long associations of the area with crime and violence. St Matthew's is still there today. It survived a bombing during the Second World War that destroyed its roof and obliterated nearly all the gravestones in the grounds; it remains a central feature of the area to the north-east of Brick Lane.[340]

The Hardiman family were very familiar with the East End and, like many families that existed on the margins of poverty, they moved around a lot. One contemporary middle-class commentator complained that the poor swam about like fish, never staying anywhere for very long, unlike the 'respectable' middle classes, who placed a greater value on settlement and the establishment of roots. Of course, working men and women on the bottom rungs of society had little opportunity to establish themselves. Most would have rented the rooms they occupied and lived a precarious existence with little security over their domestic arrangements. Landlords were notorious for upping the rent when it suited them and even a short period of unemployment or a rise in the family expenditure (caused, for example, by a growing family) led to evictions or midnight flits. The popular music hall song 'My Old Man' is a reference to the reality of working-class life and the problems those families faced in keeping a roof over their heads.[341]

People also moved to be close to their place of work. On his mother's side, several of James Hardiman's relatives worked in and around the meat and slaughtering trades. Census records show they were cattle dealers, horse slaughterers and cats' meat men so it is no surprise that when he was old enough, James followed in the family footsteps.[342] James's maternal grandparents, Samuel and Sarah Stockton, had moved around the East End living in Osborne Place, Silver Street (now Chicksand and Spelman streets, respectively) as well as Fashion Street and even in the 'worst street in London' – Dorset Street – where James's mother was born around July 1838 and where Mary Kelly was to meet her end some 50 years later. Growing up, James Hardiman had a close familiarity with the streets, alleys and courts of Whitechapel and Spitalfields. This detailed knowledge of the local geography would have been invaluable to anyone trying to avoid the clutches of a desperate police force intent on tracking down a serial murderer.

On 30 July 1873 James was 13 when his 6-year-old brother Samuel died at 24 Preston Street, Mile End New Town, which had been the family home since at least 1871. The cause of death was given as cerebritis, which would probably be understood today as meningitis.[343] By 1880 the Hardimans had relocated (without James) to 27 Hanbury Street, where Edward Hardiman, James's father, died of heart-related problems in February that year.

Shortly afterwards they moved again although this time just next door to No. 29, where Harriet was listed as the head of the household the following year.[344] Mrs Hardiman and William (James's younger brother) were still resident there when they were named in an 1888 report into the murder of Annie Chapman whose body had been found at the rear of the premises that year.[345] Harriet gave evidence at the inquest – although she had nothing substantive to say, having slept soundly until the discovery of the murder woke her up at 6 a.m.[346]

]By all accounts she sold cat's meat from a shop at the front of the premises,[347] with her son William helping out by peddling the wares further afield on a barrow. Although James was not actually living at 27 at the time of the murder, he was nevertheless intimately acquainted with the murder scene – and not just because his relations were resident there either. In 1881, he and his wife Sarah had been living at 29 Hanbury Street, while the rest of his family were next door at Number 27.[348]

James and his young bride Sarah Scott had been wed at St Thomas's Church, Bethnal Green, on 2 October 1876, only a few days short of James's 17th birthday – he was not, in fact, 19 as was stated on the marriage certificate, so they were a very young couple.

She was from Birmingham, but her family had moved south and taken lodgings in Heneage Street, at Number 20. And it was at 20 Heneage Street that James and his wife were living in 1887 while they were expecting the birth of their daughter, Harriet Maria. According to Rob Hills and Adrian Stockton, the couple had moved across the road to Number 13 by June the following year, probably renting some rooms there with other tenants.[349]

Heneage Street, as we have seen, is an important location in understanding this case for it was here that PC Spicer had his brief encounter with a man he believed to be the 'Ripper' but it is also situated at the heart of the Whitechapel murder series. In 1961, when John G. Whitby took a series of 27 photographs of 'Ripper' sites in Spitalfields, Heneage Street was among them. Philip Hutchinson was a little puzzled by this; after all it was, he wrote, 'a street with only the most tenuous of connections to the Whitechapel Murders and an unusual choice for Whitby's attention'.[350] But Whitby also photographed Swallow Gardens, the site of Frances Coles' murder, a much disputed 'Ripper' victim. As Hutchinson points out, Whitby's ability to identify the location of Coles' murder so accurately (and 'four decades before the rest of Ripper historians caught up with him') suggests he may have benefited from a little local knowledge gleaned from those with long memories.[351] So perhaps that same local intelligence led him to Heneage Street?

In 1888 James Hardiman earned his living as a cats' meat man – a purveyor of cheap meat that was supposedly sold to feed London's huge population of cats and dogs. However, as Chapter Seven has suggested, not all the meat was destined for pet food – quite a bit of it may have found its way into the diets of the very poorest in Victorian society. James's involvement with the meat trade seems to have meant that he, like his parents before him, moved around a lot. In 1885 he and Sarah were living at Cudworth Street, close by the slaughterhouse in Coventry Street, which was destined to become part of the Harrison, Barber empire. James Hardiman's uncle John was also an established dealer in horseflesh, who ran the Bricklayer's Arms, a pub on the corner of Collingwood Street and Somerford Street, which was a stone's throw from the Hardiman family home. His son, (James's cousin) also named John, helped with this and eventually went on to take over the licence on his death. James had been listed as a 'knacker' or horse slaughterer in the 1881 census and it is likely he moved to Cudworth Street to be closer to his work. It seems then that James was someone who was well-versed in the meat trade, both as a slaughterman and someone who sold cheap cuts from a barrow. His would have been a familiar face indeed as he walked the streets of east London, supplying his customers with cooked and processed horseflesh.

James's life had not been without incident. He'd lost his younger brother Samuel as a child, his father when he was 20, and he had been present at the death of his 26-year-old elder sister Sarah, who succumbed to epilepsy in January 1885 at 29 Hanbury Street.[352] Then, probably sometime in the late spring of 1887, his only child, Harriet Maria, was born at 20 Heneage Street.[353] What should have been a cause for celebration, however, turned out to be anything but, as just one year later the sickly child too would be dead. The official cause of death was given as *Tabes Enterica* (six months)/*Marasmus,* which would probably be recorded now as *Tabes Mesenterica* or childhood tuberculosis of the mesenteric lymph glands with wasting and emaciation. On the day of her death, 18 June 1888, the child's mother herself was admitted to the London Hospital suffering from paraplegia.[354] She would never leave her hospital bed as, just three months later on 13 September 1888, she died aged about 28, the seemingly unambiguous cause of death in her case being *phthisis pulmonaris*/exhaustion – pulmonary tuberculosis.[355]

Although there is probably little reason to doubt the cause of death as far as the mother is concerned, the determination in the case of the child is perhaps rather more open to question. Without recourse to modern diagnostic tests, a correct diagnosis of *Tabes Mesenterica* can still be a difficult one to make which, in no small part, is due to the similarity of the infection's symptoms with those of other congenital diseases.[356] Indeed, tuberculosis is almost as well-known for its ability to mimic different conditions as the other 'great imitator' we touched upon earlier, syphilis. Many of the symptoms likely displayed by Harriet Maria can just as easily be caused by congenital syphilis as by congenital tuberculosis. Particularly, these include hepatosplenomegaly (simultaneous enlargement of liver and spleen) and lymphadenopathy (swelling of the lymph nodes), although pneumonia, jaundice, fever, respiratory distress and rashes (which can occur in cases of tubercular sepsis) are often also present.[357] A failure to thrive with muscle atrophy (wasting) and lack of energy can also be indicative of syphilis, as we have seen in a previous chapter, and could be consistent with the *marasmus* noted. In fact, even the paraplegia with which Sarah was admitted to hospital (probably transverse myelitis rather than *tabes dorsalis* of tertiary-stage syphilis) can be taken as both a manifestation of syphilis as well as that of tuberculosis infection.[358] Indeed, the very term 'paralysis' was known at the time as a euphemism for syphilis as syphilitic paraplegia had been recognised in patients from the early 1880s at least and was not uncommon. Paralysing the sufferer from the waist down, it would have been a devastating development for both James and his wife coming on top, as it did, of their only child's death.[359]

At the time of the murders the link between tuberculosis and infected raw cow's milk had not been discovered and although we now know that tuberculosis can be transmitted from mother to child *in utero* through the umbilical cord, or at birth via the birth canal,[360] it had been shown in 1882 to be an airborne bacterial infection, rather than an inherited condition. Given then that the child would most likely have been symptomatic from birth or within the first few weeks of life, James may well have suspected syphilis to be the cause at that juncture if he and his wife had been so infected. We already have several clues to suggest that James very likely *was* afflicted by syphilis such as the 'rosy cheeks' and 'sunburnt appearance' noted by Constable Spicer and Ada Wilson in their encounters, and the scar or abscess evident on the suspect's neck at the time of Annie Farmer's assault. While it is impossible to know anything conclusive about the Hardimans' marriage and any extra-marital activity they may have engaged in, prostitution was endemic in the period and given the nature of James's work – which brought him into contact with all sorts of people over a wide geographical area – it is hardly speculative to suggest that he might have contracted a sexually transmitted disease from sexual encounters with local women. Indeed, other indications will present themselves later, as we shall see. Moreover, if *he* was infected then it is almost inconceivable that he wouldn't have shared his misfortune with his wife who could then have passed it on to their unborn child during pregnancy.

In fact the spectre of syphilis could explain the gap of some 10 years or so between the marriage of James and Sarah and the birth of their daughter. Although pregnancies of those with active tuberculosis can result in miscarriage and stillbirths, it is also a definitive feature for women with untreated syphilis. In a recent television documentary, sexual health consultant Dr Peter Greenhouse of the British Association for Sexual Health and HIV explained how it can take such a time for the disease to 'clear' before an infected woman can start having healthy children following a succession of miscarriages, stillbirths and deaths shortly after birth.[361] Moreover, paediatric consultant Dr Vas Novelli also stated that in cases where *marasmus* was present in surviving children, a diagnosis of congenital syphilis could be a distinct possibility, given the disease's prevalence around the turn of the century and the difficulties of diagnosing tuberculosis infection.[362]

James then may well have had little doubt regarding his (or his wife's) culpability for their child's condition and the disease responsible for it. In fact Sarah's death from pulmonary tuberculosis with the likely previous sighting of James in apparent respiratory distress (*see* Farmer case) strongly suggests that the pair of them were suffering from *both* diseases at this time. Indeed, we know that James, like his wife, would die of pulmonary tuberculosis some time later.[363] If he had been looking for an outlet for his anger at this point, there were no obvious scapegoats to be had as far as tuberculosis was concerned – even on the off-chance that he *did* believe it the cause. In the case of syphilis, however, prostitutes would have been obvious targets for any retribution he might have had in mind, given their reputation as the principal spreaders of the disease and the most likely source of his own infection. In any event, from the moment Sarah had entered the London Hospital, James would have been home alone at 13 Heneage Street with time to reflect on his own sorry feelings about life and without any responsibilities or supervision. Indeed, even if he had visited the hospital on a regular basis following her admission, he would still have had considerable freedom of action in the three months preceding her death as Sarah's death certificate confirms his residence there at this time.[364]

A year later from the day that Sarah passed away, on 13 September 1889, a man calling himself 'John Arnold' gave himself up to the police investigating the discovery of another 'Torso' victim in Pinchin Street, Whitechapel. Is it unreasonable then to ask whether this 'John Arnold' and James Hardiman could have been the same person? There could well be a strong motive here and when this is coupled with both means and opportunity, this presents us with the sort of individual who might have taken out his anger and frustrations on a group of women he mistakenly blamed for the tragedy that blighted his life. John Arnold will be explored in more detail later, in Chapter 12.

If James Hardiman did have syphilis it could certainly go some way towards explaining his subsequent behaviour and so we will later examine the possible psychopathology of this man in more depth. Syphilis, as Chapter Five demonstrated, is a degenerative disease but is not always one that will directly bring about death. We know that James would later die of tuberculosis, another deadly Victorian disease, but syphilis undermines the immune system and would have left him vulnerable to contracting tuberculosis in the first place. Syphilis is also known to affect the mental health of a sufferer, especially if mercury is used to treat it. If we combine the medical evidence with psychological profiling, it seems very reasonable to suggest that Hardiman, riddled with syphilis himself and having probably infected his wife and unborn child, could have been raging against the world in general following their deaths – and against the perceived carriers of the dread disease in particular.

If this hypothesis is correct it seems very likely that James would have sought some help from the medical profession. It is unlikely, however, that he would have received it at the nearby Royal London due to both its admission policies and its limited facilities. One place he could have obtained it, though, was at the Charing Cross Hospital on Agard Street at the western end of the Strand. This hospital (which now serves as Charing Cross Police Station) was located next to Harvey's Buildings, which was run as a common lodging house in the 1880s and was the address where the man calling himself 'John Arnold' claimed to stay. The hospital itself was a large 'charitable' establishment that catered especially for the needs of the poor, and treated diseases such as syphilis and tuberculosis that workhouse infirmaries would not touch. It had been founded in the early nineteenth century by Benjamin Golding, the first new hospital in the capital for 80 years. Its patients were described in a report to the Prince Regent in the early 1820s as 'mostly Irish labourers, costermongers and characters of doubtful calling'. It moved to the site Hardiman would have known in 1834.[365] Under the direction of Dr John Astley Bloxham, Charing Cross became an important centre in the pioneering plastic surgery undertaken for the reconstruction of facial deformities, such as 'saddle nose', which were associated with syphilitic ulceration.[366] Teaching and research hospitals required subjects to examine and this no doubt would have led many poorer sufferers, such as Hardiman, to its doors.

The London Hospital did treat syphilis sufferers on its Hannah Ward, under the direction of Sir Jonathan Hutchinson, but this was a very small unit and it could only accommodate seven patients at a time, mostly acute cases in the tertiary stage of the disease. It was also a condition of admission that a patient either had the means to pay for their treatment or, if not, were recommended on a 'no fee' basis as a 'deserving cause' by a trustee of the hospital – a seemingly unlikely route in Hardiman's case. If he had been seeking cheap or even free treatment then, Charing Cross would appear to have been the more likely choice – although another eminently suitable institution in the area would have been the London Lock Hospital in Dean Street, Soho. This establishment had been opened in 1867 as the world's first V.D. clinic specifically for men and was less than a brisk 10-minute walk from the Harvey Buildings on the Strand.[367]

Treatment for syphilis at the time almost invariably involved remedies using mercury, or 'quicksilver' as it was known, most commonly in the form of tablets ingested orally. Mercury, as we now know, is highly toxic and a common side effect of this 'treatment' was the appearance of ulcers on the patient's face and throat. In several of the witness descriptions given for sightings of the 'Ripper' or suspicious persons associated with the Whitechapel or Thames Torso murders series, ulcers or lesions were noted as being present on the left side of the suspect's face or neck. Blemishes such as this are a common side effect of mercury poisoning, as is a marked reddening of the cheeks, something that could easily explain the 'sunburnt face' and 'rosy cheeks' described by both Ada Wilson and PC Spicer in their descriptions of the suspect they saw.

James Hardiman may also have been exhibiting the distinctive symptoms of late-stage neurosyphilis, *locomotor ataxia*, as a report in the London edition of the *New York Herald* concerning a later murder attributes a 'shuffle' to the suspect's gait, as we shall see. It is possible that other manifestations of the disease could have been responsible, for example, some related arthritic conditions or gummatous tumours associated with syphilis's tertiary stage. The FBI profile of 'Jack the Ripper' from the late 1980s suggested that the perpetrator would quite possibly have suffered from some type of physical deformity, illness or skin condition. It also alludes specifically to the distinct possibility that he could have been syphilitic.[368] It would certainly seem plausible then that James Hardiman, having contracted syphilis from a local woman, could then have gone on to exact an awful vengeance on the class of women he believed responsible for the death of his daughter. What is more, he would not only have had a clear motive for the murders – his work equipped him with the means and opportunities for their commission as well.

As regards the FBI's interest in the case, their 'Jack the Ripper' offender profile was produced in 1988 by Supervisory Special Agent John E. Douglass of the Bureau's National Centre for Analysis of Violent Crime. It was commissioned by the Cosgrove-Meurer Production Company for the television programme *The Secret Identity of Jack the Ripper* which aired shortly afterwards. Psychological profiling involves closely analysing the behaviour of an offender around their victim(s) using all available sources such as crime scene investigation, autopsy findings, background reports, etc., in an effort to identify the 'type' of person most likely to have committed the crime(s) including their motivation and general characteristics such as gender, age race, marital status and education. This, in theory, enables investigators to concentrate their efforts in the most appropriate areas. The FBI were at the forefront of this relatively new discipline at the time. The producers of the programme were keen to see if such modern 'cutting edge' techniques could be used to shed light on the historic unsolved 'Ripper' murders despite the comparatively poor-quality Victorian 'evidence' available to the profilers. Specifically, they hoped to be able to narrow down a list of several top suspects to just one 'prime suspect'. The study however only encompassed the 'canonical five' victims. The programme was staged in the US, with live feed from London, and comprised a panel of five 'experts' with five suspects to choose from (including Sir William Gull of Royal Conspiracy fame). Although the viewer phone-in poll at the end found Gull to be the most likely candidate, the 'experts' (including John Douglass himself and an FBI colleague) plumped unanimously for one of the others, Aaron Kosminski. Although the actual report was not declassified and made public until relatively recently, much of its content was used in the programme. As we have noted throughout this book, our own 'prime suspect' in the case seems to be very well matched with many of their conclusions.

Hardiman's working life revolved almost entirely around the London meat trade. He came from a family of knackers and cats' meat vendors. He had been cutting up and selling meat from a very young age; at least from age 11 according to the census records and perhaps even for a good while before that.[369] Furthermore, he was listed as being a 'knacker' (slaughterman) in 1881 while resident at 29 Hanbury Street with his young wife, Sarah, as well as at Cudworth Street four years later.[370] He was quite literally steeped in blood and gore for most of his young life. Let us remind ourselves that Harrison, Barber & Co. were far and away the largest firm of horse slaughterers in the capital. They almost enjoyed a monopoly, owning premises at Queen Victoria Street, in the City; York Road/Brandon Road, Camden; Garrett Lane, Wandsworth; Winthrop Street, Whitechapel; Westcott Street and Tabard Street, Borough; and at 35 Green Street, Blackfriars. Other yards were located at Coventry Street and Parliament Street in the East End as well as several in the Bermondsey area and elsewhere. Moreover, the meat trade interconnected with Smithfield Market and other markets across the metropolis, including those at Coventry Street and the Metropolitan Cattle Market on the Caledonian Road. It is inconceivable therefore that Hardiman would *not* have worked for Harrison, Barber – although he may well have picked up work at smaller, independent establishments, as well as at other associated businesses. As we shall see, the location of these business premises is crucial in trying to understand how James Hardiman's working life interlinked with both the Whitechapel and the Thames Torso murders. It seems certain Hardiman would have been very familiar with both the meat trade and the general geography of the area through his employment as a cats' meat salesman, slaughterman and ancillary worker. If Hardiman worked at or visited a variety of these premises across London, we can place him close to several of the murder or torso discovery sites, as well as to locations where he could have discarded victims' body parts. The discovery of limbs in the Regent's Canal close by the Metropolitan Cattle Market and the slaughterhouse at York Road/Brandon Road could mean that Hardiman was taking advantage of the yard there to dismember and dispose of his victims. It is also possible that he could have used the Garrett Lane or Tabard Street premises for any of his activities south of the river. St George's Circus (where a strange man was seen carrying a noxious smelling parcel) was an important transport hub for Hardiman. From there, he could use the No. 12 tram that would take him west to Battersea Park and the Garrett Lane slaughterhouse, or north towards London Bridge and up into East London via the Tower Subway. Other routes serving the north bank of the river involved the crossing of several bridges from which body parts could have been thrown. Yes, he would have been taking a risk, but perhaps that was part of the thrill of it all. Concealing body parts under the very noses of the detective department must have given him 'real fits'.[371] If Hardiman's employers took advantage of his willingness to work all hours and if he had developed a bond of trust through his reliability, then he may have found himself alone in yards across London, able to dismember and destroy the women he had killed – and parcel up their bodies up for disposal. He could even have hidden them in the cold storage facility of Harrison, Barber's Garrett Lane complex if it had been operational at the time.

In and around Whitechapel, Hardiman would have worn out his shoe leather as he collected and sold parcels of cats' meat from his barrow. He would have cut a sombre figure in his blood stained workman's clothes and apron. Inured to slaughtering, his hands rough and strong, it is also likely that he enjoyed a drink or two at the end of the day. If he was in and out of the local pubs such as the Ten Bells near Christ's Church, or the Britannia over by Dorset Street, or even up his cousin's place the Bricklayer's Arms, James could have met many if not all of the 'Ripper' victims at some point. As a married man whose in-laws lived either with him or close by, it may be that James Hardiman was sometimes glad of unattached female company and probably earned enough at his various occupations to pay for sex if he was denied it at home, especially during his wife's pregnancy and later when she was ill and incapacitated. A rough man with rough manners, no doubt, but these were no barrier to securing the 'affections' of a street prostitute with one eye on her lodgings or her next alcoholic 'anaesthetic'. That is to assume, of course, that Hardiman always came across as 'rough'. If this was an individual intent on 'bettering himself', by learning to read and attending Toynbee Hall, and by earning enough money to splash out on more 'respectable' clothing, it is possible that James, as a man with 'an eye for the ladies', could cut a quite different figure when he chose. There is one more thing to note about James Hardiman, however – and that is the possibility that at some point he spent time behind bars.

Rob Hills discovered that a prisoner named Hardiman (who was described as a 'meat salesman') was interned in Wandsworth Prison sometime between 1880 and 1881.[372] The prisoner's name was recorded as 'James Alf Hardiman' with his place of birth noted as Bermondsey.[373] 'Alf' was not released until 25 November 1881, whereas James Hardiman was supposedly living at 29 Hanbury Street according to the census of that year. But what if Sarah had told the enumerator that her husband was simply at work, or otherwise not at home, and that he 'normally' lived there? This might explain the anomaly. Garrett Lane slaughterhouse was situated only a few minutes' walk from the prison and it is not beyond the realms of possibility that he could have sought work there immediately upon his release, as undoubtedly he would have been penniless and fairly desperate for any money he could get. Perhaps more significantly, although the birth of James's elder sister, Sarah, was registered in Whitechapel in 1858, the census record tells us that she was actually born in Bermondsey on the Old Kent Road.[374] Although James's birth was also registered in Whitechapel, it is just conceivable that his roots also lay in the area south of the river. For the record, it should also be noted that Tabard Street, which ran virtually as a continuation of the Old Kent Road at its western end, was also home to another Harrison, Barber premises. Another coincidence perhaps but, if so, then they are quickly mounting up.

The prisoner known as 'Alf' Hardiman had been sentenced to 12 months hard labour at Southwark Police Court for theft and embezzlement. A prison sentence would certainly have hardened James and perhaps helped to remove any lingering vestiges of humanity he might have had. In addition, he would have come into contact with the wider criminal fraternity. Embezzlement is a form of petty theft but one that is rarely committed with others. It is a solitary crime and that fits the profile we are developing of Hardiman as an individual who operated independently of others. In Wandsworth gaol he might have picked up useful titbits about avoiding getting caught in future, or new 'dodges' he might try when he got out. Importantly James might have talked to fellow inmates about more serious offences and those who committed them. Prisons have long been seen as breeding grounds for further acts of villainy and perhaps there he might have learned new 'skills' such as the ability to render a person unconscious, or worse.

Prison would also have made him reliant on any future employer's good will too; one indiscretion might be overlooked but from now on, James had to keep his nose clean and take any work he could get if he was going to support his family. Thus in James Hardiman we see a man who would travel considerable distances to find work and who would probably give up his evenings, weekends and bank holidays to earn a living. To the expanding firm of Harrison, Barber, James may have seemed to be the ideal employee – flexible, well connected and willing. For James, however, the company offered a network of locations to indulge his darker passions, locations in which he could often have been left alone with complete freedom of action. Although no official photograph of 'Alf' has been found to date, the prison did record a physical description of their charge. It reads:

Age 23 years, Height 5'4", Fair Complexion, Light brown Hair, Blue eyes.[375]

Most 'Ripper' studies close with the murder of Mary Kelly in Miller's Court and explain the end of the cycle as the result of the death, flight or capture of the suspect. But as we have seen, the killer struck again later in November even though he failed on this occasion, with Annie Farmer surviving the knife attack on her. Soon afterwards Montague Druitt (an unlikely but much-championed 'Ripper' suspect) was dragged out of the Thames. The East End thereafter had settled down and held its collective breath. Had 'Jack' stopped his bloody work, was he really dead or confined to a lunatic asylum? Sadly for at least four other women, he was not – as the following chapters will show.

12

THE KILLER RESURFACES

In the aftermath of the murder at Miller's Court, life in Whitechapel had, to some extent at least, returned to what passed for 'normal'. The police presence in Dorset Street lasted for under two weeks – at first it was welcomed by residents for the protection it apparently offered, then it was resented as unnecessary interference in their daily lives. Jack McCarthy, Kelly's former landlord, relet Number 13 Miller's Court without even bothering to redecorate it and the next tenant lived there without seemingly being notably disturbed by the fading bloodstains on the walls.[376] Journalists continued to snoop around the area and interested tourists peered into the hovels and alleyways of the 'abyss' to see 'how the poor lived'.

On the last day of 1888 a body was dragged out of the River Thames and later identified as that of Montague John Druitt, a lawyer and private school teacher. Druitt had committed suicide following his sacking as tutor at a school in Blackheath. It is possible, but not established, that Druitt may have been interfering with one or more of his pupils; all we know is that one report suggested he had 'got into serious trouble at the school'. Paul Begg's observation that Druitt worked out his notice and was not, therefore, summarily dismissed (as he undoubtedly would have been had there been any substance to any allegations of paedophile behaviour) is persuasive.[377] However, his dismissal from his position seems to have plunged him into depression. There was a history of mental illness in his family and the note he left behind him reportedly stated that: 'Since Friday I felt I was going to be like mother, and the best thing for me was to die.'[378] His candidature for being 'the Ripper' comes from his inclusion in Sir Melville Mcnaghten's famous memorandum, which named Druitt alongside Michael Ostrog and 'Kosminski' as the police's three favoured suspects.[379] Mcnaghten appears to have favoured Druitt in part because he saw the murders as a series that rose in intensity, culminating with Mary Kelly as the final victim. Druitt's suicide appeared to correspond with the end of the series, with the Miller's Court slaying being the 'tipping point' that sent the young barrister over the edge into madness. In almost all other respects there is very little that ties Druitt to the murders. Mcnaghten mistakenly thought he was a doctor and given the notion circulating at the time – that 'the Ripper' was possibly a medical man – this may have persuaded Sir Melville that, given the timing, this might just be the man the police had been looking for.[380] He was a respectable gentleman, a Sunday cricketer; he was not familiar with Whitechapel and had no real motive for the murders. If he had not killed himself, it is unlikely that anyone would have posited him as a potential killer. Druitt's candidacy has far more to do with contemporary notions of the sort of person that might be the killer than any forensic proof that he was.[381]

The Thames was to give up another secret in the months following the discovery of Druitt's body and remind the capital that any idea that the murderer had been captured, died or had otherwise stopped killing was a false one. On 4 June 1889 two workmen found a parcel near St George's Stairs, Horsleydown, and the press immediately leapt to the conclusion that it was either the work of a prankster or yet another episode in the 'Ripper' murders.[382] Disturbingly the package had become the plaything of some local children who were pelting it with stones until a nearby stevedore intervened. The package contained human remains: the lower abdomen of a young woman who, it was soon established, had been subject of an illegal abortion. A woman's left leg and thigh were then found near the Albert Bridge.[383] Dr Bond examined the two parts and confirmed that they belonged to the same person. Two days later, another section of the body appeared at Battersea, in a shrubbery, wrapped up in a piece of fabric cut or torn from a woman's burgundy-coloured dress. The gardener who found it was alerted by the stench that had been coming from it.[384] The gardener, Joseph Davis, quickly went off to find a policeman.[385] This upper torso (which lacked both head and arms) was found in bushes high on the foreshore at Battersea Park, just 200 yards from the previous discovery under Albert Bridge. This was found to have considerable damage to the rib cage. A gipsy traveller then reported finding a right foot and part of the leg near Wandsworth Bridge on the Friday, with more parts being washed up at Limehouse and near Bankside. On 8 June a woman's buttocks and pelvis were taken out of the mud of the river between the Battersea and Albert bridges by a Thames Police officer. Curiously, a piece of cloth 'probably a handkerchief' had been rolled and inserted into the victim's rectum and vagina.[386]

All the various body parts were sent to the Battersea mortuary to be examined together by the police surgeon Dr Kempster, who had previously worked on the Rainham case. He was of the opinion that the victim had been killed about 24 hours earlier and that the thigh had only been in the water a short time. The piece found over the river on the Chelsea Embankment, had been in the grounds of Sir Percy Shelley's house (the son of Mary Shelley, the author of *Frankenstein*) apparently thrown over a fence, but this macabre link to a cultural legend of body-dealing was less significant than another coincidence – two of the discoveries were made close to the Harrison, Barber slaughterhouse in Queen Victoria Street.

The furthest upstream find was discovered near Wandsworth Bridge, on the southern foreshore. This was less than a kilometre from the confluence with the River Wandle and less than a 20-minute walk from the Harrison, Barber slaughterhouse in Garratt Lane, which stood on the riverbank. Garratt Lane had the largest cold store in London at the time – capable of storing 250 horse carcasses.[387] Although it appears that the Whitehall torso had decomposed naturally, evidence suggests that elements of the Rainham one had perhaps been preserved – the body parts discovered over a period of nearly a month showed similar levels of decomposition. The lack of skin wrinkling evident in the remains that were found in central London suggested that they had not been placed there simultaneously. If they had been somehow preserved in the meantime, could the cold store at Harrison, Barber's Garrett Lane yard, or another like it elsewhere, perhaps provide the answer? The possibility is intriguing.

Unlike the previous Torso cases, all the body parts (except the head, heart and lungs) had been recovered and a partial reconstruction had been attempted as an aid to identification. And this time a positive identification eventually occurred, with the victim's mother coming forward to name her as Elizabeth Jackson, a 24-year-old casual prostitute who had recently fallen from grace and who had taken to sleeping rough on the Chelsea Embankment.

The press was particularly shocked to learn that Jackson had been pregnant when she died and that her killer had seemingly performed some sort of abortion on her. They were also disturbed by the news that the body had been abused in some unnatural manner, with the invasion of her vagina and anus. When Dr Bond examined her, he noted that the uterus had been deliberately cut open and the foetus removed. It goes without saying that the absence of the heart (as perhaps had been the case with Mary Kelly) and the concentration on the uterus (as with Chapman, Eddowes and possibly the Whitehall torso) has clear echoes to the other murders in the series. Again, as with the other victims, the cause of death may well have been asphyxiation due to garrotting prior to severance of the carotid artery. Noting the latter, the doctors who examined the remains, concluded it was probably the work of a *horse slaughterer or butcher* rather than a surgeon.[388]

Interestingly, when the police investigated Jackson's movements prior to her death some of her acquaintances came forward to give evidence. This established that she had been alive up until 24 hours before her body parts began to surface in and around the river. According to 'Ginger Nell', Jackson was homeless and was known to sleep rough in Battersea Park after closing time. The park was a notorious location for sex workers and their clients but also a dangerous place to be found at night. It would have provided a serial killer ample opportunity to select a suitable victim and carry out such a gruesome murder and mutilation. The arm recovered at St George's Circus, and which was connected to the Torso series, had been covered in lime. In the absence of any evidence to suggest that James Hardiman was a keen gardener, we must ask ourselves where the killer could possibly have come across such material. It is interesting that although the park's soil is now considered pH neutral in most areas, it is still somewhat acidic in others, particularly the wooded ones. Almost certainly this would have been the case for the entire park before certain areas had been treated with lime to aid plant growth – the park had been open for about 30 years at the time of the murders. This is of particular interest given that the upper torso, the heaviest portion, which was discovered by the gardener in the shrubbery, was found very near to where any lime that was being used in the park was most likely to have been stored – the works yard. As with the Whitehall torso case, there would have been no shortage of tools in the workshops, including the carpentry saws which would have been so essential for the killer's activities that night. In addition, there would have been plenty of places in the vicinity to store some of the smaller body parts for later retrieval and distribution.

Some months later, on Thursday 13 September, and thus on the first anniversary of Sarah Hardiman's death, a pickle jar containing a human foetus was found. Although at the time Dr Kempster

Gustave Doré, *Wentworth Street* (1872). This engraving gives a good idea of the miserable conditions in the East End of London.

This 'poverty map' of London in 1889 shows dark squares for the lowest level of existence. Social reformer Charles Booth drew maps to link poverty, unemployment and crime. The River Thames is in the lower right corner, with Victoria Embankment curving along its bank. The Whitechapel area, which had even high levels of poverty, is further to the right. In areas where people struggled to find paid work, women sometimes sold sex on the streets as a means of earning enough to pay for a night's accommodation.

MAP DESCRIPTIVE OF LONDON POVERTY, 1898-9
(SW 10 SHEETS)

THE STREETS ARE COLOURED ACCORDING TO THE GENERAL CONDITION OF THE INHABITANTS, AS UNDER:—

Lowest class. Vicious, semi-criminal.

Very poor, casual. Chronic want.

Poor. 18s. to 21s. a week for a moderate family.

Mixed. Some comfortable, others poor.

Fairly comfortable. Good ordinary earnings.

Middle class. Well-to-do.

Upper-middle and Upper classes. Wealthy.

A combination of colours—as dark blue and black, or pink and red—indicates that the street contains a fair proportion of each of the classes represented by the respective colours.

Map Descriptive of London Poverty, 1898–9. This image is of areas south of the Thames River. Note Battersea Park, shown in the upper centre of the map. It was here that the Horsleydown Torso was found in a shrubbery on the foreshore.

Left: Buck's Row, where Polly Nichols died.

Below: Berner Street. The gates to Dutfield's Yard are below the cartwheel. Elizabeth Stride was found dead just inside the gates.

Above: An artist's impression of Mitre Square, where Catherine Eddowes was found.

Right: The entrance to Goulston Street Buildings, where the famous graffito about 'Jewes' was discovered.

The entrance to Miller's Court, where Mary Jane Kelly had been living.

The windows through which Thomas Bowyer saw Mary Jane Kelly's body in her room at No. 13 Miller's Court. He had been sent to collect her rent, which was in arrears.

Dorset Street, Whitechapel, known at one time as the 'worst street in London'.

The London Hospital, Whitechapel: the facade. Engraving, c.1836. It was here that Emma Smith was taken after she was assaulted close to Whitechapel Church on 3 April 1888, and where she later died of internal injuries. It was also where James Hardiman's wife, Sarah, spent her last days. Evidence was found near the hospital after another killing at the end of September 1888. (Wellcome Collection)

Above: Berner Street, Whitechapel, where Elizabeth Stride met her death in September 1888.

Left: A later image showing the hand barrow used in a trade that flourished in the late 1800s, that of the cat's meat man. Horseflesh was cut up and threaded onto skewers to be fed to pets. Some of the very poorest families may have eaten this meat themselves but would not have let their neighbours know.

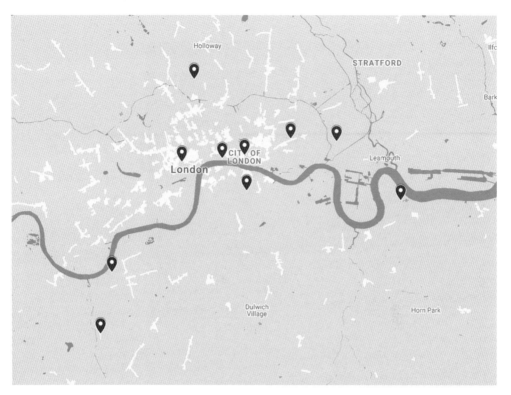

Harrison, Barber & Co. removed horses that were injured or had died in the streets of London. By 1889 the firm had expanded and had several yards, shown on this map.

Pinchin Street looking west towards Backchurch Lane. The torso was discovered in the bricked-up arch with the small windows near the end. The London and Blackwall Railway lines ran along the top of the arches. (Authors' collection)

The Tower
Subway
from a map
of 1895
showing its
position in
relation to
the Tower
of London
and Tower
Bridge,
which was
completed in
1894.

Inside the
Tower
Subway –
although it
was dark
and damp,
it provided
quick access
from one side
of the River
Thames to
the other.

South London tram map showing the route of the No12 connecting Garratt Lane, Wandsworth and London Bridge (Tower Tube) via Battersea Park and St. George's Circus (March 1914).

Ingleside, Wandsworth, where Polly Nichols had once worked. In April 1888 she had written to her father to tell him of her good fortune but by August she was back in digs in Thrawl Street, having run away from her new opportunity with some of her master's property.

Looking east along Heneage Street, towards Brick Lane, showing The Pride of Spitalfields pub (formerly The Romford Arms).

Heneage Street today. (Authors' collection)

Sir Charles Warren, the retired Metropolitan Police Commissioner. He was in charge during the Whitehall murder series and had a difficult relationship with some sections of the press. He resigned as the head of the Met after Mary Kelly's inquest.

Sir Robert Anderson, Assistant Commissioner, Metropolitan Police. (*Windsor Magazine*)

Left: Sir Melville Macnaghten, Assistant Chief Constable C.I.D. Sir Robert and Sir Melville both wrote memoirs in which they presented their theories of who 'Jack the Ripper' was.

Below left: Sir Henry Smith, the Acting Commissioner of the City Police. He believed he had been close on the trail of the killer shortly after he had killed Kate Eddowes when he found a bloodied water trough in a close off Dorset Street, in which he assumed the killer must have washed his hands.

Below: Inspector Frederick George Abberline. He and the rest of H Division investigated the series of murders that soon had the press in a frenzy of speculation.

Above left: Detective Inspector Edmund Reid. He was a central figure in the investigation of several of the killings. *(Police Review)*

Above right: Dr George Bagster Phillips attended the scene of Elizabeth Stride's murder and later performed a post-mortem.

Above left: Dr Frederick Gordon Brown examined the body of Catherine Eddowes after she had been murdered and said whoever had cut up her body knew what he was doing.

Above right: Dr Thomas Bond said the Rainham torso belonged to a 'well-nourished stout woman' of around 25 and it had been in situ for about three days before it was found.

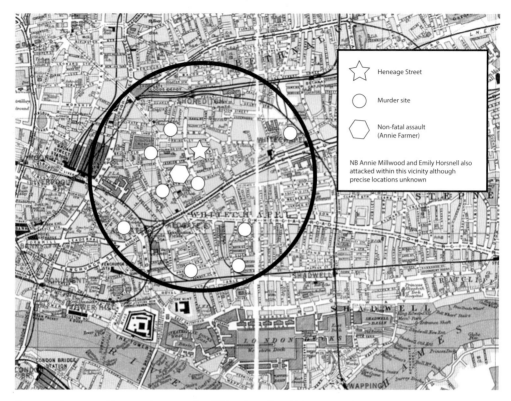

Heneage Street and its proximity to the Whitechapel and Torso attack sites, 1888-1891.

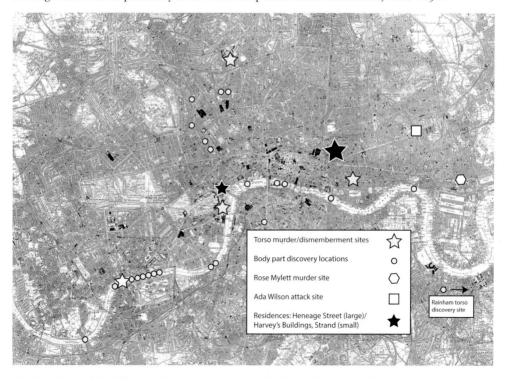

The locations of the Thames Torso body parts, and other related assaults.

suggested that it was probably not related to Jackson, we find the discovery potentially significant. The Horsleydown torso was, along with the Rainham and Whitehall cases, the third of the 'Thames Mysteries' to baffle the police in 1887–9 and while most researchers have been content to treat these and the Whitechapel killings as separate entities, we think there is ample evidence to suggest that they were the work of just one individual. Some elements of the press certainly believed it was possible and while the body parts were being discovered, a letter was published in the newspapers that purported to come from the killer. The police ignored it, presumably having become inured to the various cranks who had sent countless missives to them but this one did at least appear to offer some inside knowledge of events:

I see you have been finding the pieces.
How is it you have not caught me yet?
Look out for more pieces

It was signed 'Jack the Ripper'.[389]

Jackson was not the killer's final victim, or even the last of the Torso murders in 1889. Just as London started to settle down again, the murderer struck once more in the Whitechapel area. Running parallel to Goulston Street and intersecting with Wentworth Street is Old Castle Street, in the heart of Spitalfields. In 1889 it was simply 'Castle Alley', a notoriously poor and degraded narrow passageway with a desperate reputation at the time for vice and crime. On 17 July 1889, PC Walter Andrews was patrolling along the alley at a 12.15 in the morning when he noticed something or someone lying between two coster barrows. That 'something' was a woman's body and the police constable immediately called for assistance. Help arrived in the form of his sergeant, Edward Badham,[390] and eventually Inspector Edmund Reid, soon to be joined by Dr Philips, who had examined several of the previous Whitechapel murder victims.[391] In fact, there were to be two medical examinations and they came to quite different conclusions.

As with the attack on Annie Farmer, it became apparent that some elements within the police were keen to establish that the 'Ripper' murder series had ended in Miller's Court. Some of the findings, however, would soon suggest otherwise.

The murder victim was identified as Alice McKenzie, a 40-year-old woman who had been living with her partner, John McCormack, at Mr Tenpenny's lodging house at 52 Gun Street, Spitalfields, close to Dorset Street and the scene of Kelly's murder.[392] Indeed, it seems that she too was known to use the name 'Kelly' on occasion.[393] On the night of her murder she had been seen out and about and, between 11.30 and midnight, she was last spotted in Flower and Dean Street, heading towards Brick Lane.[394] Her throat had been cut, with two incisions. The cause of death was believed to be severing of the carotid artery, as in most of the previous murders where it was believed the cause could reasonably be established. It could, of course, have been preceded by a garrotting, as was potentially the case with several of the other victims. Dr Bond, the second of the two medical examiners, reported that the abdomen had also been attacked with a series of jagged cuts, extending from the chest to the vagina. He believed that the attacker had lifted the woman's clothes (she was found with her legs pushed up) with his left hand and then mutilated her with his right.[395] Bond was adamant that he was looking at another 'Ripper' victim while, just as vehemently, Phillips disagreed.[396] Bond's report ended with the statement that he saw 'evidence of similar design to the previous Whitechapel murders'. He noted 'sudden onslaught' on the throat of the victim, and mutilations, which indicated 'sexual thoughts and a desire to mutilate the abdomen and sexual organs'.[397] Thomas Bond was perhaps the foremost forensic expert of his day, and was 'often brought in when other medical evidence was in doubt'.[398] The fact that the new Chief Commissioner of the Met, James Munro, chose to place plain clothes detectives on the streets of Whitechapel for the next two months suggests he probably concurred with Bond's analysis, or at least felt there was reasonable grounds for caution.[399]

In fact, McKenzie fits the profile of a 'Ripper' victim in several ways and we find it impossible to exclude her from the series. She was an occasional street prostitute, just like some of the other murdered women; she was murdered in the heart of the East End – on the streets of the 'hot zone' around Flower and Dean Street – by someone who knew the movements of the local police and could easily escape. Her injuries were similar to some of the others: more severe than Stride, when the killer was interrupted, although not as marked as Eddowes and Kelly, when he had more time. But the nature of the killing and the mutilations would seem entirely consistent with someone intent on expressing anger against a class of women held responsible for the destruction of family life.

Alice McKenzie, forever known as 'clay pipe Alice' because when she was examined an old clay pipe was discovered within the folds of her clothing, was definitely killed and mutilated on the street, putting to bed an idea that the killer carried out his 'street' murders somewhere else and then dumped the body, something which had been suggested as early as the Buck's Row murder.[400] The pavement below Alice's body was dry, and it had started raining in Whitechapel just as PC Andrews had turned into the alley and stumbled upon her body. This shows she was killed in the street. The killer had struck again in Whitechapel after an absence of eight months and the press were quick to make the association that 'Jack the Ripper' was back.[401] The press returned to speculating on the identity of the suspect and to ridiculing the police's attempts to catch him. The police had apparently varied their beats in order to 'fog' attempts by the killer to work these out (clearly unsuccessfully) and they still had no clue as to the murderer's identity. They believed perhaps he might be a foreign sailor – such as a Lascar or a Portuguese, both noted for their love of knives and their ability to use them – who was hitting the streets of the capital when his ship came into port. In one of many letters sent to the papers and police, Dr Forbes Winslow complained that the police had ignored his advice on how to catch the 'dangerous homicidal lunatic' he believed the person to be, and that he would be shown to be correct when the killer was eventually apprehended.[402] There was even another letter, this time sent to Mr Albert Backert of the Whitechapel Vigilance Committee, promising that the attacks would recommence in July with the police reporting that they had received several similar letters in previous weeks.[403] Naturally we do not want to make too much of the letters, most of which were almost certainly penned by misguided if not completely deluded individuals. But within these press reports are the vestiges of truth – the killer had not stopped in November 1888 and we should view the Castle Alley murder as very much a part of his continuing campaign against the capital's 'unfortunates'.

Almost two months later, on 11 September 1889, the police received a letter from somewhere in south-west London. It referred to a close encounter the author had just had with a policeman. The writer (who signed himself 'JMS Clarke, Not Jack the Ripper') stated that 'I must confess I was as nere cought this morning as possible. PC passed me while i was carring my deadly parcel to the arch off cable st or nere there' [*sic*]. He went on to suggest that he was tired of killing and wished he was 'ded'.[404] A week or so earlier, on Tuesday 3 September, another note had been found behind the London Hospital on Whitechapel Road (where Sarah Hardiman had spent her last weeks) in which the author intimated responsibility for the previous murders and indicated his intention to begin killing again soon. Were these the work of the same person, or yet more examples of hoaxers enjoying the small amount of publicity that the publication or news of these letters brought? As far as the authors are concerned, not only do we believe these to have been the work of the same person, we think they offer further possible evidence that James Hardiman was a serial killer.

The one received by the police on 11 September would appear to be yet another example of the rampant game-playing which characterised this killer's actions – the initials 'JMS' being a contraction of Hardiman's given name, James. A play on his surname however was perhaps too risky even for him, so he was forced to find an alternative. Even here, though, instead of choosing something random, he seemed compelled to offer a taunting clue with personal significance. 'Clarke', we should remember, was the name of the builder in whose yard he had murdered Rose Mylett the previous year – an event perhaps still very much on his mind. As regards the letter found behind the London Hospital, the first anniversary of his wife's death there was also only 10 days away – the predicted resumption of hostilities, therefore, was probably no coincidence at all. Although the timing of the signed letter was no doubt designed to confuse, there may have been a grain of truth in the sentiment expressed regarding his weariness with killing. By this stage he had probably murdered at least 11 women and seriously injured several more.

On the following Sunday, the 8th, it was noticed that a well-known Whitechapel prostitute, Lydia Hart, was missing from her usual haunts in the area. All seemed quiet, however, until a patrolling policeman made a particularly grim discovery on his Whitechapel rounds during the early morning of Tuesday 10 September. PC Pennett was new to his beat. At 5.25 a.m. he turned into Pinchin Street from Christian Street. Along one side of Pinchin Street was a row of railway arches (that are still there today) underneath which rough sleepers often made their beds. By a broken-down hoarding, PC Pennett noticed a package on the ground inside one of the arches. When he investigated he discovered it was a decomposing human torso lying on its stomach, minus the head and legs. Summoning help, Pennett waited for the police operation to swing into action and, by 6 a.m., Dr Philips' assistant, Dr Percy Clark, arrived on the scene and examined the body. After this preliminary check, the torso was piled onto a cart and taken to the nearby St George-in-the-East mortuary for further investigation. The torso belonged to a woman, probably aged 30 to 40 and about 5 foot 3 inches tall. Dr Phillips believed the woman had died as a result of having her throat cut and while there was some speculation that a certain degree of surgical skills was evident in the way the head had been separated, Philips was of the opinion that this was simply the work of someone adept in butchery. To see what Pinchin street looks like today, *see* the plate section.

Also present at the post-mortem were Doctors Clark and Hebbert; the latter had examined the remains of Elizabeth Jackson. They concluded that the victim had never borne children but was not a virgin.[405] They could also detect no evidence of a wedding ring having been worn or hard manual work having been undertaken on a regular basis, although the police noted that both elbows were discoloured as if continually leant upon. Although there was a large gash on the abdomen she had not been eviscerated and all the organs (including the uterus) were present and healthy. The liver showed signs of alcoholism.[406] Dr Phillips also noted that certain aspects of the dismemberment showed similarities with the mutilations sustained by Mary Kelly. Both Phillips and Hebbert agreed that blood loss was the most likely cause of death, with Phillips of the opinion that this had been rapid – probably due to her throat having been cut. Judging by the attending advancement of *rigor mortis* and decomposition, Clark estimated the time of death to have been in excess of 24 hours previously, early Monday morning or late Sunday night – a timeframe subsequently adopted by Police Commissioner Monro in his official report. It needs to be acknowledged that Monro was sceptical that this was a murder committed by the Whitechapel killer. He thought the wounds looked different and suggested that if the torso hadn't been found in Whitechapel no one would have associated the death with 'Jack the Ripper'. Noting that one cut had seemed to target the 'organs of generation', he saw this as either a slip of the knife or a deliberate attempt to divert attention away from the real killer and onto the man associated with all the other deaths in the district.[407] However, Monro was open to the idea that the Pinchin Street discovery was connected to other Thames Torso murders. Perhaps he simply couldn't accept the idea that the cases were interconnected, or else he supposed that one serial killer had now chosen to place himself at the heart of the police investigation into another. It is entirely possible of course, but is it probable?

Given that the murder had not occurred at the spot on Pinchin Street where she was found, but probably nearby, the police began a house-to-house search of the area. Crowds gathered in Pinchin Street as they had in previous murder investigations and the press immediately began to connect this latest discovery with the Whitechapel series and the other Thames Torso murders. Were they right to do so, or was this incident entirely unconnected to the other killings?

In the course of the police investigation, three men found sleeping rough under the arches were quickly eliminated from the enquiry. Likewise, the involvement of several barrows and carts found there, stacked up against the walls, was also discounted.[408] Commissioner Monro believed the torso had been placed there between 5 a.m and 5.30, given that the crime scene was passed every half-an-hour by a patrolling beat officer. They established that a handcart or barrow was the most likely means of transport. This was hardly contentious; someone in the street carrying a dead body slung over their shoulders would, after all, be bound to attract attention. It remains rather a mystery, therefore, that no one that morning, especially numerous policemen in the area, seems to have heard or seen such a barrow or cart clattering its invariably noisy way across the cobbles of the otherwise quiet and deserted streets. Unless of course that was such a familiar sound for the district and therefore one that simply passed unnoticed.

There was one piece of tangible evidence that might have helped the police in their enquiries, had they had the means to decipher it. A blood-stained segment of underwear was lifted from Hooper Street, where it seems to have been stuffed through a hole in a fence about 120 metres north from Pinchin Street on Backchurch Lane. Sadly the late-nineteenth-century police lacked the forensic science available today and they could do very little with this find, and so, like the row of carts at the scene, this too was dismissed by the police as inconsequential. The location might be important, however, given the case we have tried to build against Hardiman. In 1889 Hooper Street was the site of a hydraulic pumping station that brought LBR wagons down to ground level to enable their entry into the Commercial Road goods depot following an elevated approach above Pinchin Street. The road is much changed today and the railway has long gone. Now Hooper Street runs seamlessly into Leman Street, but it seems that this wasn't necessarily the case in 1889. Although a rail bridge may well have been in place then, which enabled travel on an underlying road for much of the time, this was not, it seems, always possible due to the railway traffic which periodically crossed it.[409] It may not, therefore, have served the killer as an escape route that night (or indeed on the night of the 'double event' the previous year) and it is entirely possible that on this occasion, having deposited the torso and the piece of underwear, he made his way north instead towards Commercial Road. This could explain why no one had seen him in the upper reaches of Back Church Lane immediately following the discovery. Having quickly ducked into Hooper Street, he could then have proceeded up the much quieter (and darker) Gower's Walk running alongside the goods yard if Heneage Street had been his destination. Once on Commercial Road it was a short hop across into Osborn Street and Brick Lane before he reached the sanctuary of home. Indeed, having extensively walked the area, the authors believe that a quicker route to Heneage Street is hard to find and his route would have taken the killer no more than 10 minutes to complete. Alternatively, if destined for Charing Cross, he may have crossed the railway tracks at Hooper Street or made use of the railway tunnel, as we believe he may have done following Stride's killing. In fact, we think that he had already used the tunnel once before that night during the commission of this crime – a point we will return to in just a moment. If the bloodied rag had been a clue, it seems that yet again the police had been unable to profit from it.

There were several suggestions as to the identity of the murdered woman whose headless body was found under the Pinchin Street arches. At first it was suspected to be that of Lydia 'Lyddy' Hart, the missing streetwalker, but she turned out to have been on something of a drinking spree and was otherwise unharmed. It was also reported in a Mexican newspaper that the torso might be that of Emily Barker, a young woman who had gone missing from her hometown of Northampton, but the police rejected this idea.[410] In the end the remains were buried in a tin container at the East London Cemetery in early October and her identity remains unknown. There was to be one further twist in the Pinchin Street story, however, something which recent researchers have chosen to skirt around or ignore but one which is crucial to our case. It is necessary, therefore, to set it out in some detail.

In the early hours of the previous Sunday morning (8 September) a man had walked into the offices of the *New York Herald* in Fleet Street claiming to have information about the murder of a woman in Back Church Lane. Giving his name as 'John Cleary' or 'Leary' and what turned out to be a false an address at 21 White Horse Yard, Drury Lane, Covent Garden, the man had said that he had been told by a police inspector that a body had been discovered there by a policeman at 20 minutes past 11 that night – Saturday 7 September. Two reporters from the *New York Herald* raced over to Back Church Lane to investigate his story and, although they had asked him to accompany them, he had very quickly disappeared. Finding nothing untoward at the scene they made their way to Leman Street Police Station to find out what, if anything, was going on. No one there had any knowledge of a body being discovered and the whole episode was dismissed as a hoax. Things all changed two days later, however, with the discovery of the torso in Pinchin Street and frantic efforts began to try to trace the informant. The police were frustrated by the fact that the man had given a false name and address.[411] On the day after the discovery, Wednesday 11 September, the *New York Herald* published a description of the person who had presented himself at their offices that night:

> Circa 25–28 years, approx. 5' 4" in height, Medium build,
>
> Light complexion, Fair moustache, Blue eyes.
>
> Inflamed spot on left cheek (healing boil?), wearing dirty White handkerchief around neck and a round, stiff, black felt hat.
>
> Walked with a shuffle and spoke like, and resembled, a 'developing' Whitechapel resident.[412]

This description bears strong comparison with some of the other witness sightings of men associated with the Whitechapel series. Notable is the reference to a mark on the cheek and the handkerchief around the neck – possibly to hide skin abrasions associated with syphilis. If we add the 'shuffle' of his gait then it might indeed point towards someone suffering with the so-called 'French disease' and its associated symptoms and maladies. The inflamed spot or boil on the left side of the face is very like the scar or abscess that witnesses Ellen Marks and Philip Harris noticed on the left side of the suspect's neck or throat at the time of Annie Farmer's assault 10 months earlier. As well as possessing very similar physical characteristics, the specific type of hat described in both cases and the handkerchief around the neck give rise to the strong possibility that this could be the same man. It also bears a striking resemblance to the description of the mysterious prisoner James 'Alf' Hardiman who had been incarcerated at Wandsworth – right down to the colour of the eyes.[413] As has been previously stated, the age on James's marriage certificate was wrong. The prison authorities may well have believed him to have been aged about 23 on admission but he was 21 then, and 22 on discharge. This would have made him 29 at the time the *New York Herald* issued their description – only a year older than their upper estimate.

Despite extensive enquiries the police were apparently no nearer tracing 'John Cleary' when, two days later, a person resembling his description and claiming to be the wanted man, walked into their headquarters in Whitehall Place, Great Scotland Yard. He gave his name this time as John Arnold and his address as No. 2 Harvey's Buildings on the Strand. Recanting his previous story that a police officer (or ex-police officer) had told him about the body, he stated that a person resembling a soldier outside the King Lud pub in Fleet Street, where he had been selling copies of the *New York Herald*, had given him the information. He explained that he'd given false details as to his identity so that his wife would not discover his whereabouts. It should be noted that both his visit to the newspaper offices and the likely death of the Pinchin Street Torso victim (8 September) occurred on the first anniversary of Annie Chapman's murder – a point which was not overlooked by the police at the time.[414] The day on which he gave himself up, 13 September, was the day that the pickle jar containing the foetus in the case of Jackson had been found and it was also the first anniversary of the death of James's wife, Sarah.

The location of his surrender is also noteworthy from a psychological perspective. It seems that Hardiman had chosen to give himself up not at any old police station, but at the very nerve centre of the organisation that was hunting him. Furthermore, it was only 350 metres or so along the Victoria Embankment from where he had so humiliated the police the previous year with the discovery of the torso in their fledgling new headquarters. Was this in fact the latest sneering episode in an increasingly cynical production – a further chapter in the psychological war that characterises many a serial killer's campaign of terror? In fact it seems that 'Arnold' was actually known to the police of H Division (under what name though is hard to determine) as something of a drinker and gambler who had served 21 days behind bars for 'wife desertion' although he was not thought to be dishonest.[415] Although deeply suspicious of him following his 'confession', the police had no real alternative but to let him go, as they must have let so many potential 'Ripper' suspects slip through their fingers. We should not be surprised at this, however; Peter Sutcliffe (the 'Yorkshire Ripper') was questioned on no less than nine occasions in the period that he killed 13 women in the north of England.[416] The fact was that the police were not really looking for a cats' meat man at all, they were on alert for a violent sailor, a deranged Jewish butcher or maybe even a medical man with a Gladstone bag. Nevertheless, it seems that for a time at least, he would have been considered a top suspect in the case and kept under close observation as a result. If we are right, the culprit, it seems, may well have been under their noses for some time – hiding, as the saying goes, in plain sight.

This was not the first time that Harvey Buildings, where 'Arnold' said he lived, had cropped up in the police investigation. Although his testimony subsequently proved to be false, a certain William Brodie who also claimed to reside there had confessed to the murder of Alice McKenzie some two months previously.[417] Given its relative remoteness from the Whitechapel crime scenes and the similar timeframe involved, it is certainly intriguing then that two characters associated with the murders should have apparently been living there. Another coincidence among many perhaps?

Now let us concentrate on Pinchin Street, as it has particular significance for both the Whitehall *and* the Torso murders given its location and the nature of the associated killing. The discovery there represented a 'cross-over' point between the two sets. On this occasion, a 'Torso' victim had been found on 'Jack's patch' in Whitechapel – near where Elizabeth Stride's body had been discovered a year earlier. But what was it that would have attracted Hardiman there in the first place, given that there were no slaughterhouses in the immediate vicinity? The answer could lie in the fact that the cats' meat trade and Harrison, Barber was not the only common association between the two sets of murders. At various times as we have seen, the previously mentioned cart maker, Arthur Dutfield, had maintained business premises in both the eponymous Berner Street yard of Stride's demise, as well as in nearby Pinchin Street where the torso was discovered. We believe that one of the keys to solving the case lies in the probable association between this business, Hardiman and the closely related horse-slaughtering one of Harrison, Barber & Co.

In 1886, two years prior to Stride's death, Arthur Dutfield had moved his operations from Berner Street to new premises beneath the arches at 10–18 Pinchin Street, a notorious night-time haunt of prostitutes. He was located here at the time of both murders (Liz Stride and the Torso victim) with his previous premises in Berner Street seemingly remaining unoccupied at the time of Stride's demise. However, a sack manufacturer, W. Hindley, had still operated there. Hardiman was familiar with Pinchin Street and its environs at the time of Stride's murder as he appears to have used it as an escape route on his way west to kill Eddowes in Mitre Square. Had he also used his knowledge of Dutfield's former premises in Berner Street to evade capture on the occasion of Stride's death? Many people, then and now, believe the killer may have been hiding somewhere in the yard immediately after the murder or used a secret escape route from it to evade capture. It seems very likely that, given the availability of possible targets, Hardiman had picked up his 'Torso' victim in Pinchin Street itself in 1889. Had he also picked up Elizabeth Stride there the previous year? As we have seen, the witness testimony certainly suggests that this could have been the case.

Commissioner Monro thought that the Pinchin Street victim was likely to have been killed and dismembered on the Sunday evening in private premises the killer either had legitimate access to, or could otherwise gain entry to.[418] He believed, however, that the torso had probably been placed under the arch between 5 and 5.30 on Tuesday morning – primarily it seems on the strength of Constable Pennett's testimony, which he accepted.[419] Had Constable Pennett been somewhat economical with the truth, though, in order to cover up a degree of complacency on his part? Does his contention that it was the torso's smell that first caused him to cross the road and investigate imply that he normally walked on the opposite, pavement side, of the road? If so, how could he have been so sure the torso was not there on previous occasions, as he had stated? Had it actually been placed there under cover of darkness around the same time the previous morning when it was not as decomposed and odorous? The sleeping drunks discovered in the adjacent arch on Tuesday morning would probably have been too far gone to notice any smell late Monday night anyway – even if one was evident.

At the time Dutfield held tenure to all the arches along Pinchin Street, running approximately from the present-day No. 12 right up to their end on Back Church Lane, although several may have been unused at the time of the 'Torso' case, or were utilised instead by a stone yard at the rear. A glance at modern satellite images reveal that it probably would have been possible to enter the stone yard from the rear of Dutfield's works and advance along the back of the arches without being visible from the street. The police apparently found no evidence of a cart having been used to approach the arch in question (wheel tracks, for example) nor footprints and, despite numerous criss-crossing police patrols, neither they nor anyone else in the area noticed a barrowman on Monday or Tuesday mornings.

In order to remove a torso from any of the locations Hardiman was associated with (the various Harrison, Barber & Co. yards, 13 Heneage Street or Dutfield's vacant premises in Berner Street) he may have needed to use a barrow or a cart. Hardiman however was a strong, stocky man by all accounts – well capable of carrying the torso an arch or two along the back and carefully laying it down on the ground, which was apparently the case. Any trace that was left could easily have been covered with stone dust. The police had expected an approach from the street side of the arches and their search for clues had naturally been focused there – the killer, however, may well have adopted an entirely different strategy. Moreover, W. Hindley's sack-making business was conveniently situated nearby and canvas sacking had been used for the wrapping and transportation of the torso.

If our hypothesis is correct it would seem to be yet another example of Hardiman's prior association and familiarity with murder sites – certainly at Hanbury Street where he had lived and most probably at places such as Bucks Row, which he would have been acquainted with through his employment. After Pinchin Street, however, the trail went cold and London might have been forgiven for thinking that 'the Ripper' had disappeared as quickly as he had entered the public consciousness. Consigned to the chapters of horror stories, he had become a 'bogeyman' to warn naughty children of the perils of not saying their prayers or disobeying their parents. As 1889 faded into 1890, a year passed without a 'Ripper' killing for the press to get agitated about. Then, just before Valentine's Day in 1891 one final murder shook the capital. 'Jack', it seemed, was back.

13

THE END GAME

The mystery surrounding the death of the last of the Whitechapel murder victims is perhaps the most curious of all. For the first time since John Pizer (the man believed to be the mysterious 'Leather Apron') the police had a man in custody who seemed to be a good fit for the murder. The victim Frances Coles, like Mary Kelly, was younger and so her premature death seemed all the more tragic. Added to this, it appears that she had successfully concealed her life as a prostitute from her elderly father, who still believed she held a respectable position at a chemist's.[420] The preamble to her death had involved almost 24 hours of drunken excess as she and the person initially accused of her murder went on a wild pub crawl across the East End, taking in several of the pubs associated with previous 'Ripper' victims. Coles had been seen talking to a man shortly before her body was found, with one witness claiming that just such a man had sold him a knife on the morning of the murder. She had also recently bought a new hat (an echo of Polly Nichol's 'jolly bonnet') and had been refused a bed in her usual lodgings due to the lack of the necessary funds. There had also been an odd clue at the murder site – two shillings were found nearby, having been concealed there for no apparent reason. Finally, the policeman who found the murdered woman's body reportedly heard footsteps moving away and forever regretted not pursuing the person he later believed to have been 'Jack the Ripper'.

Thus, in some respects, the final murder in the Whitechapel file offers a view of the whole series in microcosm – a young woman cruelly slaughtered, a series of witness sightings of her and possible suspects, a tragic life of degradation, and a police force that was just as baffled at the end as it was at the beginning. Let us unpack some of these themes and see how they might fit with the explanation of the case we have outlined thus far.

At around 2.15 in the morning of Friday 13 February 1891, a probationary constable walking his beat alone for the very first time, made a startling discovery. Having turned right into Chamber Street from Leman Street, PC Ernest Thompson was heading in the direction of Mansell Street when he became aware of the sound of footsteps ahead. He could not be sure whether they were coming from Swallow Gardens and trailing away towards Rosemary Lane (now Royal Mint Street) or heading off in front of him in the direction of Mansell Street. Leman Street Police Station was only a couple of minutes' walk away but, as with Pinchin Street, the railway arches that Thompson approached were a notorious spot for local prostitutes. Indeed, earlier that night, police had already cleared three women away from the area. Today Chamber Street remains a shady back street with a railway bridge running across it and somewhere that would be best avoided after dark.

As he walked through Swallow Gardens, PC Thompson noticed a bundle halfway down the alleyway that ran through the railway arch from Royal Mint Street to Chamber Street. Shining his torch, he could see that it was the body of a woman. She had been attacked, her throat had been cut and there was blood flowing from her neck, but she was not dead.[421] PC Thompson claimed he saw her eyes flicker and despite the sounds he had heard of retreating footsteps, his duty told him he had to stay with the injured woman.[422] Thompson's frantic appeals for help were soon answered as several officers appeared on the scene and a local doctor was raised from his bed. Dr Oxley arrived too late to save the woman's life but he did suggest that the wounds to her throat had been made while she had been on the ground.

This was also the opinion of Dr Phillips who later performed the autopsy. He told the subsequent inquest that in his opinion the throat wound had been inflicted while the victim had been face down on the ground and had been caused by three separate slashes, from left to right. He thought it probable that the murderer, standing to his victim's right side, had held her head back by the chin with his left hand while executing the cuts with his right. Furthermore, the way the body had been tilted suggested to him that the killer had been at pains to avoid becoming bloodstained. As had been the case with the Berner Street murder, there were no abdominal mutilations and her only other injuries seemed to be trauma marks to the back of the head, caused, as Phillips thought, by her being thrown down onto the street. The killer may have been surprised to hear the tramp of PC Thompson's boots on the cobbles or perhaps his energies by 1891 were not what they once were. It seems a tired killing by comparison to some of the earlier ones and possibly reflects the reality that the murderer was himself quite unwell.

Officers searching the vicinity found two shillings wrapped in newspaper as well as a black crepe hat. The money might have been Coles' payment from her client but initially the police thought it might be unconnected, as it was found 18 yards from Frances' body.[423] The provenance of the hat was quickly established once the police began making their house-to-house enquiries. Frances Coles was a young woman of about 25 who lived in and around Thrawl Street who had survived by prostitution since giving up her job at a wholesale chemist's in the Minories. She was described as a drinker who had 'let herself go' from being a very attractive and respectable young woman. Her father, James Coles, lived in the Bermondsey workhouse and she visited him regularly and seemingly kept up a pretence that she remained on the straight and narrow.[424]

On the day and night before she was found in the street, she had been drinking with a sailor named James Thomas Sadler, someone she had known for a while.[425] The pair were seen at a variety of pubs including the Princess Alice and possibly the Britannia on Dorset Street, both close to Commercial Street and to Frances' digs on Thrawl Street, where they ended up and where Sadler later said that he spent the night.[426] One incident seems to have soured their relationship that evening, however: Sadler was attacked on Thrawl Street by a local woman and up to three men, being robbed of both his money and watch and badly roughed up. What seems to have most irritated him was that Coles just stood by and let it happen. She had protested that there was little she could do to help, but Sadler took some time to reconcile himself to her.[427] By 11.30 p.m. the two were back at the lodging house where Sadler got cleaned up but, because they had no money, they could not stay there. It seems that Sadler left first, leaving Coles to doze at the kitchen table. He then managed to get into a fight at the docks as he tried to get back aboard his old ship, the SS *Fez*,[428] before attempting to find a place to sleep in East Smithfield – eventually winding his way back to Spitalfields at around 3 a.m. He was again refused entry to a lodging house, presumably because he still didn't have the doss money, before he tried and succeeded in getting himself admitted to the London Hospital where his various wounds were dressed and he was allowed to get some sleep.

Meanwhile Coles was reportedly talking to Ellen Callana on Commercial Street at 1.45 a.m. shortly before a man attacked Callana (who was also, it seems, a prostitute) after she had refused him trade. Coles, with no money and still the worse for drink, seems to have been less discerning, and had led the man off in the direction of the Minories. At around 2 a.m., or just after, three men passed through the railway arches at Swallow Gardens but didn't notice anything unusual – just a man and woman on the corner of Royal Mint Street, at the end of the Minories. The witness, the colourfully named Carman William 'Jumbo' Friday, later said that the man looked like a 'ship's fireman' (which was Sadler's occupation) and the woman was dressed in black and wearing a black bonnet.[429] However, the police found Friday's testimony far too vague and contradictory, as he claimed to have seen another couple that evening also. Nevertheless, it did prompt the police to hunt for a sailor and Sadler was later arrested at the Phoenix pub on Saturday 14 February 1891 where he seems to have been expecting the pull. He vigorously protested his innocence of Frances's murder, however.

There was little real evidence against Sadler until a man presented himself at Leman Street claiming that he had been sold an 'American' knife by a man he later identified as Sadler. The whole process of identifying James Sadler appears to have been very improper, with Paul Begg even suggesting that the witness (Duncan Campbell) might have been paid to provide his evidence.[430] Nevertheless, Sadler was charged with Coles' murder and attempts were made to link him to others in the Whitechapel series. One of the key witnesses who saw someone talking to Catherine Eddowes in Mitre Square was called to see if he could identify Sadler as the same person. Joseph Lawende failed to do so, however, and the case subsequently collapsed. At his pre-trial hearing at Thames Police Court, the prosecution admitted they had no case to pursue and later that evening Sadler celebrated his freedom in an East End pub.[431]

For a while then it seems that the police believed Sadler was 'Jack the Ripper' but once it was established he was not in the country at the time of several of the other murders, because he away from the capital serving in the merchant navy, they were back to square one. Sadler, like 'Leather Apron' and several other false leads, was yet another wrongly accused individual. Meanwhile the real killer had quietly escaped and was never to be brought to book for his crimes. Although no reliable eye-witness accounts of suspects at the scene seem to have been forthcoming, an interesting observation was offered by Mrs Hannah Hague, the landlady of Wilmot's Lodging House on Thrawl Street where Coles had previously stayed and which she had visited on the morning prior to her death. Mrs Hague stated that she had seen Coles later that day in a pub in Montague Street talking to a man who had treated her to a drink. This man was not Sadler, because she was asked to identify him later. Although brief, the description of the man is interesting and fits several other descriptions, which might help construct a photo-fit image of James Hardiman: 'A Fair Complexion and a Light Moustache'.[432]

Although many then and since have discounted Coles as a 'Ripper' victim it is almost impossible to dismiss such a notion, especially when one factors in the figure of James Hardiman.[433] The killing 'signature' and MO in the Coles case accords almost exactly with most of the other 'street' killings where we believe the victims were probably garrotted prior to having their throats cut. Even if the victim was merely unconscious rather than dead, careful handling would have enabled her murderer to avoid the arterial spray that would mark him out were he unfortunate enough to be trapped by the tightening cordon of Metropolitan and City police. Coles' murder is also another example of our killer's prior association with a murder scene or discovery site. On the night of the 'double event', he may well have used Chamber Street and, conceivably, even Swallow Gardens itself, while *en route* between Stride's and Eddowes' murders. This local knowledge was vital both in avoiding the police patrols and finding fresh victims and places to kill – it is highly unlikely that someone unfamiliar with the dark streets and alleys of the East End would be able to operate in this way.

Two questions remain, however. Firstly, why was there such a gap between the murders of Alice McKenzie, the unknown victim found in Pinchin Street, and the murder of Frances Coles? Secondly, why did the killer then apparently stop altogether? In the penultimate chapter we will endeavour to provide answers to both these questions as we sum up our theory to solve these long-standing mysteries. Before doing so, however, we should perhaps examine certain aspects of the crime scenes, which, in recent years, have given rise to theories concerning everything from Freemasonry to 'black magic'. Indeed, can we be certain that anger and revenge were Hardiman's only drivers? To try to answer this question in the context of *both* sets of murders it will be necessary to venture into the disciplines of modern criminology and forensic psychology. Be warned that this journey will not be a comfortable one. In attempting to determine 'Jack's true nature we must depart from the traditional, somewhat 'sanitised' portrait of the killer to plumb the depths of depravity we believe he reached.

14

THE PSYCHOPATHOLOGY
OF 'JACK'?

Throughout his campaign of terror the Whitechapel murderer seems to have chosen victims who had been drinking, probably expecting them to be easier targets. The 1988 FBI profile report into the case suggests that the killer himself was also likely to have frequented local pubs prior to the murders, in order to steady his nerve.[434] It is even possible that both killer and victim drank together. Furthermore, it is likely Hardiman was already acquainted with some of the women either as their client, as in the case of Annie Farmer, or knew them as customers for his cat's meat. So what if the killer was someone the women knew, or at least someone who was a familiar face, someone known in the locality, perhaps an occasional client? This was the case in Suffolk in the first decade of the twenty-first century. Steven Wright admitted to using prostitutes at his trial in 2008 when he was subsequently convicted of killing five women. He had slept with at least three of them and was known to the community. This familiarity enabled Wright to get close to his victims and to inveigle them into his car, where he was then in control. A similar scenario may well have been the case in the Whitechapel and Torso series. The killer must have approached his victims, or allowed himself to be propositioned by them, and some agreement was reached. In some circumstances we have witness testimony that might support this. Annie Chapman was seen by Mrs Long with a person who commented 'You will say anything except for your prayers' and Catherine Eddowes was identified as a woman seen with her hand on a man's chest by Mitre Square, possibly negotiating for her services. In most cases, it seems that the killer had first probably garrotted his victims from behind before cutting their throats when they were on the ground dead or unconscious. Due to the nature of the injuries, however, only in the case of Rose Mylett was there surviving evidence of the initial garrotting.

The subsequent severing of the carotid artery would have been a technique very familiar to Hardiman in the slaughtering trade, and, as it was not necessarily required to kill his victims (he would simply have needed to apply the ligature a little longer to achieve this) it was no doubt done with another purpose in mind – to drain the body of blood for evisceration. But was this the only additional purpose it served? Although no evidence was officially recorded at any of the crime scenes that would suggest a sexual motive for the murders, modern forensic psychology tells us that the mere act of cutting flesh can be sexually arousing for certain individuals who indulge a form of paraphilia known as picquerism. Indeed, the FBI report ascribes this diagnosis to the killer in categorising the attacks as 'lust murders'[435] while Dr Bond at the time believed the killer suffered from satyriasis – his actions being due, he thought, to episodes of 'homicidal and erotic mania'.[436] Bond may even have been familiar with the work of the Austrian psychiatrist Richard Freiherr von Krafft-Ebing whose *Psychopathia Sexualis* had first been published in 1886. In a later edition Von Krafft-Ebing suggests the Whitechapel murders may have had a sexual motive and argued that cutting up their victims was an important part of their depraved behaviour.[437] Picquerism – the penetration of skin with sharp objects for sexual gratification – is a form of sadism in which, in many cases, the breasts, buttocks and groin are targeted – often as a form of 'punishment'. Likewise, evisceration, as practised on several of the 'Ripper' victims, is classified as sexual mutilation also – with the perpetrator again deriving sexual pleasure from the act of cutting.[438] This is considered a secondary method for achieving violence-related sexual satisfaction – the primary method being sexual assault.[439]

A University of Texas study, cited earlier in this book, found that six of the 11 victims in the Met's 'Whitechapel' file (the 'canonical five', plus Tabram) exhibited the characteristic 'signatures' of picquerism, mutilation and body posing. It declared, however, that these types of murders were very rare; evident in only 0.05 per cent of all cases in its database of several thousand. Moreover, the number of these involving prostitutes was zero.[440] Furthermore, targeting of the genital area in such cases was rarer still – recorded in less than 1/10 of 1 per cent (0.001 per cent) of all murders. These six killings, therefore, were almost undoubtedly the work of one man. Due to the absence of common 'signatures' in the other five cases, the Pinchin Street torso victim included, they could not be attributed to the same killer.[441] We believe, however, that Rose Mylett, Alice McKenzie and Frances Coles could certainly have been victims of this individual – the killer, as with Stride, simply being disturbed on these occasions before being able to inflict the tell-tale mutilations. Indeed, the last two victims were discovered by policemen just moments after he had struck. Moreover, one of our surviving victims not included in the study, Annie Millwood, displayed wounds indicative of picquerism, which were very similar to those of one of the designated six, Martha Tabram.

Interestingly, people are not the only victims of picquerism. This paraphilia is also apparently perpetrated against animals with practitioners often developing an interest in this area before 'jumping' the species barrier to humans.[442] The American serial killer Jeffrey Dahmer had a fascination with dead animals from an early age and enjoyed killing, skinning, dissecting and preserving them. Hardiman of course had been immersed in the slaughtering and cat's meat trade from an early age too – had his experiences led him down an equally disturbing path? Indeed, the FBI profile speculates that the killer may well have been an abuser of animals in childhood.[443]

Furthermore, the *Diagnostic and Statistical Manual of Mental Disorders* (DSM-5) lists a subset of people who engage in necrophilia-related paraphilia. Among these are necromutilomaniacs – people who derive pleasure from masturbating either during, or immediately after, the mutilation of a corpse. Both Dahmer and the British serial killer, Denis Nilsen, indulged in this behaviour with the latter claiming it was fuelled by a combination of heightened emotions and alcohol. It seems that many of these people ejaculate during the stabbing or slashing process without the need to touch their genitalia.[444] This could explain the lack of such evidence at the crime scenes. Inspector Abberline did supposedly find traces of semen at one such murder scene, however – significantly, perhaps, the most horrific of those discovered – that of Mary Kelly.

Considering the proximity of neighbours in Kelly's case, Hardiman would have been taking a very big risk and, no doubt, was acutely on edge. Her unexpectedly spirited (and potentially very noisy) defence, therefore, would have seen them both engaged in a life-or-death struggle – with her desperate to avoid the knife – and he the gallows. As with Nilsen, though, had the exceptionally potent cocktail of adrenaline, testosterone and alcohol that night left him so aroused in 'victory' as to explain the subsequent 'orgy' of destruction that followed? Indeed, any forensic clues found by Abberline on this occasion may well have been in evidence at the private 'Torso' crime scenes, had they been uncovered. Another very specific example of sexual mutilation involving Kelly was the removal of her breasts – a likely indication of the killer's desire to completely 'defeminise' his victim.[445] This has similarities with a particularly horrific twentieth-century New York double murder involving a mother and her teenage daughter, which we will return to consider in a little more detail later.[446]

Another paraphilia practiced by both Dahmer and Nilsen – fetishistic necrophilia – may well also have some bearing on our suspect. This particular perversion sees killers remove clothing, objects, and/or body parts from a corpse for subsequent sexual purposes – in Dahmer's case he retained victim's heads for later use as a masturbatory aid. Given that the heads of the Torso victims (unlike most other body parts) were never recovered, it begs the question as to whether Hardiman had shared this penchant for 'trophy' collecting as well. Had he still enjoyed access to 13 Heneage Street he could well have kept them there. It is possible, and perhaps most likely, that he had simply retained them to prevent identification of the victims and thereby any association being drawn with himself – but it remains nevertheless an alternative explanation for their absence. Whatever the case, in the context of 'trophy collecting' we should certainly remember that rings had been removed from Annie Chapman's fingers. Jeffrey Dahmer was fond of preserving body parts such as genitalia in acetone, which has parallels with the pickled 'foetus-in-a-jar' in the Elizabeth Jackson case and the spirit-preserved kidney portion sent to George Lusk. All of which brings us around to the taboo subject of cannibalism.

Anthropophagy – the consumption of human blood or flesh – is also a well-documented behaviour among serial killers, something noted by Von Krafft-Ebing in his seminal study of criminal sexual behaviours. One of the cases he cites is the example of Vincenzo Verzeni who murdered several women in Italy in the early 1870s. Verzeni abducted, strangled – 'garrotted' is the term Von Krafft-Ebing uses – mutilated and cannibalised his victims. He admitted his crimes and his detailed confessions revealed that he had begun to enjoy the sexual sensation he felt when he was a boy 'while wringing the necks of chickens.' His case is compared by Von Krafft-Ebing with one described by the Italian criminologist Cesare Lombroso. Lombroso wrote of another Italian killer, Gruyo, who murdered six prostitutes, ripping out their intestines and kidneys through their vaginas.[447] Among the parts Jeffrey Dahmer preserved were organs such as livers and hearts, which he kept for later consumption – perhaps the ultimate expression of power. In the 1950s it was suggested that Robert Maudsley had eaten part of the brain of one of his four victims, although this was later dismissed. It was widely suggested that Mary Kelly's heart was missing and it is acknowledged that the killer took away the uteruses of both Chapman and Eddowes, as well as the latter's kidney. In the Lusk letter, the writer claimed to have eaten the other half of the kidney he sent – is this really so hard to believe given what we now know about such killers? We can only speculate about the 'Torso' victims – given the state of the bodies when dragged from the River Thames, from canals or found at the other discovery sites – but it is certainly not impossible that Hardiman was cannibalising his victims.

Like Dahmer and Nilsen, it is also possible that Hardiman was a necrophile. Forensic psychiatrist Professor Stephen Hucker of the University of Toronto considers picquerism to be not only closely related to other sexual sadisms such as rape, torture and vampirism – but also to necrophilia as well.[448] Von Krafft-Ebing also made this link and notes that when other evidence of violation (such as mutilations or the removal of organs) is absent this might indicate that the 'lifeless condition [of the corpse] itself forms the stimulus for the perverse individual.'[449] With this in mind, we can only imagine what horrors the 'Torso' victims may have suffered in private – both post-mortem and in life. In the previously mentioned New York case, the killer's intention was to torture his victims prior to killing them, having first rendered them unconscious. This opportunity had been denied him, however, when the initial assaults proved fatal. He seems to have compensated for this lost opportunity by indulging in hours of sexual deviance with the bodies. Both were eviscerated, had objects inserted into them and were posed. Incised genitalia were placed in or on their mouths and faces and the mother had her breasts removed. The killer also drank their blood and had sex with the bodies.[450] Of particular interest with regard to James Hardiman is the fact that in New York the killer had engaged in picquerism post-mortem in order to fulfil the torture fantasy that had been denied him.[451] In the Pinchin Street Torso case the victim had also displayed signs of possible torture through specific bruising and the manner in which an item of her clothing had been removed. The bruising to her arms and spine suggested that she had been struggling violently while tied to a hard, flat surface by the hands and feet. The chemise in which her torso was wrapped had also been cut down the arms and central front – a necessary procedure for its removal had she been so restrained. Was Hardiman fulfilling a similar such fantasy in private here – targeting the face and eyes perhaps, as had been seen previously with Eddowes? If so, could it be then that, like the New York case, the mutilation of his Whitechapel street victims was inflicted in substitution for the torture fantasy he knew he would be unable to fulfil on these occasions?

Whatever the reality, the report regards the hallmark of these assaults, the posing of bodies with legs spread and genitalia exposed, as being indicative of the killer's need to dominate and control his victims. The placing of viscera outside the body served to increase the shock value even further, it seems, and highlighted his ability to do virtually anything, anywhere, unchecked, and we can see this in 1888 in the display of Annie Chapman's body in the back yard of 29 Hanbury Street, at the very heart of Hardiman's world. This need to dominate and control is a common thread running through serial-killer psychopathology and often stems from feelings of inadequacy and low self-esteem. Dahmer and Nilsen both suffered from this and the sense of empowerment their behaviour afforded them both during and after their victim's death compensated for it.

Low self-esteem is also considered a significant trait among necrophiles, the onset of which can often be traced to a significant loss. In this context, we should not forget that James Hardiman's world had recently fallen apart with the death in quick succession of both his child and his wife. We should also not ignore DI Swanson's observation that the main police suspect for the Pinchin Street Torso murder was known to them not only as a gambler but also as a heavy drinker. Both Dahmer and Nilsen in fact were known for abusing alcohol and most of their killings took place in drink- and/ or drug-fuelled circumstances, with Nilsen actually garrotting his inebriated victims first – a likely (albeit usually unseen) hallmark, we believe, in many of Hardiman's attacks.

In conclusion then, even with the limited 'evidence' available in our case, it seems clear that strong motivating impulses of a sexual/sadistic nature were very likely driving Hardiman. Although his primary motivation (initially at least) was non-sexual – revenge – once he had decided to embark on his 'crusade' the opportunities to indulge latent sadistic tendencies (probably derived from his slaughterhouse experiences) became apparent and manifest at the murder scenes. It would appear that the killer had jumped the species barrier in these cases with the women subsequently becoming the targets of his unbridled misogynistic sadism. If the family deaths and the start of the killings signalled the onset of this behaviour, which seems likely, then he would probably be considered an 'opportunistic necrophiliac' – one not normally engaging in such behaviour but nevertheless taking advantage of opportunities to do so should they arise. This would accord with the 'sexual sadist' label afforded the killer by some commentators at the time. Walter Dew thought it likely that the murderer (the 'Ripper' – he didn't think the two series were connected, of course) was at the very least mad, and quite possibly suffering from some sort of 'sex mania'.[452] Of course, having found his actions sexually gratifying when applied to people, these impulses may have taken over as the killer's primary motivation at some point – perhaps being responsible even for keeping up the momentum of his campaign and prolonging it. As 50 per cent of necrophiles are also believed to have pre-existing personality disorders, it is quite possible that Hardiman was a psychopath as well.

Driven by hatred and contempt for these women, the killer's primary objective was to exert maximum power and control over them and to humiliate them – in life as well as in death. In effect, he dehumanised his enemy, seeing them as worthless, sub-human adversaries – worthy targets of his righteous campaign. His preferred theatre of operations would have been a private setting, as per the 'Torso' victims, his actions during the street attacks being necessarily constrained. In a private environment he would have been free to express the full force of his anger by indulging his punishment-driven torture fantasy unchecked. All this would have required care with the initial assault (the garrotte attack) to ensure unconsciousness rather than death. This strategy would also have been contingent on the availability of potential pick-up points near secluded, non-residential locations where privacy would be guaranteed such as the parks, industrial premises and building sites we have noted. As it is likely that some or all of these locations were previously known to Hardiman or reconnoitred beforehand, it seems that an element of pre-planning had been present in the Torso cases at least. In the event of no such location being available, however, the victim's own abode, if she had one, was deemed acceptable. As we have seen with the Kelly case, though, this was a much riskier proposition due to the prying eyes and ears of neighbours. In the absence of either option, however, the killer was content to make do with the streets and alleyways he knew so well.

As to why the killer had apparently targeted the uteruses of the 'Whitechapel' victims Chapman and Eddowes, we believe the Torso victim Elizabeth Jackson provides the answer. The removal of the foetus from her womb post-mortem suggests that Hardiman never lost sight of his original, non-sexual, motive for his killing, which was revenge.[453] In Hardiman's eyes these women had deprived him of his progeny and he would now be sure to deprive them of theirs. An 'eye for an eye', no less. Women such as these had destroyed Hardiman's world, leaving him humiliated and alone. He had resolved to treat them likewise it seems – even in death.

15

CONCLUSIONS: UNMASKING THE KILLER

How can we identify a killer from the past? In 2006 James Bailey mused on the 'art of profiling' in the context of the 'Ripper' and concluded that the murderer was a male Caucasian aged 26–31, who may have been 'known' to the police, or have had previous convictions; he 'probably knew or developed a brief relationship with the victims'. Not surprisingly Bailey believes the killer would have been strong and 'most likely had some type of psychological problem'. He also 'had a distinctive signature of cutting the throat and post-mortem mutilation by evisceration' but Bailey reminds us that the 'signature of a criminal is different from a modus operandi, the latter can change with circumstances.'[454]

It has now been more than 130 years since the serial murderer known to history as 'Jack the Ripper' terrorised London in the late summer and autumn of 1888. The official police case was closed in 1892, a year after a mortally wounded Frances Coles was found by PC Thompson in Swallow Gardens. Much of the evidence associated with the case has been lost, destroyed or stolen in the intervening years. No doubt less fastidious policing methods in the late nineteenth century meant that clues were lost forever, but souvenir hunters have also since removed evidence and, as a result, what remains, for public viewing at least, is a rather sad set of microfilms at the National Archives (NA) in Kew and the London Metropolitan Archives. The Luftwaffe were responsible for destroying some of the City of London's records during the Blitz so what we are left with is, at best, a partial history of the murders from the official sources.

This can, of course, be supplemented by the huge coverage given to the case by the newspapers in the 1880s, a medium that had grown from the 1860s to become omnipresent in late Victorian society.[455] There are reams of newspaper articles about the case and it is quite easy for the researcher, academic or amateur, to become overwhelmed by the amount of newsprint dedicated to it and, to a lesser extent, by the Thames Torso series. Part of the problem we have is in determining how reliable newspaper sources are, especially when we have relatively little information about who created them. Unlike today, nineteenth-century newspaper stories rarely carried the name of the journalist who penned them, 'from our own correspondent' was as close as they came to naming their writers, many of whom were freelance or 'penny-a-line men' who wrote in sensationalist prose in the hopes of attracting an editor's eye. Throughout this book we have tried to be conscious of the nature and limitations of the sources of 'evidence' we can draw upon.

There is also a tremendous amount of previous history written about the 'Ripper' murders and, to a much lesser extent, the Torso ones as well. From 1888 onwards, authors have written their versions of the 'facts' of the case and offered solutions to the mystery. Perhaps the most famous of the early 'Ripperologists', Leonard Matters, offered up a medical 'Ripper' ('Dr Stanley') in his 1929 book *The Mystery of Jack the Ripper*.[456] While the book contained several factual inaccuracies, the idea that 'Jack' was a doctor captured the public imagination as it echoed contemporary beliefs that the killer 'operated' on his victims for some foul purpose. In Matters' view, Dr Stanley was seeking revenge (his son had supposedly contracted syphilis from Mary Kelly) and while we think that while Matters was wrong about the identity of the suspect, there is something in his identification of motive.

But let us continue to reflect on sources for a moment; since Matters there have been hundreds of books (and probably thousands of online articles) that have attempted to solve the case. The worst simply present ill-thought-out and unsubstantiated claims based on minimal evidence, using very selective sources. The best, however, have endured although quite often they do not posit a thesis on who the killer was. We have shamelessly mined these works for our facts about the case and so recognise the debt we owe to Paul Begg, Donald Rumbelow and Phillip Sugden especially, all of whom have studied the case for many years. We have examined the police files in the National Archives and the newspapers but we have also looked carefully at three key areas of evidence that surround the case. At the end of it all, we have a suspect in the frame for which we are particularly indebted to Rob Hills and Adrian Stockton, who first mooted him as a person of interest regarding the Whitechapel series some years ago.[457] In building on their work, we now believe this person could have been responsible for upwards of 16 attacks on women (with at least 13 being fatal) between 1887 and 1891 – assaults encompassing both the Whitechapel and Thames Torso series. We could also possibly add another four fatal assaults to this list, giving a total of 20 attacks with 17 fatalities in all. Their inclusion would be tentative, however, as the supporting evidence for these is much sparser than for the others. Most writers attribute five or maybe six murders to 'the Ripper', so we recognise that we are going out on a limb in suggesting that our man possibly killed and mutilated more than three times as many as previously thought. However, think of the alternative for a moment – that in 1888 there were two serial killers operating in the capital *at the same time*. One killed five or more prostitutes in Whitechapel while the other murdered and dismembered four or five other women, dumping their remains in the Thames and elsewhere. Of course, it is not impossible that two such killers were active at the same time – but statistically it is most improbable. This is even less likely when we consider the similarity of the victims (all probably prostitutes) and the close proximity of the murders themselves.

In support of our contention then that these killings were the work of one man – James Hardiman – we would offer the following observations:

- The marked similarity between suspect descriptions in the 'Whitechapel' assaults, and that issued by the *New York Herald* regarding Pinchin Street 'Torso' suspect 'John Arnold'.
- The possible 'double event' of the Whitehall 'Torso' victim and Martha Tabram, which would represent a direct 'cross-over' between the two sets of murders.
- The indirect 'cross-over' of a 'Torso' victim being found in the killer's 'Whitechapel' territory (Pinchin Street).
- Hardiman's prior familiarity with Pinchin Street from its likely use as a transit route after Elizabeth Stride's 'Whitechapel' killing.
- Hardiman's likely association with Arthur Dutfield's business, which was located both in Pinchin Street where the 'Torso' was found and in Berner Street prior to Stride's 'Whitechapel' killing there.
- The uterus had been targeted on 'Torso' victim Elizabeth Jackson, which was also the case with some of the 'Whitechapel' women.
- Doctors believed the same person was responsible for the killing/dismemberment of all four 'Torso' victims – including the Pinchin Street ('Whitechapel') one.
- Doctors believed that, like most of the 'Whitechapel' victims, throat cutting had been used on all four 'Torso' cases with the possibility that they could also have been garrotted first.
- Dr Bond believed that, as with the 'Torso' victims, the killer of the 'Whitechapel' victims, Annie Chapman and Mary Kelly, had also attempted to decapitate them.

- The Rainham Torso body parts discovered in the canal at Camden were close by the Metropolitan Cattle Market and the adjacent Harrison, Barber slaughterhouse in Brandon Road.
- The tram network south of the river gave access to the East End via the Tower Tube and linked 'Torso' discovery sites at Whitehall, Battersea Park and St George's Circus with the residence of Pinchin Street ('Whitechapel') 'Torso' suspect 'John Arnold' at Charing Cross.
- Four of the Whitechapel victims (Polly Nichols, Annie Chapman, Catherine Eddowes and Frances Coles) are known to have had connections in the Bermondsey/Lambeth area south of the river – the latter two having visited there immediately prior to their deaths.

Even though we have considerably 'upped the ante' in respect of the killer's tally, there are plenty of examples of serial killers in history who have killed more than a dozen victims: Gesche Gottfried, for example, poisoned 15 relatives and friends with arsenic before she was hanged in Bremen in 1831. Burke and Hare murdered (or 'burked') 16 victims in Edinburgh and sold their bodies to Dr Knox.[458] Dr William Palmer was widely believed to have killed up to 10 people when he was convicted of murder in 1856[459] and in 1866 Joseph Phillipe was guillotined for the murder of seven prostitutes and a child in Paris. Mary Ann Cotton reportedly killed 21 individuals between 1852 and 1873, most of them babies and children in her care; while Amelia Dyer may have killed as many as 400 in her career as Britain's most notorious 'baby farmer'.[460] In a case that has closer links to our own, Francisco Guerrero Pérez raped, strangled and then cut the throats of 20 prostitutes before throwing their decapitated bodies into the Consulado River in Mexico.[461] In France, Joseph Vacher (the 'French Ripper') killed at least 11 and possibly more than 20 women, girls and boys, disembowelling their bodies before he was caught and executed in 1898.[462] So, in the nineteenth century it seems that there are several well-documented examples of serial killers with body counts as high, if not higher, than 13.

What of the modern age though, a period in which serial killing has become a central focus of research and concern for police, crime authorities and criminologists? Here the figures can be quite staggering. Ted Bundy is known to have killed 35 and John Wayne Gacy 33 but they are relatively low statistics: Gary Ridgway (the 'Green River Killer') confessed to killing 71 women, many of them prostitutes. In England, the highest number of deaths can be attributed to Dr Harold Shipman who was convicted of killing 15 patients but is believed to have actually murdered between 218 and 250 using diamorphine. Fred and Rose West killed at least 12 young women between 1967 and 1987, and Peter Sutcliffe (the 'Yorkshire Ripper') was convicted of killing 13 women (12 of whom were prostitutes) in the space of five years (1975–1980).[463] Depressing as these bare statistics are, they are merely the tip of the iceberg when it comes to serial murder; there are hundreds of killers and thousands of victims and the more one looks at the topic of serial killing the more widespread it appears to be. So, we should not be surprised that one man could be responsible for the murders of between 13 and 17 women in a period of four years. In the context of what we now know about serial murder, this killer does not seem to have been exceptional at all.

In adding the name of James Hardiman to this sorry list we will devote the rest of this chapter to setting out the case against him by examining the three factors that underpin all murder investigations – means, motive and opportunity. Proving Hardiman was responsible is, of course, impossible but we hope to demonstrate that he is, at the very least, an eminently plausible candidate. It certainly seems that he had the means and opportunity to attack, kill and mutilate these women – and in his tragic family life story we believe we can also unpack his motive.

One of the keys to understanding this case in is provided by the work of David Canter and his research into criminal mapping and the movements of killers.[464] As he shows, by plotting the murder sites on a map it is possible to trace their geographical pattern and thereby determine a killer's likely 'centre of operations'. With 'Jack' it appears that 'his Whitechapel and City killings were clearly circumscribed within a limited area; this is especially clear with the "canonical five".'[465] Canter concludes that this was because the killer lived within this part of a closely defined district; it was familiar territory, he knew it and its workings – the movements of police, prostitutes and other members of the public. While to some it might seem dangerous to commit such serious crimes so close to home, to Hardiman it represented familiarity and relative safety. If one joins the dots on Canter's map of Whitechapel in the 1880s the focal point is somewhere to the west of Brick Lane's lower reaches, on the other side of Commercial Street around the Middlesex Street/ Petticoat Lane area.[466] Using similar techniques of geographical profiling in 2006, Dr Kim Rossmo of the Centre for Geospatial Intelligence and Investigation at Texas State University placed the killer's likely residence a little further east, in a tightly defined 'hot zone' centring on Thrawl Street and Flower and Dean Street, just off Brick Lane.[467] Indeed, it is in this area where interest has traditionally been most closely focused, both then and now. Rossmo had previously included Heneage Street itself in his zone and, more recently, an American geographic profiler and forensic psychologist, Wesley English, has also included it in his sphere of interest.[468]

Our own calculations place Heneage Street very much at centre stage and it was most interesting to find someone such as Hardiman living there at the time of the murders. Martha Tabram, Polly Nicholls, Annie Chapman, Alice McKenzie and Mary Kelly were all killed within easy walking distance of Heneage Street. Liz Stride and Catherine Eddowes were a little further away but no real distance from this base, as was also the case with the Pinchin Street and Swallow Gardens murders. Poplar (where Rose Mylett died) was further out but, as we have shown, the distance would not have been problematic for Hardiman had he used the public transport available and familiar to him.

We need to remember what this man did for a living. He was a cats' meat man and a slaughterhouse worker, who may also have delivered carts and barrows to such places for Arthur Dutfield, moving around East London and indeed the wider capital during the course of his work. In so doing, he familiarised himself with the neighbourhoods, getting to know the short cuts, alleys and courts like the back of his hand. He knew who lived where and presumably established contacts with customers for the meat he sold. The idea that the killer could have been a cats' meat man is not a new one. It has been suggested that the Torso murderer was just such a tradesman. Mei Trow believed the man responsible for the Thames Torso murders was a 'socially competent' individual who 'lured his victims to his slaughterhouse, won them over, perhaps with alcohol' before killing them. While we don't agree with his hypothesis that the two sets of killings were distinct, we do agree that this sort of person fits the profile of the kind of man that could do this sort of thing.[469] Hardiman's family had lived in the area for many years and when James married, he had stayed close to his support network, as many people did in the 1800s. But, as we have said, he also appeared to have ranged further away and was comfortable doing so. This took him out of the East End on occasion, to the west and perhaps even across the river to Wandsworth and Battersea in the south. Indeed, when the police investigation into the Whitechapel murders became a little too close for comfort (probably during the house-to-house searches of October 1888) Hardiman seems to have taken himself off to digs in central London, far from the prying eyes of H Division in the east.

As we have hopefully shown, Hardiman's ability to move around was aided by two important factors – the capital's burgeoning transport network and the expanding business empires of John Harrison and Arthur Dutfield. As we have set out in previous chapters, these developments would have made it very easy for a man such as Hardiman to get around London without arousing suspicion. The fact that many 'Torso' body parts had been found in the river throughout the city could naturally be seen to contradict the notion that the killer was a Whitechapel native. As we have seen, however, Hardiman's London was a much larger area, given his ability to roam the capital in the course of his work and seek out victims as he went. It made him much harder to catch and while the police almost certainly did 'catch' him on two occasions at least, they let him go again not suspecting that he was the killer. Unfortunately, this sort of error in policing is almost inevitable; in the 1970s Peter Sutcliffe was questioned several times about the series of murders in Yorkshire before he was finally arrested and charged.

London's tram routes in particular would have allowed Hardiman to travel across the city with ease and at relatively low cost. A portion of the Whitehall Torso corpse was found close by St George's Circus, Lambeth, on the route that connected Battersea Park and London Bridge. Near Battersea Park (and on the route itself) was the Harrison, Barber & Co.'s slaughterhouse at Garrett Lane, and from London Bridge it was but a short walk to the entrance of the Tower Tube. At night this would have brought the traveller up within striking distance of the East End without arousing the inquisitive gaze of passers-by.

Part of the Rainham Torso was dragged from the Regent's Canal at Camden Town, conveniently situated near the Metropolitan Meat Market and another Harrison, Barber yard in Brandon Road. Although Ada Wilson and Rose Mylett were both attacked some distance from the 'hot zone' of Spitalfields and Whitechapel, these locations were close to a Harrison, Barber depot at Tredegar Terrace, off Burdett Road, and other premises located in the vicinity of Poplar High Street. Mary Nichols was murdered on Buck's Row which, as well as being close to Hardiman's home in Heneage Street, was also a mere stone's throw from Barber's yard in Winthrop Street. What's more, the Hardimans had all lived at 29 Hanbury Street where Annie Chapman was killed. Not only was James Hardiman intimately acquainted with that location and well known to the locals there, one of Barber's yards was just a few doors down too. It is crucial to remember that our killer not only had to have a sound knowledge of his environment, he also had to be able to blend in; this is why so many of those put forward as suspects fail to pass muster – as a recent documentary has suggested, the killer in fact was likely to have been no more than just 'an ordinary man'.[470] This particular ordinary man's occupation had endowed him with the extraordinary skills necessary to efficiently cut and mutilate his victims. Indeed, one of the first conclusions that the police investigation reached was that the killer could have been someone involved in the slaughtering trade. Hardiman, as we have seen, was well versed in dissecting flesh and bone and was no doubt inured to the sight of dead meat. He must have spent almost the entirety of his childhood and working life around the carcasses of dead animals, as his family had been steeped in the business for years. Most people who encountered him in the immediate vicinity of his home would have expected him to be spattered in blood and to have blood on his apron or work clothes. Despite previous musings over the wrapping of a Whitehall torso body part, the police in nineteenth century found it impossible to distinguish between human and animal blood so even if they did have suspicions about a blood-covered man, they were not really in a position to investigate further.

So then, we have seen how his job gave him the perfect cover story if he was stopped and questioned by a suspicious 'bobby'. More than this – the distribution of Harrison, Barber slaughterhouses meant Hardiman had a variety of locations in which to hide – and conceivably even, murder and dismember his victims.[471] Safely inside premises where he was trusted, and perhaps working late or at weekends alone for extra money, he would be free to clean himself up, dispose of or hide weapons or do whatever else he wished, emerging later as a 'respectable' man with ambitions to 'better himself'. Delivering carts to such premises for Arthur Dutfield may well have also afforded him similar opportunities.

Indeed, we believe it was opportunities such as this that had allowed him to acquire the anatomical knowledge necessary for the removal of Annie Chapman's uterus and Catherine Eddowes' kidney. As Dr Philips noted in examining Chapman's corpse, it was almost inconceivable that the killer could have executed the procedure so deftly in the time available without a good deal of knowledge and prior experience. We should remember, though, that the Rainham and Whitehall torso victims had both been killed prior to Annie Chapman's death. Although it seems that the Whitehall victim had met her end on the building site, as previously stated, the possibility exists that the Rainham victim could have been killed at just such an establishment, the slaughterhouse in Brandon Road at Camden perhaps, which was near to where her legs were discovered in the Regent's Canal. There would have been no shortage of potential victims in the locality given the known prostitute haunts of nearby King's Cross station and the taverns surrounding the meat market. It was, after all, at another station, in Liverpool Street, that PC Spicer had seen the 'good doctor' pestering women following his encounter with him in Heneage Court. If this were the case then, it would seem likely that the building site and slaughterhouse had served as the killer's very own private mortuaries prior to Chapman's demise – quiet sanctuaries in which he could hone his skills at leisure. Dr Phillips may well have been right in one respect – the killer had possessed a good deal of anatomical knowledge. The knife in question though had been a slaughterman's all along – and not that of a doctor. With the Battersea Park workshops having apparently served a similar purpose in respect of Elizabeth Jackson, it would seem both possible and plausible that Dutfield's premises in Pinchin Street had been used to hold, torture and kill the unknown victim found there.

Indeed, if she had been killed and dismembered elsewhere, the obvious question to ask would be how she had actually got there without anyone noticing? Reasonably plausible explanations perhaps are that he could have used his cats' meat barrow or one of the slaughterhouse recovery carts that were always kept on standby. The mundane and everyday sometimes becomes so familiar as to be rendered almost invisible. Curiously though, there were no traces at the scene of any such conveyance having been used. And of course the archway premises themselves would have made a perfect base for Hardiman's activities in the east and so, as well as the torso found there, it could also have served as the pick-up point (and intended murder site) for at least one other victim – Elizabeth Stride.

If we are correct then, we would seem to have identified the four likely killing sites the killer used for his 'Torso' murders and noted the ready availability of suitable victims (mostly women whom he believed to be prostitutes) at all of these locations. We believe all of the sites would have had one additional thing in common that would have been essential for the killer's activities there – the availability of saws for dismemberment. In the case of the building site, Battersea Park and Pinchin Street these saws would have been of the carpentry type, whereas the slaughterhouse at Brandon Road would have been home to plenty of the butchery variety.

In relation to the Pinchin Street victim, we think it likely that in the late evening of Saturday 7 September, Hardiman picked up his victim around the arches and enticed her into Dutfield's barrow yard. Either he had legitimate access to the premises during normal weekend closure or he was otherwise able to effect entry. Having rendered his victim unconscious, he then tied her by the arms and legs to a hard, flat surface before torturing and killing her and leaving the premises around midnight to head in the direction of the City and Harvey's Buildings in the Strand – probably via the railway service tunnel which we believe he used following Liz Stride's killing. Realising a further opportunity to taunt the police, he presented himself at the offices of the *New York Herald* in Fleet Street (just before it turns into the Strand) around 1.15 on Sunday morning, claiming to be 'John Cleary' and reporting the discovery of woman's body in Back Church Lane. Stating his source as a serving or former police officer, he had then apparently absconded rather than accompany the reporters to the alleged scene. Following this, he may then have gone back to his lodgings to sleep but, as killers often do, he may well have returned independently to Pinchin Street to witness any activity there which he had generated. Indeed, had he retraced his route, he could have observed the coming and goings at Leman Street Police Station before re-entering the tunnel and making his way back to Dutfield's premises. Once safely inside he could even have taken great delight in the dismemberment of his victim under the very noses of his adversaries – an undoubted thrill which would have been entirely in keeping with his previous contemptuous behaviour. He could then have waited for things to quieten down before carrying the torso around the back to its final resting place, as previously suggested. On leaving the scene, he could have discarded the bloodied cloth behind the fence in Hooper Street before heading back to his bed for the night – either across the railway tracks and west to the Strand, or north in the direction of Heneage Street via Gowers Walk. He could, however, have used the tunnel for a third time that night if he was destined for Harvey's Buildings at Charing Cross. All of this could have been accomplished before people arrived for work again on the Monday morning.

In any event, the torso would have remained undiscovered throughout Monday until the patrolling policeman was altered to its presence by the smell early on Tuesday morning. It was on the following morning, Wednesday 11, that the *New York Herald* issued a description of the 'wanted' informant who had attended their offices – a description which bore marked similarities we should remember to those of prisoner James 'Alf' Hardiman and the suspect in several Whitechapel attacks. Two days later, on Friday 13 September 1889, on the anniversary of his wife's death, Hardiman gave himself up as the 'wanted' man at Great Scotland Yard which was a mere stone's throw from his lodgings at Harvey's Buildings, Strand where he now said he resided – rather than an address previously given to the *New York Herald*. He gave a different name to the one used previously as well however and changed his story to say that it was a soldier who had given him the information rather than a policeman.

The smell that first alerted the patrolling constable is also likely to be significant in terms of timings. Although apparently not an exact science, lack of stiffness of the torso (indicating the passing of rigor mortis) combined with the odour of early stage decomposition, would probably suggest today a time of death in excess of 36 hours, as opposed to the best estimate Dr Clarke was able to give of 'at least' 24 hours. As such, this would indicate that the victim was killed sometime before 6 p.m. on Sunday. If Hardiman had picked his victim up on the Saturday night, which would seem most likely, it could be that she was probably killed around midnight that evening prior to him turning up at the *New York Herald* office at 1.15a.m. on Sunday. We cannot completely discount the slight possibility that she was actually left there alive (bound and gagged) during this time, only to be killed and dismembered on his return.

The post-mortem found extensive bruising (caused while the victim was still alive) to the fronts of both forearms, the backs of both hands and to the spine – injuries which could be consistent of course with someone struggling violently to free themselves while bound to a hard surface by the hands and feet. The victim, it seems, could have been tied to a workbench, the floor or similar such hard surface at the premises, although it is interesting to note that the discovering officer, Constable Pennett, had noticed an abandoned barrow in nearby Splidts Street with a board attached to the top. It had been there he thought since the start of his shift at 10 o'clock on Sunday night. Could Hardiman have used this? He would certainly have finished the killing and dismemberment process by then and it could have been used for the subsequent disposal of body parts elsewhere.

Whatever the case, it is interesting to note that if Dutfield had moved to Pinchin Street a full 16 months prior to the Rainham killing as opposed to the minimum of four, it would have coincided almost exactly with John Harrison's takeover of his six competitors in January 1886, which had left him with a virtual monopoly of the market. Was Dutfield's move related to this – did he need larger premises to fulfil a burgeoning contract for the newly enlarged John Harrison empire? If so he would have needed reliable people to deliver his barrows and carts to slaughterhouses right across London. Who better for this role than Hardiman – a man who was familiar with many of these yards. For Hardiman to have been confident of avoiding detection, the murders and dismemberment he carried out needed to have been well planned (or as well organised as they could be) requiring him to be fully cognisant of the variable police beats in the area. Beats remained the same but the personnel changed on a monthly basis, to avoid any possible temptations towards corruption.[472] To this end he would have required a suitable vantage point (and a valid reason to be there) from which to observe these over time, as with the other murder locations. It would certainly make sense then if Hardiman had been engaged by the company in some capacity or other. Furthermore, perhaps there had been an additional game-playing element here on the part of the killer. When 'Arnold' handed himself in he said that his informant was a soldier. Was this an attempted red herring to try to refocus attention on the prime suspects in the Tabram case – the London-based guardsmen? John Leary, the name Hardiman may have used in the newspaper office, had been the name of one of the suspect soldiers in that case.

Before leaving Pinchin Street, we must not forget the railway line that ran across the top of its arches. If Dutfield's business was now expanding to serve a wider area, which seems possible, likely even, then the means to efficiently distribute its products would have been paramount. For its customers in the north-east, south and east, the Whitechapel goods yard of the London and Blackwell Railway – a mere stone's throw from Pinchin Street – would have provided the perfect solution. From here Dutfield could have serviced customers south of the river via the Greenwich ferry, the 11 slaughterhouses in Poplar High Street to the east, as well as those to the north-east around Stratford, the 'spiritual home' of John Harrison's business empire. As we have said, Hardiman had attacked Ada Wilson in Burdett Road where there was a slaughterhouse as well as an

LBR station. We also think he killed Rose Mylett in Poplar High Street – another location with a plethora of slaughterhouses and a LBR station. A couple of stops further, in fact, was the line's terminus at Blackwall Pier – a popular destination at the time for Londoner's keen to take in the pleasure steamer trips and bracing air – a spot he and his wife could well have been familiar with in the years prior to her death. Furthermore, as previously mentioned, the LBR Millwall extension through the Isle of Dogs afforded access, via the ferry, to the Greenwich Peninsular slaughterhouse on the seemingly eponymous John Harrison Way.[473] This lies directly across the river from where some of the Rainham body parts were found, in the vicinity of the Royal Victoria Dock, at the beginning of our story.

It is time to move on to other considerations. Although we certainly hope to have convinced you that Hardiman possessed the means to kill his victims, had he in fact possessed sufficient opportunities to do so? He was a married man after all, so wouldn't his wife or someone close to him have noticed if he was acting strangely in some way? It is a reasonable question to ask but we hope it is one that we have already managed to answer. As we have said, in June 1888 the Hardimans had suffered the very real tragedy of the death of their daughter Harriet Maria. At the same time Sarah Hardiman had been admitted to the London hospital. From then on, James would have enjoyed an unfettered freedom of action, domestically at least. Indeed, it was at this point we believe that the 'autumn of terror' began to unfold as there was no one to ask awkward questions about his movements. So long as he played the dutiful husband and continued to visit Sarah in hospital there was little to raise suspicion or connect him to the murders – initially at least.

It is difficult to determine exactly where Hardiman was living later in 1888 and 1889, as we have no census records for the gaps between decades. However, if, as we believe, John Arnold and James Hardiman were the same man, then by late 1888 or early 1889 he had probably moved out of Heneage Street to the relative safety of the Harvey's Buildings at Charing Cross – or at least had started to use the accommodation there on an occasional basis. Indeed, he may have started using other such 'doss-houses' in the East End as well if his neighbours in Heneage Street had been growing suspicious of him as the murders progressed. This strategy, coupled with the adoption of an assumed name(s) would have made him much harder to pin down if the police had been minded to seek him out for any reason. It would also have allowed him to be close to a medical care centre, as we have seen. In any event, it would have allowed him to detach himself from the intense Whitechapel 'heat', which the killings had generated and allow him to concentrate on his next moves.

In a recent television documentary, a forensic psychologist, Laura Richards, stated her belief that the Whitechapel murderer was, in all probability, a calculating risk taker.[474] He would have been intelligent or cunning enough to balance the risks he faced but would also have had to enjoy an element of luck at the same time. In Richard's opinion, the murderer would have been socially skilled, at least enough to establish short-term relationships with people – a cats' meat man developing a customer base for example, or a casual worker trying to engender trust in return for work or access to business premises. He may even have possessed some charm and was almost certainly a good liar. All these characteristics would have helped Hardiman avoid arrest or answer difficult questions should he have needed to. Crucially, though, it would also have made it much easier for him to persuade his victims to place themselves in dangerous positions in the first place. Indeed, one of the issues that is rarely tackled explicitly in the many histories of 'Jack' is how the killer managed to inveigle these women into situations where he was then able to kill them. Yes, they were all street prostitutes, or poor homeless women, and all were probably desperate for money, but it is likely that their murderer came across as non-threatening and 'ordinary', not as someone who looked dangerous or who fitted any of the contemporary portraits of the Whitechapel assassin. Hardiman was not an immigrant Jew,

'Champagne Charlie' or, a mad doctor; he was an ordinary resident of Whitechapel and probably someone many of the girls knew – and may have done business with previously. In fact, it is probably this very connection with the area's street prostitutes as we have said, that explains why he was driven to kill in the first place. Determining the motivation of serial killers is fraught with difficulty but in a previous chapter we have done our best to suggest the triggers that were likely responsible for the onset of Hardiman's behaviour as well as considering some latent impulses he may have had which could subsequently have driven him on.

To reiterate, Hardiman was almost certainly infected with syphilis and had very likely passed this on to his wife, who may then have infected their unborn daughter. This was probably his belief, in any event. About a year after her birth, the daughter had died; then at this time his wife also went into hospital, where she died three months later. This was a personal tragedy for Hardiman; to lose his child and perhaps even his wife apparently to a scourge ravaging nineteenth-century society at all levels, and it must have been devastating for him. As we have seen syphilis affected not only the physical but also the mental health of the sufferer. While Hardiman, did not die of syphilis – it was TB which apparently claimed him in December 1891 – it must have nonetheless played with his mind, and health. The guilt that Hardiman felt would undoubtedly have been overwhelming and it is not unreasonable to think that he would have needed an outlet for his grief, self-loathing and anger. Aged 20, he had lost his father and assumed the role of the head of the family, starting on his own in the process. In losing both Harriet Maria and his wife Sarah in quick succession, however, Hardiman had palpably failed that family. In late 1887 James Hardiman was aged 28 and he and Sarah had been married for 11 years, but their first live-born child did not arrive until then. They had waited so long for a son or daughter and then she had been born sickly and destined for an early grave. Hardiman was probably in little doubt as regards his own responsibility for this but, like many disturbed abusers and killers, he sought to redirect that anger away from himself. His daughter's fate was the trigger for the terrible revenge he took on the prostitutes he blamed for giving him the infection in the first place. Indeed, it was soon after Harriet Maria's birth that the unknown victim's dismembered torso was washed up in the Thames at Rainham.

There are many other connections that link events in Hardiman's family life to the murders. On 13 September 1888 Sarah Hardiman died and a year later, to the day, a pickle jar containing a human foetus, possibly taken from the person whose body was found at Horsleydown, was discovered by the police. Was this Hardiman's way of memorialising his wife and child's deaths? On 8 September 1889, exactly a year after the murder of Annie Chapman at 29 Hanbury Street, a location closely associated with the Hardiman family, a man walked into the London offices of the *New York Herald* claiming to have information about another 'Ripper-style' murder.[475] This man, who called himself John Cleary, was described as being aged 25 to 28, 5 foot 4 inches tall, of medium build with a 'light complexion, fair moustache, [and] blue eyes'. The paper added that he had 'an inflamed spot on his left cheek' and had covered his neck with a dirty handkerchief, perhaps to conceal abrasions there. He had a stumbling, 'shuffling' gait and resembled a 'developing' resident of Whitechapel. Who was this mysterious man and why had he chosen the anniversary of one of the Whitechapel murders to come forward?

We believe the answer is that Cleary (or John Arnold as he later professed himself to be) was in fact James Hardiman. By now he was residing at 2 Harvey Buildings on the Strand, close to a medical centre providing care for those suffering from sexually transmitted diseases such as syphilis. He had surrendered himself to the police on the 13 September – two days after the Pinchin Street torso had been found by PC Pennett and a year to the day after the death of his wife. These could, of course, all be coincidences but let us return to the various descriptions we have of our suspected killer. Taken together, they would appear to give a picture of him roughly as follows: Aged 25 to 30, 5 foot 4 inches to 5 foot 8 inches tall – although most likely between 5 foot 5 inches and 5 foot 7 inches – stocky, with light brown hair, a fair moustache and blue eyes. His complexion was fair but with a 'sunburnt' or 'blotchy' appearance. He had an ulcer or boil on his left cheek or his neck and walked with a 'shuffling gait'. This certainly comes close to matching the description of James 'Alf' Hardiman, the man imprisoned in Wandsworth between 1880 and 1881, in addition to being comparable (accepting the acknowledged problematic nature of witness statements) with suspect sightings around Hanbury Street, Berner Street and Mitre Square. Moreover, the identifications of a boil or ulcer chime specifically with the descriptions given by Ellen Marks and Phillip Harris of the man who had attacked Annie Farmer in Spitalfields. The reddening of the cheeks that left the impression of him being 'sunburnt' in several instances could be explained by the use of 'quicksilver' (mercury), a well-known quack cure for syphilis. If Hardiman was self-medicating then this would certainly explain his complexion. In 1888, Mitre Square had close associations with the trade in quicksilver; the local prostitutes knew this and Hardiman may well have bought the element there and discovered for himself what an ideal spot for a murder the dark and mostly unlit square was. It was also at the heart of London's Jewish community, which, as has been noted, probably also served another purpose for the killer in his attempts to avoid capture by throwing the officers chasing him off his scent.

Hardiman was almost 28 years old when the murder series started and 31 when it stopped in 1891. Thus, he fits perfectly into the age profile of such killers. And what of the gap of some 17 months between the discovery of the Pinchin Street Torso and the murder of Frances Coles? We should remember that following his 'confession' regarding the former, 'Arnold' was the Met's top suspect and would undoubtedly have been placed under close surveillance. For how long he would have been accorded this status is impossible to determine but in the absence of suitable alternative candidates (other than Sadler of course who was eventually discounted) it could well have been for some time – certainly long enough to explain such a lull in his activities. Indeed, the FBI report states that the killer would very likely have ceased his activities if he believed he was close to being identified.[476]

One conundrum needs to be overcome, however – serial killers rarely stop killing of their own accord; they usually die or get caught. Hardiman was no exception to this rough rule of thumb. Following the death of Frances Coles, no further murders were recorded that could be associated with either 'Jack the Ripper' or the Thames Torso murderer and in 1892 the Met closed the case files completely, with the killings remaining unsolved. By the close of the previous year, however, Hardiman had been riddled with TB and it seems he was about to enter his very own 'end game'. Coles had been murdered in February and shortly thereafter Hardiman's ill health had effectively taken him out of circulation. By then he had moved back to 29 Hanbury Street with his mother and brother William where he was to die on 22 December 1891, at the age of 32.

James Hardiman would appear to present as a very plausible suspect for both the 'Ripper' *and* Torso murders; he was a local man with a good knowledge of his environment who had previously been associated with several of the murder sites. He also possessed the requisite skills, freedom of movement and opportunity. As far as any motives are concerned, we would suggest that although he probably had a deep underlying psychological condition that predisposed him to murder, it was the birth of his daughter and the subsequent death of her and her mother from a disease he had given them, that triggered his descent down this pathological path. That he got away with the killings was due to his local knowledge, his cunning and his ability to 'hide in plain sight', which his dual trades in both horseflesh and the carts that carried it afforded him. No doubt harbouring animosities towards the police from previous dealings, once having embarked on his 'crusade', he was able to take great delight in taunting them at every opportunity the killings offered. He probably fully expected to get caught and was surely astounded at the inability of his adversaries to catch him, despite coming to light on at least two occasions – once even as their chief suspect 'John Arnold'. Hardiman had nothing to lose, though. He was dying anyway and would hang for just one murder so why shouldn't he carry on doing something he found sexually gratifying?

We recognise that any candidate presented to as well-informed an audience, as is the worldwide fraternity of Ripperologists, would be unlikely to convince everybody. We also accept, and agree, that a 'conviction' after 130 plus years is all but impossible, and we are not so arrogant as to suggest that we have 'solved' the two murder series where others have struggled to do so. Nonetheless, we think that if James Hardiman had been arrested today the police would certainly have some serious questions to ask him about his activities.

Convincing though we believe the case against Hardiman is, one particular part of the puzzle however remains problematic. Three more killings attributed to the Thames Torso series were recorded prior to the Rainham case at the beginning of our story. Although, given the paucity of information, it is hard to make an objective assessment of the first two torsos found in the Thames in 1873 and 1874, we believe it is difficult to attribute these to our suspect considering he would have been aged 14 or 15 at the time – even given the fact he was dealing cat's meat by age 11. Far harder to discount though is the third case which came to light somewhat closer to the others, in 1884.

On 25 September that year, human bones thought to have belonged to a young female, were discovered in the ornamental gardens at Mornington Crescent, Camden. More remains, which had either been placed on or thrown over railings, were found a little later further south, at Fitzroy Square. Further south still, on 23 October, a skull and an arm (wrapped in brown paper) were found at Alfred Mews and Bedford Square respectively, the latter, again, apparently thrown into gardens over railings. Although there appears to have been no consensus as to whether the parts belonged to just one or more than one woman, Dr Samuel Lloyd was of the opinion that the victim(s) had been killed in April of that year. The case has generally come to be known as the 'Tottenham Court Road Mystery' given that most of the finds occurred in close proximity to that thoroughfare. It is also known as the case of 'the girl with the rose tattoo' due to the fact that a recovered arm exhibited such adornment.

As was the case with the killer's other victims, the tattoo could suggest that the deceased had also been a prostitute. It is interesting to note as well that on two occasions the remains had been thrown or placed over railings as happened in the case of Elizabeth Jackson, the Horsleydown torso, and the Lambeth discovery, the Whitehall torso. The parcelling of the arm in such a fashion is also reminiscent of other torso discoveries. These body parts themselves also appeared to have been covered in lime, which had been the case previously at Lambeth. What is more, a quick look at the map and an appreciation of the north/south axis of these discoveries should serve to increase our interest further. Continuing in a north-easterly direction from the northernmost find at Mornington Crescent, our killer would have passed King's Cross and St Pancras stations – well-known soliciting haunts. Eventually, he would have come out in Camden Town – an area notable for the presence of the Harrison, Barber slaughterhouse at Brandon Road, which was close to where the body parts had been discovered in the Regent's Canal. At the southern extremity of the finds, was the one-time residence of a certain 'John Arnold' at Harvey Buildings on the Strand.

If this had also been the work of Hardiman at this earlier juncture, however, it begs the question as to what could have triggered his offending on this occasion. Although we believe that it was the tragic events of 1887/8 that had precipitated his main crusade – could earlier happenings have initiated a precursor event one wonders? His elder sister Sarah had died in January 1885 and he may well have been in a bad way around the time of the killing if her death had been protracted. Had the scourge of syphilis been evident in some way here too, one wonders? It seems the jury on this one will have to remain out for a while longer yet.

In summary then, from the Rainham torso find in May 1887 to the death of Frances Coles in February 1891, the *probable* and *possible* murders/assaults we associate with our killer are as follows, with the *possible* ones in Italics:

25 September 1884 'The Girl with the Rose Tattoo'
11 May 1887 Rainham Torso
5 November 1887 Emily Horsnell
Oct – 26 December 1887 'Fairy Fay'
25 February 1888 Annie Millwood (Non-fatal)
28 March 1888 Ada Wilson (Non-fatal)
30 April 1888 Emma Smith
7 August 1888 Martha Tabram
31 August 1888 Mary Ann Nichols
8 September 1888 Annie Chapman
11 September 1888 Whitehall Torso
30 September 1888 Elizabeth Stride
30 September 1888 Catherine Eddowes
9 November 1888 Marie Jane Kelly
20 November 1888 Annie Farmer (Non-fatal)
20 December 1888 Rose Mylett
4 June 1889 Horsleydown Torso (Elizabeth Jackson)
17 July 1889 Alice McKenzie
10 September 1889 Pinchin Street Torso
13 February 1891 Frances Coles

As we have said, reasonable doubts exist regarding the indicated 'possible' victims. Doubts have also traditionally been expressed in respect of some of the other victims, such as Millwood, Wilson and perhaps even Rose Mylett who met her end some way off the 'Ripper's' usual patch. Hopefully, however, we have been able to convince you that it is entirely possible that they *all* could have succumbed to the same man's hand – that of local resident, horse slaughterer and cat's meat man, James Hardiman.

Before we leave the Hardimans, an interesting postscript to the story also exists. It seems that James's younger brother William, or 'Bill' as he was known, who was resident at 29 Hanbury Street on the night of Annie Chapman's murder, had been continuing the family tradition on the cat's meat barrows when he joined C. R. Ashbee's Guild of Handicraft at Toynbee Hall in 1890.[477] He also moved with them, it seems, when they relocated to new premises in the Mile End Road a little later.[478]

He rose to be their top metalwork modeller and produced exquisite pieces that command premium prices at auction today. The embossed leather wall panels for Ashbee's Chelsea townhouse, which he also crafted, are now housed in London's Victoria and Albert Museum. Although generally regarded as a simple-minded yet kindly soul, it had been noted by those around him that he was becoming increasingly unstable. When the guild moved again to the Cotswold town of Chipping Campden in 1902 he once more moved with them although by this time the management considered him to be 'hopelessly insane'.[479]

Believing there to be a conspiracy against him and preferring to work alone, he finally left the guild in 1905 and returned to Whitechapel – accusing his foreman of 'getting the detectives on to him'.[480] He committed suicide later that year, at the age of 33, by drinking hydrochloric acid.[481] But when exactly and why had the police first taken an interest in Bill and what was it that had preyed on his mind and tipped him over the edge? Had he too been suffering the progressively grim symptoms of tertiary syphilis recorded by Alfred Fournier – had his encroaching blindness perhaps been too much for the gifted craftsman to bear? Or had he known something more, perhaps, of events in Whitechapel all those years ago? Indeed, had his mother, Harriet? She, by all accounts, passed away at the Hackney Union Infirmary a few years later. As with much else in the case – this is probably yet one more question for which we will never have a completely satisfactory answer.

16

POSTSCRIPT – A REFLECTION ON 'HISTORY', 'TRUE CRIME' AND 'RIPPEROLOGY'

There's something inherently seedy and salacious in continually picking the scabs off these crimes, peering at mutilated bodies, listing the undergarments, trekking over the tainted ground in quest of some long-delayed occult frisson.

Iain Sinclair, *White Chappell, Scarlet Tracings* (1987)

In a recent PhD thesis, Matthew Thompson explored the effect of 'the Ripper's legacy' by studying almost 130 years of Ripperology. He traces the evolution of the 'Ripper figure' and its connection to popular culture, social concerns and politics. In his final sections, Thompson addresses the modern manifestation of the 'Ripper' myth in television, literature – including graphic novels and comics, and in video games and cinema. He references a particularly unpleasant example of a Japanese adult film from 1976 about murder and sexual violence and states:

The fact that such films invoke the Ripper's name to communicate graphic violence and titillation only reinforces the notion that the Ripper figure is in danger of becoming trivialized for shock value.[482]

In this final section we explore the nature of Ripperology, of the myth-making associated with the 'Ripper' murder series, and the exploitation of it by countless authors – including us, of course – as well as tour guides, and the broader entertainment industry. There are consequences that occur from the misrepresentation or exploitation of history, and the current furore around 'fake news' (about which there is nothing 'new') serves as a reminder that the casual dissemination of unchecked or unsubstantiated 'facts' can be dangerous. We live in a world where 'news' is increasingly contested and the public now no longer knows whom to believe. Historians are not the keepers of some sacred flame, nor are we the only trustworthy individuals on the planet, but academic history is concerned with a deeper analysis of the past (and the present, for that matter) than is often the case with journalists who are required to file a breaking news story to meet an editorial deadline. We have the luxury of more time and the related academic skills of source analysis, interrogation and historical context, which might allow us to engage more deeply. This is not to set academia up as something special; plenty of the so-called 'amateur' histories written about the case are equally grounded in recognised historical processes.

Ripperology has garnered something of a bad press over the years, much of it (if not all) undeserved. The public perception of Ripperology is probably very far from the reality; most people will have some idea of the 'Ripper' murder case and one or two of the most prominent theories but few will have actually read more than one book on the subject, if that. Popular cultural representations of 'Jack the Ripper' are therefore much better known and understood than the history of the Whitechapel murderer case itself, or indeed its victims, and the context in which the murders happened. In this final chapter then we will look at the phenomenon of Ripperology, at what it means for history, and offer some suggestions for ways in which academic history and amateur history could work together to address some of the undoubted problems that exist within the (broadly defined) Ripperology community. Why is this necessary?

Well, we only have to look at Matthew Thompson's quote above, with other examples that we shall explore, to suggest that it is.

The 'Ripper' phenomenon and the creation of a cultural monster

Writing in 1988, with more than a nod to the centenary of the Whitechapel murders, Deborah Cameron noted that: 'Jack the Ripper has been thoroughly sanitised, turned into a folk hero such as Robin Hood. His story is packaged as a bit of harmless fun: only a spoilsport would be tactless enough to point out it is story of misogyny and sadism.' Some years later, Robin Odell wrote a useful retrospective of 'Ripper writing' that detailed the ways representations of the case (and the emergence of a succession of suspects for the murders) had evolved from the 1880s to the present.[483] While Odell's work was not intended, as Cameron's may have been, to undermine the industry created by the unsolved mystery, his analysis does reveal how the anti-hero of the 'Ripper' was able to emerge in the manner she described. More recently Thompson's 2017 PhD thesis also offers a helpful overview and explanation for the creation of the cultural 'monster' that most people associate with 'Jack the Ripper', even if, as one eminent Ripperologist has said, he gets plenty of things wrong in the process.[484]

Much has to do with the way the case was presented and represented at the time in the late nineteenth century. Michael Diamond has described the 'Ripper' murders as the 'greatest murder sensation of the Victorian era'; the brutality, the serial nature of the killings, and the failure of the police to catch anyone, all contributed to making it the biggest story of its day.[485] One of the first published accounts of the murders was written in 1888 and so, at least superficially, would appear to be a useful primary source. The *History of the Whitechapel Murders: a full and authentic narrative* was published in New York in 1888.[486] However, it takes as its primary source the reportage of the contemporary London press. As a result, it lists the nine murders that the press had linked together to create the narrative of a single assassin, something that almost all subsequent studies have started with. But the New York publication also makes several errors and this is typical of many of the writings that have surrounded the Whitechapel series. So, for example, it states that the killer had removed organs from Tabram's body and that Nichols had been killed elsewhere and then left in Buck's Row later – neither of these 'facts' are accepted today. The reality is that subsequent narratives of the murders have built on previous retellings, cannibalising information and taking the whole back catalogue of 'Ripperology' as sacrosanct. In the 1920s an author named Tom Robinson penned his 'authentic account' of the murders and like Leonard Matters, who is often seen as the first Ripperologist,[487] he drew on a personal connection with the area.[488] However, like Matters he committed errors in his narrative that have clouded future research. Robinson said that he lived in Whitechapel during the 'autumn of terror' and claimed that Emma Smith was a 'Ripper' victim and that local girls had complained of being 'molested by a dark-bearded man of such a frightful aspect, that at his approach they ran away'.[489] Interestingly neither of these early 'authentic accounts' makes reference to the 'writing on the wall' although we have contemporary accounts (from Sir Charles Warren, no less) that confirm its existence.

Leonard Matters' 1948 work was later picked up by William Stewart (who believed 'Jack' was a woman, whom he dubbed 'Jill the Ripper') and his research was clouded by the same repeated mistakes that Matters had made. As Phillip Sugden reminds us, it is quite common for authors to perpetuate these errors by simply borrowing 'facts' from each other. Sugden's evident indignation is well justified; 'for far too long these myths have clouded our understanding of the character and background of the victim, the details of the crime, even the appearance of the murderer.'[490] Sugden was writing about the death of Annie Chapman but his views are relevant for the whole series of the murders reviewed in our book.

Lee Perry Curtis claims that what 'transpired in London during the autumn of 1888 was not just a series of five sadistic murders but a serial story combining mystery and sensation-horror spread out over almost four months and cobbled together by a metropolitan press eager to boost sales.'[491] Darren Oldridge argued that the way the Victorian press handled the case, linking together the murders of Emma Smith to those of Tabram, Nichols and then Chapman, established the idea of the lone killer and side-lined competing explanations that the murders were the work of a criminal gang of prostitutes' 'bullies', or 'pimps' to use modern terminology.[492] Thereafter this is the only narrative that has been generally accepted and forms the basis for all the 'solutions' offered by researchers, including – to a large extent, at least – our own.

Not only did the press of the day help construct a narrative of the murders they also set down the framework for identifying the killer and in the process they helped establish 'many of the distinctive features of Ripperology'.[493] This point is emphasised by Christopher Frayling in a seminal essay in which he argues persuasively that ever since 1888, we have been searching for an archetype of the killer rather than the killer himself. But Professor Frayling goes further, suggesting that the police hunt for the murderer was undermined from the very start because Detective Inspector Abberline and the men of H Division were chasing a cultural stereotype rather than a serial murderer.[494] Let's explore this for a moment because it offers us a useful insight into how the 'Ripper' myth has developed. Layers of research have often served to obfuscate rather than illuminate the case, partly because they start with a false premise.

Frayling's typology of the 'three ready-made models of the sort-of-person-who-might-do-such-things' included the 'English Milord', 'Mad Doctor' and 'Deranged Jewish Immigrant', and reflected contemporary fears of the 'other'. That these arose is in part explained by contemporary fears (about the decadent aristocracy, the emerging medical profession, and high levels of migration from Eastern Europe) but also by the paucity of official source material. As a result, certain surviving documents – including a number that surfaced decades after the murders ceased – have been given undue significance in much the same way that artefacts supposedly associated with 'the Ripper' have, such as the diary, Eddowes' shawl, or Abberline's walking cane. This is the conclusion reached by one author, Spiro Dimolianis, who suggested that the Mcnaghten Memorandum (which named three suspects – Druitt, Ostrog and Kosminski) as well as the 'Swanson marginalia' and Sir Robert Anderson's memoirs have all done more to obscure the truth than they have to provide 'historical closure'.[495] Anderson apparently favoured the idea that 'Jack' was Jewish but given his well-known dislike of 'aliens' and his lack of direct knowledge of the case, should this not be treated with considerable scepticism given that, as Dimolianis points out, this merely 'conveyed an entrenched racial prejudice of the time'?[496] This scepticism with 'official' accounts is also shared by Craig Monk, who reminds us to be cautious of autobiographical accounts from those such as Anderson, Mcnaghten and Henry Smith (the Chief Superintendent of the City of London Police from 1885–1890) because like 'the authors of all life narratives, they each construct individual truths that have but an uncertain relationship to verifiable fact'.[497] In other words – as anyone penning their own diary, memoir, or indeed version of a traffic altercation can attest – personal accounts of events are imbued with personal bias, self-justification and, in some cases, ignorance. Academic and other trained historians are generally adept at picking a path through contested or subjective primary material but some less-well-informed works are apt to accept contemporary accounts at face value.

It seems that Sir Melville Mcnaghten preferred Montague Druitt as a candidate. As we've seen Druitt, a lawyer and school master, had thrown himself into the Thames shortly after Mary Kelly's murder in November 1888 and a suicide note he left declared that he was scared of going mad 'like mother'.[498] Mental instability chimed with a popular contemporary notion that the killer must have been someone that manifested a split personality (decades before psychiatry could better explain mental illness) and suggested that a 'civilised' 'gentleman' had somehow lost control of himself and reverted to his primeval roots. This fitted nicely with late Victorian fantasies born out of Robert Louis Stevenson's novella about a doctor who experimented with an alter ego. In the autumn of 1888 as 'Jack the Ripper' evaded the police in the East End, a West End stage was playing host to the American actor Richard Mansfield's portrayal of *Dr. Jekyll and Mr. Hyde* in an all-too-real representation of the beast-within-man for contemporaries to cope with. Mansfield closed the show after widespread protests and threats and instead put on a benefit performance of a musical comedy to raise money for the poor.[499] Ideas that the killer was a 'slumming' aristocrat – a 'champagne Charlie' or 'Burlington Bertie' – also reflected late Victorian distaste for the excesses of the rich, while the infestation of the East End by hordes of newspapermen helped expose the desperate poverty of the residents of the 'abyss' and emphasised the huge gulf in wealth between the two halves of the capital of the empire. For some then, the 'Ripper' symbolised the callous disregard of the poor by the rich in late Victorian Britain. It rather neglected, however, the uncomfortable reality that a West End 'slummer' or 'toff' (and certainly a member of the aristocracy being ferried about in a coach) would find it less easy to melt into Whitechapel's labyrinth of streets, alleys and courts, which even the police found difficult to navigate in 1888.

The press fanned the flames of division between the classes in Victorian London as they raised concerns that the neglect of poverty in the East End of London might lead to bloody revolution in England, as it had elsewhere on the European continent. Despite the 1848 revolutions taking place more than a generation earlier, the Paris Commune and the rise of the rival Communist Internationals in the 1870s had kept the spectre of revolution on the agenda of commentators. There were similar echoes closer to home and empire, as John Marriott has noted, and the 'reading public were reminded that events in Whitechapel were strikingly similar to the atrocities of the Indian revolt of 1857, when British subjects were mutilated by alien savages unrestrained by Christian influence.'[500] No less a figure than George Bernard Shaw, writing to

The Star newspaper in September 1888, described the murderer as an 'independent genius'. Referring to his own political stance (as a Fabian, a democratic Socialist) he wrote:

> Whilst we conventional social democrats were wasting our time on education, agitation and organisation, some independent genius has taken the matter in hand, and by simply murdering and disembowelling four women, converted the proprietary class to an inept form of communism.[501]

William Morris made a very similar point in *Commonwealth*, suggesting that 'a fiend-murderer may become a more effective reformer than all the honest propagandists in the world.'[502] Central to understanding the effect of the 'Jack the Ripper' phenomenon on late Victorian society is the way in which the case was used by overlapping and sometimes competing interest groups – from philanthropists and social commentators, to radical politicians, left and right, and, of course, the purveyors of popular culture and entertainment.

Much has been made of the 'positive' influence the murderer supposedly had on social reform, particularly in the immediate aftermath of the killings when swaths of slum housing was cleared away to build new, clean 'model dwellings' for the poor. This had been at the heart of Canon Barnett's campaign of 'urban renewal' and bore some fruit after legions of newspapermen had shone their lights on the squalor of the area.[503] However, before we get carried away with the notion that the 'Ripper' did some good it is important to understand that this is itself part of the mythology surrounding the murders. While Odell declared that after the murders Britain 'at last woke up to the poverty on the doorstop of its capital city, and much-needed reform quickly arrived' he neglects to mention that the attempts to alleviate poverty were both partial and short-lived.[504] Slum clearance simply moved the problem elsewhere and subsequent model dwellings housed the 'respectable' poor – those with a regular, if small, income – not the casual poor who relied on the cheap lodging houses that Barnett was so keen to bulldoze in Flower and Dean Street.[505]

So not only did the popular press seek to exploit a 'crime news story' by the use of sensational language, drawing on the ways that William Stead's *Pall Mall Gazette* had exploited the scandal of child prostitution in the capital in 1885,[506] the London and nationally focused papers also painted a picture of Whitechapel's degraded state – helping build an image of a netherworld that can be seen in the writings of contemporaries such as Walter Besant, Octavia Hill and Andrew Mearns.[507] This is important because the reality was that Whitechapel and Spitalfields was a far more mixed environment than these reports suggested. One only has to study Charles Booth's poverty maps, which are easily available for all to examine online, to see that the East End was far from being completely degraded. Booth's survey revealed a very different picture of the area. He says, with additional quotes from Frayling: 'Only 1.2 per cent of the East End population were in the category of "loafers and semi-criminals", while well over 60 per cent tried to lead "decent, respectable lives" ("questions of employment permitting"). The rest were not so much "debased", as living in conditions of almost perpetual poverty, and even so trying to support one another.'[508] The local press, for example the *East End Observer*, often refuted or played down claims that the area was the cause of the murders and that its inhabitants were in any way 'degraded'. It was not in their interests to peddle an image of the East End as 'an abyss', bereft of any culture, humanity or decency. However, the idea that Whitechapel was so far removed from the rest of London as to be almost a separate country has persisted and to this day, nearly all books, TV documentaries or movies which represent Victorian East London routinely trot out the same narrative of it as a place forever synonymous with poverty and crime. One of the key myths that needs challenging then, is that of the East End itself. The degraded streets and slum housing depicted by Mearns in his *A Bitter Cry of Outcast London* (1883) or in all the newspaper reports of Whitechapel doss houses, infested with drunken men and women in search of cheap sex and the next pitcher of gin, have helped to create an image which has stuck with us. Another American visitor, Jack London, was one of several contemporary authors who wrote in graphic detail of the terrible state of poverty and immorality he found in Whitechapel.[509] John Tenniel's image of the 'Nemesis of Neglect' is another excellent illustration of how contemporaries portrayed the East End, but again it is not an accurate picture of the reality of the area.

In nearly all movies about 'the Ripper', London is dark and foggy, the smog caused by thousands of coal fires gives it a spooky gothic horror feel. But, as we've shown, none of the murders occurred in the middle of the night in the midst of fog. Just as the killer never wore a top hat or swirled a black cape, we have invented an image of the streets that fits our imagination of the murders rather more than the reality of them. So, as Clive Bloom insists, 'The East End was more than a place, it was a living symbol,' a symbol of the worst side of Victorian society and, by implication, the failure of Victorian civilization.[510]

Modern popular cultural representations of 'Jack the Ripper's' London

So we can see how myths about 'Jack the Ripper' and the area he 'haunted' have developed over the 130+ years since the murders occurred and these have been fuelled by ongoing speculation brought about by the lack of a clear and universally accepted protagonist. Put another way, because the Whitechapel murderer has never been caught, the search for 'Jack the Ripper' has become *the* quintessential murder mystery and this has been further exaggerated by the attempt to establish who he was. The list of suspects is endless and is added to with every new book on the subject – including this one! – Doctors (such as Sir William Gull, D'Onston Stephenson, Dr John Williams, or Francis Tumblety) and 'gentlemen' (like Montague Druitt, the Duke of Clarence, James Maybrick or Walter Sickert) along with the 'mad', 'bad' or simply dangerous crew of 'others' (Aaron Kosminski, George Chapman,

William Bury, Joseph Barnett) all compete for our attention. But, as Frayling reminds us, this is to miss the point. None of these men – and it is almost invariably men – (although there is a case made for a 'Jill the Ripper'[511]) can be proven to have been the killer since insufficient forensic material survives from the period to establish anyone's guilt beyond doubt, but perhaps not beyond 'reasonable doubt'.

What we are left with instead is a mythologised version of the killer as someone (or 'something') symbolic of modern popular, rather than academic, understandings of the late nineteenth century. Clive Bloom has suggested that the 'Ripper' murders are 'the final frenzied acknowledgement of the coming of the age of materialism'.[512] He sees 'Jack' as a timeless monster, not bound in the age of Victorian gaslight but able to travel and impact our own world, a sort of malign Dr Who if you will.

While academic history has largely ignored the 'Ripper' murders, other disciplines have been less quick to turn up their noses. Cultural, literature and film studies have all found something interesting to say about 'Jack', his representation and our fascination with him. Thus Gary Colville and Patrick Luciano dedicate an entire volume to the study of the cultural impact of 'Jack the Ripper' on the entertainment industry.[513] Similarly Clare Smith has explored the symbolism in movie representations of 'Jack'.[514] Colville and Luciano argue that: 'It is not so much *who* the Ripper was [...] that fascinates the public as much as it is *what* the Ripper was, and continues to be: a pervasive representation of ancient evil loose in a progressive, technological world.'[515] Matthew Thompson's recent thesis is another welcome academic intervention into the world of Ripperology that seeks to analyse the various ways in which the figure of 'the Ripper' has been hijacked for a multiplicity of purposes.[516] This was apparent from the very start of Ripperology, in the days, weeks and months following the murders of the five canonical victims in 1888's 'autumn of terror'. Suggestions that the killer was a monster, inhuman and certainly 'not English' arose from popular superstitions and prejudices. It was easy to point the finger at the Jewish immigrant community with their ritualised butchery and 'foreign' customs. Or at the Irish whose 'Fenian outrages' had been grabbing headlines throughout the 1880s. These all played into deeply ingrained folk traditions. Moreover Victorian Britain had an established tradition of mythic characters that were drawn from centuries of folklore. As London filled up with tens of thousands of migrants from within the British Isles, and with agricultural workers rendered obsolete by the mechanisation of farming, they all brought with them an oral tradition of fairy stories. In addition to the canon of folk devils, new characters such as Spring Heeled Jack and Sweeney Todd helped forge a modern urban mythology that blended with Celtic folklore and the myths brought by more exotic migrants from Eastern Europe (the Golem for example) and beyond. These mutated and merged with fears about this developing 'modern' industrial and urban society. As Smith has written: '*Fin-de-siècle* literature produced the male characters that still dominate our cultural imagination. Dr Jekyll and Mr Hyde, Dracula, Sherlock Holmes and Dorian Gray all emerged at the end of the nineteenth century along with Jack the Ripper.'[517] With *Jekyll and Hyde* playing on the London stage – and a waxworks exhibition featuring the mutilated bodies of Tabram, Nichols and Chapman appearing on the Whitechapel Road – it is not hard to see how the boundaries between reality and myth, history and fiction, were blurred from the very beginning of the 'Ripper drama,' as Judith Walkowitz dubs it.[518] In 2014 the British Library staged a major exhibition of the Gothic tradition covering 250 years of art and culture which featured the infamous 'Dear Boss' letter, thereby firmly cementing 'Jack the Ripper' in popular literature and culture forever.[519]

The 2001 movie *From Hell* (directed by The Hughes Brothers) was itself inspired by the graphic novel of the same name, written and drawn by Alan Moore and Eddie Campbell.[520] Moore and Campbell's novel utilises a cast of hundreds from London's history to blend mythology with history and politics and to reveal that the murders were part of a conspiracy to uphold the State and patriarchy. This was a popular representation of the murders that took root in the 1970s and reflected other conspiracy theories popular at the time, for example, the 'faked' Moon landings or the assassination of John F. Kennedy. Quite apart from the fact that it bore no relationship to the realities of the murder case as we understand them, both the graphic novel and the film version of *From Hell* continue to perpetuate the myths of the case and a vision of Victorian London which owes more to fiction than it does to history. This is echoed in two other fictional works that draw on the 'Ripper' myth for inspiration. Both Peter Ackroyd and Iain Sinclair deploy psychogeography in their novelised versions of the capital.[521] This alchemical blending of sources to paint a mythologised version of the past has been a literary form since at least the period of the murders themselves. In the 1880s, as Kate Lonsdale has written, the contemporary 'media also drew on cultural fantasies of the grotesque and sexually promiscuous female body; [and] the labyrinthine city, including the illicit and squalid Whitechapel setting' to establish the context for the killings.[522]

This process continues apace, with a glut of Victorianism appearing on the large and small screen in recent years. Ackroyd's *Limehouse Golem* had life breathed into it by Juan Carlos Medina and Jane Goldman, while *Ripper Street* has enjoyed five series since it first aired on the BBC in 2012. The latter used a mixture of real historical characters (Fred Abberline, Edmund Reid) and placed them in a 'real' historical setting (1880s Whitechapel) exposing them to fictionalised versions of real events while at the same time presenting us with a twenty-first-century vision of the late nineteenth century. John Logan's *Penny Dreadful* went even further. It combined fictional personalities from the 1800s with 'real life' narratives and depicted London as almost a 'steam punk' capital of empire. Here Dracula fought with Victor Frankenstein while Dorian Gray interfered from the side-lines. Less horrifically, the BBC's *Dickensian* mini-series populates mid-Victorian London with well-known characters from several of Charles Dickens' novels as Inspector Bucket of *Bleak House* investigates the murder of Jacob Marley from *A Christmas Carol*, while subplots involve Fagin and Nancy from *Oliver Twist* and Miss Havisham of *Great Expectations*. To what extent do these versions of the past, however entertaining they are, contribute to a misrepresentation of it, and does it matter if they do?

Historians or sensationalists? Ripperology and its future

In 2010 one of the co-authors of this book wrote that if there was a reason 'to continue to study the events of August to November 1888' it was 'to try to understand the reality of the lives of ordinary people living one of the most depressed corners of the British Empire.'[523] Indeed, one kind reviewer commended the study for eschewing any attempt to name a suspect when the field was already so crowded with the names of long-dead Victorians. We have made our case for ignoring our own advice and presenting the world with yet another 'whodunit', but please let us continue with this analysis of Ripperology and where it has taken us. The more recent search for the reality of the lives of the 'ordinary' (notable in the work of members of the Whitechapel Society, for example) is in stark contrast to the extraordinary and fantastical world that has been created around the murderer of five or more working-class women in Whitechapel. According to Kate Lonsdale, 'Jack the Ripper remains a definitional paradox: he is both labelled and disembodied, both historical figure and discursive presence, both representation and reality [...] He is simultaneously nobody, somebody, and everybody.'[524] For Bloom, the 'Jack' was also an 'everyman' character, an 'icon of late Victorianism'.[525] Colville and Luciano argue that through film, the character of 'Jack the Ripper has transcended mere criminality to become a representation of the dark side of ourselves, and hence the Ripper is no longer somebody, but everybody.'[526]

Self-evidently while 'Jack the Ripper', the figure created by popular culture, might be 'everyman' the Whitechapel murderer – the brutal killer of at least five 'ordinary' women – was very real. Moreover, the idea that a violent male killer was able to terrify, kill and disembowel his victims without being caught has given hundreds of serial murderers and rapists licence to replicate his crimes in the intervening century or more. Charlotte Mallinson has drawn important parallels between the representation of the murders and the profile of 'the Ripper' and a succession of male serial killers from Peter Sutcliffe onwards. The symbolic use of the historical 'Jack the Ripper' to perpetuate 'whorephobia' and misogyny in attacks on women echoes down the centuries, she argues, and it is sadly ever present in modern Ripperology and in popular culture surrounding the Whitechapel case.

In a recent exchange on social media the writer and historian Hallie Rubenhold, who has come under attack from some Ripperologists for her suggestion that they have ignored the victims of 'the Ripper' and condemned Ripperology as a whole as misogynistic, posted an image of a T-shirt being sold online which uses the stereotypical image of 'the Ripper's' top hat, cape and knives over an overtly sexualised picture of a woman's exposed vulva with her intestines 'ripped' out. This exploitation of the case might be dismissed as an example of a 'one-off' opportunistic venture that caters for a disturbed minority if it wasn't for the fact that in 2018 the London Dungeon ran an extensive advertising campaign that placed the exploitative and violent themes of the Whitechapel case at the very heart of its promotional campaign on the London Underground. The exhibit makes no attempt to contextualise the murders, or acknowledge the victims as ordinary and innocent human beings; it simply exploits a very real historical tragedy for financial gain, presenting it as entertainment, something to 'laugh' and 'scream' about.

In 2015 the Ripperology community tackled the question of sensational exploitation head on in a special edition of the monthly *Ripperologist* magazine. Adam Wood's editorial asked 'are we historians or sensationalists?'[527] He concluded with a call for common sense and decency but the recent publicity for Rubenhold's new book on the five canonical victims, and her appearance at a one day conference in September 2018, suggests there is still much work to be done to clean up Ripperology, as Wood insists the majority of those involved desire. In that issue is a thoughtful and now sadly poignant article by Kate Amin (née Bradshaw) who offers a view of feminism and its relationship to Ripperology, notably in light of the opening of the so-called 'Jack the Ripper Museum' in Cable Street that year. Amin concluded her article with the statement:

> The truth is, however, that while money continues to be made in the exploitation of the more gruesome aspects of the case and the focus of the media remains on the 'who done it' story, this will always lead feminists to argue that the really important story, that of the women, their lives, their struggles and their place in society is lost.[528]

The power of 'the Ripper' to legitimise violence against women was recognised, by some at least, as early as 1888. Like the London Monster scare of the 1790s, 'Jack the Ripper' was a useful mechanism to reassert patriarchy and define who was (and who was not) a 'respectable' or 'decent' woman. Both Walkowitz and Cameron referred to a contemporary letter published by the *Daily News* in the year of the murders. It was from Florence Fenwick Miller, who was described by Walkowitz as 'a London journalist and "platform woman".'[529] Fenwick Miller wrote that:

> Week by week and month by month, women are kicked, beaten, jumped on until they are crushed, chopped, stabbed, seamed with vitriol, bitten, eviscerated with red-hot pokers and deliberately set on fire – and this sort of outrage, if the woman dies, is called 'manslaughter': if she lives, it is common assault.[530]

In 2007 Judith Walkowitz wrote:

> The Whitechapel murders have continued to provide a common vocabulary of male violence against women,

a vocabulary now more than one hundred years old. Its persistence owes much to the mass media's exploitation of Ripper iconography. Depictions of female mutilation in mainstream cinema, celebrations of the Ripper as a 'hero' of crime, intensify fears of male violence and convince women that they are helpless victims.[531]

For all the progress modern society has made in addressing male violence it was only in 2018 that legislators were considering adding misogyny to the list of hate crimes, giving violence inspired by a hatred of women equal status to that currently ascribed to racism and homophobia. As Kate Bradshaw (Amin) insisted in 2015, the study of the Whitechapel murders is not inherently anti-feminist or misogynist but the glorification of the killer as a man who mutilates women and gets away with it most certainly is. There is misogyny within the Ripperology community even if it exists on the margins and with certain misguided individuals. How this is tackled is clearly a problem for a body of people which has no institutional core. You don't apply to be a member of the club; you just 'pop up' on a message board or social media site. Unpleasantness and abusive behaviour can get one banned or excluded but in the modern world of cyber space it is all but impossible to silence discordant voices. The various 'Ripper Tours' are not subject to licensing by nature of their content so this is certainly an area in which Ripperologists have struggled to be seen as respectable. Many excellent guides and walks take place every month but equally there are exploitative and overly sensational ones as well.

As Warwick and Willis declared in their introduction to the volume of essays that was to launch a greater academic interest in the subject: 'Jack the Ripper is a phenomenon that shows no sign of being incarcerated.'[532] Most recent academic authors recognise the debt they owe to Judith Walkowitz for being bold enough to take on this money-making juggernaut by challenging the ways in which we have depicted the killer. Yet the outpouring of 'Ripper' books, most of which repeat the myths and 'glorify' the killer; 'Ripper' tours, the worst of which project images of the mutilated bodies of the women onto the fabric of the modern city, in a callous repetition of the brutality of the murderer; and even the travesty of a 'museum' to the killer, are the main legacy that most people will experience when they encounter the 'history' of the Whitechapel murders. The museum in Cable Street can be dismissed as little more than 'an attraction', akin, if you like, to the waxworks that graced Whitechapel High Street in 1888. This is how one eminent Ripperologist prefers to see it. But very many visitors to the area will *only* see the Whitechapel murder case through the lens of this tawdry and exploitative venture. As Claire Hayward complains, 'the museum relies on myth and morbid imagination to sew a patchy narrative together; it lacks the information required to teach visitors much about Jack the Ripper, his victims, or the historical context in which they lived.'[533] It not only does the victims a disservice, it does Whitechapel and history one too.

Kate Lonsdale notes that 'the Ripper's victims are themselves often reduced to "stage props" in discussions of these crimes, their lives "overshadowed by repeated exhibition of their bodies" in the gruesome mortuary photos by which we have come to remember them'.[534] The Jack the Ripper Museum is the epitome of this exploitation of the victims, engaging, as some elements of the Victorian press did, in 'victim blaming' and relegating the five women to the status of 'supporting characters' in a fictionalised narrative of 'Jack the Ripper' as anti-hero.[535] There is an important role for public history, a relatively new academic discipline, in challenging the prevailing misrepresentation of Whitechapel and the 'Ripper' case. Serious questions need to be asked about how we present history and whose history we are telling when we do so. This is question that has already been applied to the history of Black British immigrants, to slavery and Imperial History, to the Holocaust and other sensitive historical topics, so why not 'the Ripper'? The Whitechapel Murders are taught in schools but often falls short of addressing some of the myths and stereotypes generated by 130+ years of 'Ripperology'. The 'Ripper' then, is clearly a topic to which public historians could bring a much-needed intellectual perspective.

Ripperology has moved on from the 1980s when Cameron dismissed it as 'pseudo-intellectual' and accused some of those involved in writing about the case of 'stupidity' and 'a barely suppressed erotic excitement with the idea of killing for sexual pleasure – and in the case of Jack the Ripper, of *getting away with it*.'[536] Now very many of those involved with the Whitechapel Society and the Casebook internet site are far more interested in finding out about the women who were killed and the lives they led. They painstakingly research the area and challenge some of the preconceived myths that surround it. They get a lot of stick from outsiders who get caught up in the case, often for their supposed obsessive interest, or for the proposal of ever more spurious solutions. But in reality much of this comes from *outside* mainstream Ripperology, as represented by the members of the Whitechapel Society and the contributors to *The Ripperologist* magazine. Indeed, as Matthew Thompson has observed: 'It is ironic that figures such as Bruce Robinson and Patricia Cornwell deride Ripperology for its half-baked facts and its obsessive willingness to keep up with various "trends" when they themselves have constructed suspects that do more to romanticise the legend of the Ripper than to analyse the horrific nature of the crimes themselves.'[537] Yet Ripperologists come in all shapes and sizes, male and female, and many delight in adopting pseudonyms inspired by the case. So we have 'Sir Robert Anderson', 'Abberline', 'Mr. Barnett', 'PC Neil', 'Saucy Jack' and 'Leather Apron' – even 'Carotid Capers' – among the many contributors to the Casebook message boards and numerous Facebook groups. You can also buy 'Ripper' merchandise and games themed on the case. In 1996 a PC game was released which allowed gamers to chase the killer through the streets of a futuristic New York. Now gamers have the opportunity to play as 'Jack the Ripper' in the most recent version of the popular video game *Assassin's Creed*. Here 'Jack' is a member of the assassins' guild and all his victims are other assassins, justifying their murders of course, and in effect, rewriting history.

We asked if any of this matters because we believe it does. The vacuum caused by the lack of academic history (crime history particularly) with the Whitechapel murder case has allowed the narrative to be driven by popular history, by Ripperology, and by the entertainment industry. This has not served the victims of 'the Ripper' very well. There is space for a proper engagement by historians with the 'Ripper' case and with Ripperology. Several prominent Ripperologists are keen to debate the case and its legacy with crime and cultural historians and there is much to be learned from them and the years of dedicated research they have invested in the minutiae of the case. Moreover, with the recent 'Me Too' campaign by women across the globe to expose the inherent misogyny of world society, 'the Ripper' needs to undergo a cultural transformation. No longer should he be presented as the 'criminal mastermind' who eluded the Met's finest, or a symbol of male dominance to inspire the next series of femicides, nor a way to justify 'whorephobia' and the continued exploitation of women to satisfy unrestrained male lust. 'Jack the Ripper' needs to be brought out of the dark shadows into the light and exposed to the full glare of academic study. His victims should be commemorated and their deaths recognised as symbolic of thousands of women who have suffered at the hands of male abusers before and after 1888. Deborah Cameron demanded this is in 1988 and we are still waiting. As she wrote then 'those who glorify the criminal should be forced to remember the victims.'[538]

Final thoughts and our justifications for taking the reader this far

There are literally dozens of books about the Whitechapel murders in print, and countless more that have long since been confined to the remainders shelves, pulped, or which exist solely in the dusty basements of library overflows, or perhaps pop up occasionally in eBay searches. Only a handful of texts have survived the test of time and those are the ones that offer the reader a little more; many of those currently available will disappear soon, to be replaced by a fresh supply. Such is our appetite for 'true crime' and for the 'Ripper' case in particular. So why bother to write this one? It's a reasonable question and one that invites us to think about the whole genre of 'true crime', 'Ripperology' and the writing of history itself. The authors of this book are not 'Ripperologists', we have not studied the case for 20 or 30 years as some have. Nor are we former murder squad detectives who are able to bring a lifetime of crime fighting to the task of solving a 'cold case'. Nor are we investigative journalists who have written countless other True Crime 'whodunnits' or exposés in the regional or national press. Instead we are academic social historians, with a special interest in the history of crime and punishment.

History, as one eminent historian wrote, 'is not just about events, it is about many other aspects of the past as well.'[539] It involves understanding events in the context of the time in which they occurred, not taking them as isolated moments. How does the Whitechapel case make any kind of sense without the contextual understanding of contemporary poverty, overcrowding, immigration and fears about radical new political ideas? The best histories of the 'Ripper' address these, while others virtually ignore them or trot out oft-repeated half-truths and assumptions. The effect of years of popular cultural representations of 'the Ripper' has been to create an image of the past that doesn't always accord with the reality.

Historians of all types, policemen and crime researchers are interested in 'facts'. Facts, some say, give us 'evidence' of what happened in the past. Yet facts and events are not the same thing – as Professor Evans reminds us, 'an event is a fact, but a fact is not necessarily an event.'[540] Furthermore, facts are not always evidence; it all depends on the context of how the historian uses them, and how they are interpreted. For example, the finding of a piece of bloodied cloth in Goulston Street on the night of the 'double event' (30 September 1888) by PC Long is a fact supported by documentary evidence;[541] how we interpret that fact is something quite different. Philip Sugden concludes that the discovery of the cloth and its subsequent match with the apron worn by Eddowes 'leaves no room for doubt that after murdering the woman in Mitre Square the killer escaped across the City boundary into Whitechapel'; but does it? Exactly when had it been placed there and from what direction had the perpetrator arrived? In their Channel 4 documentary the *Whitechapel Murders* (1996) Stuart Evans and Paul Gainey suggested that the killer ran 'back towards Berner Street and Batty Street', because that fitted the profile *they had constructed* of their suspect, Francis Tumblety. However, the finding of the cloth merely tells us that the killer, or at least the person in possession of the cloth, passed along Goulston Street sometime after killing Eddowes. Given the timing, it no more determines from where he came than the direction he took thereafter, or indeed his ultimate destination. Neither does it imply that he stopped to chalk a strange message on the portal of Wentworth Dwellings – although we believe that, at some stage, he did.

The curious Goulston Street graffito is another 'fact' that has allowed researchers to speculate wildly. Donald Rumbelow points out that there were two versions of the message, disputed by the two police forces that recorded it and he implies that Stephen Knight (who opted for PC Long's version: 'The Juwes are the men That Will not be Blamed for nothing') chose to represent the writing as evidence of a Masonic connection.[542] However, as Paul Begg demonstrates the use of the word 'Juwes', which was at the heart of Knight's thesis, was neither a contemporary local word for the Jewish community nor a collective noun for the murderers of the architect of King Solomon's Temple.[543] Nor do we have any actual proof as to whether the killer stopped to pen this himself, or whether it was the work of someone else entirely. So what does the Goulston Street graffito tell us? Well, in short, it perhaps gives us some evidence for the movements of the killer on the night of the murder of Eddowes and little more. We have had to consider it in the context of other, circumstantial evidence, in order to try and make some sense of it.

There is a more important underlying issue here, though, and that is the way in which a body of writing such as that surrounding the 'Ripper' case reinforces and recycles established 'facts' and presents them as 'evidence'. In this way, history is 'constructed', as layer upon layer of 'facts' are interwoven and then interpreted. Over the past 100 years or more of 'Ripper' writing, the narratives of the killings have become so well established that we have, to some extent at least, assumed that we 'know' what happened. In reality, we have known relatively little about how the murderer operated and less still about his motivation. It is this gap in knowledge that, paradoxically, allows a continual stream of writers to attempt to solve the case.

Beginning at the beginning then, what do we know? We can be fairly clear that several women were murdered between 1887 and 1891, by a person (or persons) unknown. From the anonymous Rainham torso dragged from the Thames, to the discovery of Frances Coles in February 1891, there are at least 16 unsolved killings that have been the subject of speculation, and five in particular that have fascinated 'Ripperologists'. Details of the police investigations into these deaths are fairly scant, however. The relevant records of the Metropolitan Police Office (MEPO) files at the National Archives contain statements and some images but even when we combine them with the memoirs or letters written by serving detectives from the period, there is surprisingly little to go on.

One scholar has noted that historical 'facts' can become 'constructed artefacts no different in cognitive origin than any man-made thing or "fiction".'[544] So much of the evidence left behind by the police investigation into the Whitechapel and Torso murders has disappeared, or has been destroyed, that the canon of previous 'Ripperology' has itself almost assumed the status of fact.

Some recent histories simply rehash previous ones while others deliberately play fast and loose with the facts to suit their own agenda, which is usually to pin the blame on their 'own favourite suspect'.[545] This situation is not helped by texts that almost entirely fail to acknowledge the source of their information, and there are plenty of those. While there is a difference between academic history and so-called 'popular' history it remains the responsibility of the writer of either to allow the reader to judge whether what is written is based on verifiable 'evidence'. In this book we have attempted to provide a trail that any future researcher can follow. It is no surprise then that the handful of 'Ripper' books or authors that have stood the test of time are those penned by, for example, Paul Begg, Donald Rumbelow and Phillip Sugden, that approach the case with the rigour it requires.

These titles set out what we know (or at least what we can agree that we 'know') about the Whitechapel murders and so it is from these writers, combined with our own primary research and a review of the archival material available to us, that we have derived our own narrative of events. But our set of events has created our own narrative, our own thesis on the killings, and we admit that we have also had to 'construct' this from the 'facts' and 'evidence' available. We have used discrete facts to support our argument and some readers might disagree with the conclusions we have drawn but hopefully it is at least clear that we have researched the context surrounding our claims. For in setting out to write this book, we had overlapping motivations.

In part we felt we had uncovered a possible suspect who, while having been mentioned before in the context of certain Whitechapel killings, had not figured prominently in previous studies or had his potential as a candidate fully explored.[546] Indeed, the circumstantial evidence emerging from our preliminary enquiries indicated that more in-depth research regarding this person was certainly warranted. Secondly, there seemed to be space to write a book that did a little more than simply return to the Whitechapel of 1888 to peer voyeuristically into the lives of its inhabitants.

So, we have taken the case as our focal point and offered an historical insight into a variety of themes, all of which link back to the life and times of James Hardiman and the crimes for which we believe he was probably responsible. Thirdly, it has given us the opportunity to explore the nature of 'True Crime' writing and in particular the sub-genre of 'Ripperology', an area which has grown exponentially in recent years, fuelled in part by the availability of internet chat rooms or forums.[547] Now everyone can be an expert, history is being written in blogs, in posts, in question and answers, by informed (and less well informed) contributors, many of whom hide behind colourful aliases. This form of history is interesting because it exists outside of the faculty (i.e. outside academic history in universities) but students and academics are increasingly using it. So, when an undergraduate, or anyone else for that matter, desires a quick answer to a question about the 'Ripper' case they invariably 'Google it'; turning to the Internet for advice as persons of a certain age might have reached for an encyclopaedia. Google may lead them first to Wikipedia but also to Casebook or thence to one of very many public blogs on the subject.

Moreover, academics, who have for so long turned their collective noses up at the Whitechapel case, are now embracing it and social and cultural history modules based upon the murders are now commonplace in British universities and the case is also part of the National Curriculum in schools. 'Jack the Ripper', we might say, has been rendered respectable, or at least has been deemed fit for academic study. Not wanting to be left out, one of our intentions was to construct our own 'Ripper' narrative using the tools of the academic social historian as our basis. Instead of a reliance on a physical artefact we chose instead to look at the interconnectivity of Whitechapel, the East End and Victorian London and to see whether our initial leads – the pinpointing of Heneage Street, the discovery of Hardiman there and the strange encounter between the 'good doctor' and PC Spicer – was worth pursuing. Thereafter we have allowed the facts, such as they are, to drive our narrative of events. In doing so, we think we have built a case against Hardiman that, we believe, merits serious consideration. The killer was, after all, likely to have been someone very close to James Hardiman's profile. Someone with a grudge, someone with the means to avoid detection, someone whom no one would necessarily suspect, someone with the freedom to move around the area and beyond. Overall, he was someone 'ordinary', a 'complete nobody who like thousands of other people in the East End lived a day-to-day existence', avoided justice and eventually died or otherwise became incapable of continuing his grisly 'work'.[548] Ultimately, whether you choose to believe that Hardiman was the killer or not will be down to both our powers of persuasion and your own particular take on the case. In any event, we hope that you will at least have finished this book knowing a little more about London's history (dark or otherwise) than when you started.

History is largely about interpretation – which is *not* the same thing as saying 'there are no right answers in history' – and that interpretation may involve some level of speculation. Academic history generally eschews speculation; it's a bit of a dirty word. But this sort of popular history allows us to explore history a little more, in much the same way that counter factuals (the 'what ifs' of history) do. The 'Ripper' and Thames Torso cases invite speculation because of the paucity of actual evidence that has survived but some writers have taken speculation to ridiculous heights. What we have tried to do is look for the *possible*, the *plausible* and to eliminate the impossible or the highly unlikely. For example, is it highly unlikely that a detective investigating a series of brutal murders would have allowed a police sergeant who was unattached to the case to take home a bloodied shawl found at the scene of one of the murders. Likewise, it makes little sense that a high-ranking Freemason would implicate himself in the destruction of evidence, the Goulston Street graffito, when he must have known it would have been ineffective anyway. The idea that a Liverpudlian businessman kept a secret diary of his crimes seems equally ridiculous to us as well. We prefer the maxim of a fictional detective, speaking at the time the murders were in the public eye, who opined that: 'when you have eliminated the impossible, whatever remains, *however improbable*, must be the truth.'[549] Truth, of course, is very hard to establish in history, let alone in a case so tangled and contested as the one we are concerned with. So, we have opted to remain within the bounds of the possible. It is possible that James Hardiman was responsible for the Whitechapel or Thames Torso killings or, indeed, as we have suggested, both sets. It is plausible because he had an underlying motive – a dislike of street prostitutes. And, importantly, he had the means both to carry out these killings and to get away with it. Furthermore, he had plenty of opportunity to feed his desire to kill and kill again, as he operated largely unsupervised following the admission of his wife to hospital and her subsequent death.

Many of the frequently proposed candidates for the 'Ripper' have serious question marks against them. Francis Tumblety was in custody when Mary Kelly was killed, he was also a very tall man with an imposing moustache – a description that runs counter to all of those we have from witnesses. Prince Albert Edward Victor was in Scotland, and Walter Sickert in France, when at least one of the series of killings took place. We are not even that sure who Aaron Kosminski really was; however, it appears that the man the police thought he was, was either out of the country at the time of the murders or dead before they finished.[550] This is not the place to offer a complete post-mortem on the hundreds of suspects out there, a visit to the Casebook site is recommended for those would like to explore this further.[551] It is perhaps sufficient to say that until someone eliminates James Hardiman from the equation, he remains a very plausible suspect for *both* sets of killings.

NOTES

1. Probably because it was supplied by the Star Brewery, Romford, Essex, which was part of Ind Coope, rather than the nearby Black Eagle brewery. In 1888 it wasn't listed as a pub but seems to have evolved from a casual beer shop into a fully operational public house at some point in the 1890s. The pub changed to its current name in the 1980s when the husband of the current landlady decided to mark their new ownership by drawing a link between the area and the beer it served (London Pride and Spitalfields). Lemmerman, M. *A Dictionary of Lost East London* (2017, no pub.) lists the Romford Arms at 3 Heneage Street as now being called the Pride of Spitalfields (p.215)

2. Booth, C. *Labour and Life of the People Volume 1: East London* (London: Williams and Norgate, 1889) p.114

3. *Daily Express*, 16 March 1931

4. Ibid

5. Morley, C. J. 'Jack the Ripper: A Suspect Guide' (E-book, 2005) from *Casebook: JTR* (accessed 13 April 2016). [https://www.casebook.org/ripper_media/book_reviews/non-fiction/cjmorley/33.html]

6. So it seems did Rosy because she apparently wrote and thanked the officer from saving her from 'Jack the Ripper' and sent him a Christmas card thereafter. Begg, P. Fido, M. and Skinner, K. *The Complete Jack the Ripper A to Z*, (London: Blake Publishing Limited, 2010), p.481

7. Drew Gray is the author of *Crime, Policing and Punishment in England, 1660–1914* (London: Bloomsbury, 2016) and has been teaching the history of crime in universities since 2006.

8. Throughout this book we've been able to draw on the excellent work of Neil Bell to enlighten our understanding of the contemporary police

investigation into the Ripper murders: Bell, N. R. A. *Capturing Jack the Ripper In the Boots of a Bobby in Victorian London*, (Stroud: Amberley Books, 2014) as well as the broader work of Emsley, C. *The English Police: A Political and Social History*, (London & New York: Longman, 1991)

9. Frayling, C. 'The House that Jack Built', in Warwick, A. & Willis, M. (eds), *Jack the Ripper: Media, Culture, History*, (Manchester, Manchester University Press, 2007), p.19

10. Begg, P. *Jack the Ripper: The Facts*, (London, Robson Books, 2004), p.283

11. Edwards, R. *Naming Jack the Ripper*, (Guilford: Globe Pequot Press, 2014)

12. Harrison, S. & Barrett, M. *The Diary of Jack the Ripper*, (London: Smith Gryphon Books, 1993); Williams. T. with Price, H. *Uncle Jack*, (London: Orion Books, 2005)

13. 'Whorephobia can be defined as the fear or the hate of sex worker', argued Thierry Schaffauser in *The Guardian* newspaper in June 2010 www.guardian.co,/commentisfree/2101/jun/23/sex-workers-whorephobia [accessed 19/7/18]

14. 'Recommenced' is accurate because the East End has endured a cycle of negativity throughout its history; there was nothing very 'new' about the reportage in the 'Autumn of Terror'.

15. Curtis, L. P. *Jack the Ripper and the London Press*, (London & New Haven: Yale University Press, 2002)

16. Oldridge, D. 'Casting the spell of terror; the press and the early Whitechapel murders,' in Warwick, A. & Willis, M. (eds), *Jack the Ripper: Media, Culture, History*, (Manchester: Manchester University Press, 2007)

17. London, J. *People of the Abyss*, (London, 1903. Centenary edition, Pluto Press, London, 2001)

18. www.casebook.org/suspects/gchapman.html [accessed 19/7/18]; Gordon, R. M. *The Poison Murders of Jack the Ripper: His Final Crimes, Trial and Execution*, (McFarland & Company, Inc., Jefferson, NC, 2008)

19. Its name was changed in 1912, as many street names have been over the last century. Begg, P., Bennett, J. and Jones, R. *Jack the Ripper* (Bournemouth: Future Publishing Ltd, 2017), p.36

20. Quoted in N. Tarn, J. N. *Five Per Cent Philanthropy: An Account of Housing in Urban Areas between 1840 and 1914*, (Cambridge: Cambridge University Press, 1973), p.22

21. Gray, D. D. *London's Shadows: The Dark side of Victorian London*, (London: Bloomsbury, 2010), pp.128–9

22. White, J. *Rothschild Buildings. Life in an East End Tenement Block, 1887–1920* (London: Routledge & Kegan Paul, 1980)

23. *The People*, 26 August 1888

24. The records of the Metropolitan Police Office, MEPO/3/140 ff.34

25. Begg, P. & Bennett, J. *Jack the Ripper: The Forgotten Victims*, (London & New Haven: Yale University Press, 2013)

26. The gallery opened in 1901 and while Freedom Press existed (it was founded in 1886) it didn't move to its modern site until the twentieth century.

27. Mearns, A. *The Bitter Cry of Outcast London: An Inquiry into the Condition of the Abject Poor*, (London, 1883)

28. Gray, *London's Shadows*, p.120

29. *PP.1884–5 Royal Commission on the Housing of the Working Classes. See* Jones, G. S. *Outcast London: A Study in the Relationship Between Classes in Victorian London*, (Oxford: Oxford University Press, 1971)

30. Briggs, A. *Victorian Cities*, (Berkeley, Ca.: University of California Press, 1993), p.226

31. Quoted in Fishman, W. J. *East End 1888*, (London: Gerald Duckworth, 1988), p.42

32. Goldsmid, H. J. *Dottings of a Dosser: Being the Revelations of the Inner Life of Low London Lodging Houses*, (London: T. Fisher Unwin, 1886); Jack London, *The People of the Abyss*, (London: Macmillan, 1903)

33. Goldsmid, *Dottings of a Dosser*, p.10

34. Booth, *Labour and Life*

35. Besant, W. *East London* (London: Chatto & Windus, 1902)

36. Keating, P. J. 'Fact and Fiction in the East End' in Dyos, J. & Wolff, M. (eds.), *The Victorian City: Images and Realities Volume 2*, (London & New York: Routledge, 1973) p.590

37. As is evident in the Bryant and May Match Girls' Strike of 1888 and the subsequent Great Dock Strike a year later. Raw, L. *Striking a Light: The Bryant and May Matchwomen and their Place in History*, (London: Bloomsbury, 2009)

38. Fishman, *East End 1888*, p.64

39. Ibid

40. *East End Observer*, 15 September 1888

41. Booth, *Labour and Life of the People*, pp.66–7

42. Miles, M. *Introduction* to Morrison, A. *Child of the Jago*, (Oxford: Oxford University Press, 2012), p.*ix*

43. Samuel, R. *East End Underworld: Chapters in the Life of Arthur Harding*, (London: Routledge, 1981)

44. Rule, F. *The Worst Street in London* (Hersham: Ian Allen Publishing, 2008)

45. Knight, S. *Jack the Ripper: The Final Solution*, (London: Grafton Books, 1976)

46. The police investigation into Coles' murder noted that she lived at 18 Thrawl Street, MEPO 3/140 ff. 119–121

47. James Greenwood quoted in Begg, P. *Jack the Ripper: The Definitive History*, (London: Routledge, 2013), p.25

48. Begg, *Jack the Ripper: The Facts*, p.43

49. Begg & Bennett, *Jack the Ripper: The Forgotten Victims*, p. 212

50. Booth, *Labour and Life of the People*, p.302

51. *The Pall Mall Gazette*, 13 May 1887

52. *The Pall Mall Gazette*, 4–6 July 1885

53. Stead received a sentence of three months and was awarded first-class prisoner status as befitted his rank in society; Jarrett was sent to Millbank Penitentiary and effectively abandoned by the newspaperman. Gray, *London's Shadows*, p.156

54. *Essex County Chronicle*, 13 May 1887; *The Essex Times* 18 May 1887

55. *The North-Eastern Daily Gazette*, 14 May 1887

56. *Essex Newsman*, 14 May 1887

57. *The Illustrated Police News* featured drawings of what the murder scenes might have looked like.

58. It was illegal to remove bodies from the dissecting room without them being accounted for and the police clearly dismissed this as a possibility at the time.

59. *The Devon and Exeter Daily Gazette*, 16 May 1887; *The Morning Post*, 16 May 1887

60. *Essex Newsman*, 17 May 1887

61. *The Essex Standard, West Suffolk Gazette, and Eastern Counties' Advertiser*, 21 May 1887. Harriet had been murdered, in 1874, by her husband Henry Wainwright, in one of the most celebrated crimes of the century. Henry and his brother Thomas, who was charged as an accessory, were convicted at the Old Bailey and the former was executed in December 1875 by the famous executioner William Marwood.

62. M. J. *The Thames Torso Murders*, (Barnsley: Wharncliffe Books, 1988), p.26

63. *Reynolds's Newspaper*, 5 June 1887

64. *The Pall Mall Gazette*, 7 June 1887

65. However, it appears that this never happened as the thigh subsequently 'disappeared', being sent instead to Ilford for a pauper's burial. *Lloyd's Weekly Newspaper*, 12 June 1887

66. *The Sheffield Daily Telegraph*, 8 June 1887

67. For examples see www.thepolicemagistrate.blog

68. *The Illustrated Police News etc*, 11 June 1887

69. *Lloyd's Weekly Newspaper*, 12 June 1887

70. *Essex Newsman*, 28 June 1887

71. SS *Princess Alice* sank in September 1878 with more than 650 deaths, when she collided with a larger ship, SS *Bywell Castle*. Many of those who died drowned in the sewage that had been recently released at Barking and Crossness.

72. *Lloyd's Weekly Newspaper*, 3 July 1887

73. *Reynolds's Newspaper*, 3 July 1887; *The Devon and Exeter Daily Gazette*, 4 July 4 1874

74. *The Penny Illustrated Paper and Illustrated Times*, July 23, 1887

75. Eddleston, J. J. *Jack the Ripper: An Encyclopaedia* (London: John Blake Publishing Ltd, 2010), p.240

76. Friedland, M. L. *The Trials of Israel Lipski: A True Story of a Victorian Murder in the East End of London* (New York: Beaufort Books, 1984)

77. *Daily News*, 8 August 1887

78. *Reynolds's Newspaper*, 11 September 1887

79. The first 'horseless' carriages arrived in 1896. Jackson, L. *Dirty Old London: The Victorian Fight Against Filth*, (New Haven and London: Yale University Press, 2014), p.45

80. Gordon, W. J. *The Horse World of London*, (London: David & Charles Reprints, London, 1893/1971)

81. *Pall Mall Gazette*, 12 March 1889

82. Gordon, *The Horse World of London*, p.183

83. Kelly's *Post Office Trades Directory* 1889

84. Gordon, *The Horse World of London*

85. Mayhew, H. *London Labour and the London Poor: A cyclopaedia of the condition and earnings of those that will work, those that cannot work, and those that will not work, Vol. III* (London, 1851), p.181

86. Dickens, C. *All the Year Around* (February 27, 1863), p.253

87. Gordon, *The Horse World of London*, p.189

88. Buck's Row was renamed in 1892, just a year after the murders officially ceased. The name was changed as the result of a petition by local residents who wanted to escape the associations of their homes with the 'Ripper' case. While some other locations (Berner Street, for example) have also had name changes, Buck's Row was the only one to change as a result of the actions of the people that lived there. Begg, Bennett and Jones, *Jack the Ripper*, p.49

89. *The Essex Times*, 18 May 1887

90. Chisholm, A., DiGracia, C-M. & Dave Yost, D. *The News from Whitechapel; Jack the Ripper in the Daily Telegraph*, (Jefferson, NC: MacFarland & Co, 2002), p.21

91. Yorkshire police interviewed Peter Sutcliffe on five occasions. *Yorkshire Post*, 2 June 2006

92. 'Annie Millwood' *Casebook: JTR* [https://www.casebook.org/victims/millwood.html] (accessed 23/6/16).

93. Begg & Bennett, *Jack the Ripper: The Forgotten Victims*, pp.24–5

94. *The Standard,* Friday, 24 February 1888

95. http://forum.casebook.org/showthread.php?p=119805 [accessed 29 October 2014)

96. Begg & Bennett, *Jack the Ripper: The Forgotten Victims*, pp.28–9

97. *East London Observer,* 31 March 1888

98. Begg & Bennett, *Jack the Ripper: The Forgotten Victims*, p.25; Paul Begg, *Jack the Ripper: The Uncensored Facts, a Documented History of the Whitechapel Murders of 1888,* (London: Robson Books, 1988), p.31

99. Evans, S. and Skinner, K. *The Ultimate Jack the Ripper Sourcebook,* (London: Robinson, 2001), p.4; Bell, *Capturing Jack the Ripper,* pp.114–5

100. Westcott, T. *The Bank Holiday Murders: The True Story of the First Whitechapel Murders,* (Crime Confidential Press, 2013)

101. The police file on Emma Smith's murder is no longer in the public domain. According to the National Archives records it 'was noted as missing' in December 1983. MEPO 3/140

102. Begg & Bennett, *Jack the Ripper*, p.39

103. According to evidence given at the inquest into her death. Westcott, *The Bank Holiday Murders*, p.109

104. Taylor, H. 'Rationing Crime: The Political Economy of Criminal Statistics since the 1850s', *Economic History Review*, 51 (1998)

105. Indeed, it cannot be stressed enough how difficult it was for the police to glean any useful information from the community of the East End. Police historians such as Clive Emsley and Robert Storch have, in different ways, described the animosity towards force in London and other English cites in the 1800s. Emsley, *The English Police*; Storch, R. D. 'The Policeman as Domestic Missionary: Urban Discipline and Popular Culture in Northern England, 1850–1880', *Journal of Social History*, 9:4 (1976)

106. Sugden, P. *The Complete History of Jack the Ripper, New Edition* (London: Constable & Robinson, 2002), pp.5–6.

107. Begg, Fido, and Skinner, *The Complete Jack the Ripper A to Z*, p.162

108. Cullen, T. *Autumn of Terror,* (London: Bodley Head, 1965)

109. *New York Tribune,* 11 November 1888

110. Sugden, *The Complete History of Jack the Ripper*, p.5

111. Pickersgill, P. *Hansard* 14 November 1888

112. Federal Bureau of Investigation report 'Jack the Ripper' (1988 – SSA Douglass, J. E), (https://vault.fbi.gov/Jack%20the%20Ripper/view) [last accessed 26/5/16]

113. Begg & Bennett, *Jack the Ripper: The Forgotten Victims*, p.25

114. MEPO 3/140/34 ff.34

115. Quoted in Begg, *Jack the Ripper: The Definitive History*, p.4

116. Brown, K., Keppel, R. Weis, J. and Welch, K. 'The Jack the Ripper Murders: A *Modus Operandi* and Signature Analysis of the 1888–1891 Whitechapel Murders', *Journal of Investigative Psychology and Offender Profiling*, Vol 2, 2005, pp.1–21

117. Neil Bell, via email August 2018

118. Westcott, *The Bank Holiday Murders*

119. For a carefully considered overview of policing in the East End, *see* Bell, *Capturing Jack the Ripper.*

120. Haille Rubenhold suggests we should seriously rethink this assumption; *see The Five: The Lives of Jack the Ripper's Women*, (London: Houghton Mifflin, 2019).

121. Ditmore, M. H. (Ed), *Encyclopedia of Prostitution and Sex Work, Volume 2*, (Santa Barbara, Ca.: Greenwood Publishing Group, 2006), p.432

122. There has been much written on prostitution in the nineteenth century and so readers who want to dig a little deeper into some of the issues raised by this and the following chapter are urged to seek out the work of the following: Bartley, P. *Prostitution, Prevention and Reform in England, 1860–1914*, (London: Routledge, 2000); Laite, L. *Common Prostitutes and Ordinary Citizens: Commercial Sex in London, 1885–1960*, (Basingstoke: Palgrave Macmillan, 2012); Walkowitz, J. R. *Prostitution and Victorian Society: Women, Class, and the State*, (Cambridge: Cambridge University Press, 1980).

123. Hempel, S. *The Strange Case of the Broad Street Pump: John Snow and the Mystery of Cholera*, (Berkeley, Ca.: University of California Press, 2007)

124. Matthew, C. (ed.), *The Nineteenth Century: The British Isles, 1815–1901*, (Oxford: Oxford University Press, 2005), pp.62–3

125. Quétel, C. *History of Syphilis*, (translated by Judith Braddock and Brian Pike), (Cambridge: Polity Press, 1990), p.141

126. Arrizabalaga, Henderson, J. & French, R. *The Great Pox: the French Disease in Renaissance Europe*, (New Haven & London: Yale University Press, 1997), p.1

127. McNeill, W. H. *Plagues and Peoples*, (London: Penguin, 1976, 1994), pp.166–7, p.220

128. Arrizabalaga, Henderson & French, *The Great Pox*, p.18

129. Siena, K. P. *Venereal Disease, Hospitals and the Urban Poor: London's 'Foul Wards', 1600–1800*, (Rochester, NY: University of Rochester Press, 2004), p.15

130. Quétel, *History of Syphilis*, p.115

131. Siena, *Venereal Disease*, p.23

132. Quétel, *History of Syphilis*, p.117
133. Michel Corday, *Venus*, quoted in Quétel, *History of Syphilis*, p.117
134. Quétel, *History of Syphilis*, p.160
135. Haslam, J. *Observations on Madness and Melancholy: including practical remarks on those diseases*, (London, 1809), p.259
136. Ibid, p.167
137. Acton, W. *Prostitution considered in its moral, social and sanitary aspects in London and other cities, with proposals for the mitigation and prevention of its attendant evils*, (London, 1857–70)
138. Showalter, E. *Sexual Anarchy: Gender and Culture at the Fin de Siècle*, (London: Virago, 1992), p.197
139. Quoted in Walkowitz, *Prostitution and Victorian* Society, p.49
140. Acton, *Prostitution*
141. Walkowitz, *Prostitution and Victorian Society*, p.44
142. For the history of the CDAs and their opposition *see*: Bartley, *Prostitution, Prevention and Reform in England*; Walkowitz, J. R. *City of Dreadful Delight: Narratives of Sexual Danger in Late-Victorian* London, (London: Virago, 1994); Weeks, J. *Sex, Politics and Society: The Regulation of Sexuality after 1800*, (London: Longman, 1981).
143. Showalter, *Sexual Anarchy*, p.193
144. Ibid, p.112
145. Ibid, pp.192–3
146. Ibid
147. Photographic portraits of patients with syphilis show damaged skin on their faces. *See* Fox, G. H., *Photographic Illustration of Cutaneous Syphilis* (1891). Stanley B. Burns, M.D., and the Burns Archive. www.http://publishing.cdlib.org/ucpressebooks/view?docId=ft7t1nb59n;chunk.id=0;doc.view=print [accessed 20/10/2014]
148. Hall, L.A. 'Venereal diseases and society in Britain, from the Contagious Diseases Acts to the National Health Service', in Roger Davidson and Lesley A. Hall (eds), *Sex, Sin, and Suffering: Venereal Diseases and European Society since 1880*, (Basingstoke: Macmillan International Higher Education, 2012), p.122
149. Josephine Butler also campaigned for women's suffrage, better education for women and the abolition of child prostitution.
150. In terms of the CD Act of 1864 women found to be infected could be interned in locked hospitals for up to three months, by 1869 it was up to one year.
151. Quoted in Hall, 'Venereal Diseases and Society in Britain', p.124
152. Showalter, *Sexual Anarchy*, p.192
153. Quoted in Quétel, *History of Syphilis*, p.128
154. Quétel, *History of Syphilis*, p.163

155. Federal Bureau of Investigation report 'Jack the Ripper'

157. Humphries, S. *Hooligans or Rebels? An Oral History of Working-Class Childhood and Youth, 1889–1939*, (Oxford: Oxford University Press, 1981); Pearson, G. *Hooligan: A History of Respectable Fears* (Basingstoke: MacMillan, 1983); Davies, A. 'Youth gangs, masculinity and violence in late Victorian Manchester and Salford', *Journal of Social History*, (Winter, 1998); Archer, J. E. *The Monster Evil: Policing and Violence in Victorian Liverpool* (Liverpool: Liverpool University Press, 2011); Davies, A. *Gangs of Manchester*, (Wrea Green: Blake Publishing Limited, 2009); Macilwee, M. *Gangs of Liverpool. From the Cornermen to the High Rip: The Mobs that Terrorised a City* (Wrea Green: Blake Publishing Limited, 2006)

158. Gray, D. D. 'Gang Crime and the Media in Late Nineteenth-Century London: The Regent's Park Murder of 1888', *Cultural and Social History*, 10, 4 (2013)

159. One of the supposed unshakable 'facts' of the Whitechapel murder case is that all the killer's victims were street prostitutes. A recent reinterpretation of the case by Hallie Rubenhold has questioned this and this certainly deserves careful consideration. However, in the formal surviving police report of the killing of Martha Tabram she is described as a 'prostitute'. MEP 3/140/35–36

160. Matters, L. *The Mystery of Jack the Ripper* (Arrow Book, 1964)

161. Quoted in Begg, *Jack the Ripper: The Definitive History*, p.90

162. Rumbelow, D. *The Complete Jack the Ripper: Fully Revised and Updated*, (London: Penguin Books, 2004), p.25

163. MEPO 3/140 ff. 239–241

164. MEPO 3/140 (Inspector Abberline's report)

165. Sugden, *The Complete History of Jack the Ripper*, p.39

166. *The Times*, 8 September 1888

167. Quoted in Magellan, K. *By ear and eyes; The Whitechapel Murders Jack the Ripper and the Murder of Mary Jane Kelly*, (Derby: Longshot Publishing, 2005), p.30. Magellan's quote is from the report of the inquest in the *Woodford Times*, on the 7 September 1888.

168. MEPO 3/140 (Special weekly report on the murder of Mary Ann Nichols at Buck's Row, Inspector Davis, 7/9/88)

169. Quoted in Rumbelow, *The Complete Jack the Ripper*, p.28

170. *East London Observer*, 1 September 1888

171. MEPO 3/141 ff.139–144

172. Quoted in Fishman, *East End 1888*, p.261

173. *Northern Echo*, 1September 1888

174. *The Pall Mall Gazette*, 4 September 1888

175. Rumbelow, *The Complete Jack the Ripper*, p.34
176. Census records 1881 and 1891
177. Begg, *Jack the Ripper*, p.152
178. www.casebook.org/ victorian_london/weather.html [accessed 13/9/2018]
179. Sugden, *The Complete History of Jack the Ripper*, p.96
180. Dave Yost notes that Long's timings were slightly out and although she told the inquest that she'd seen a man and a woman in conversion at 5.30 that conflicts both with the testimony of Albert Cadoche (who later heard the killer and his victims in the yard) and the opinion of Dr Philips as to how long it took the murderer to complete his mutilation of the corpse. Annie Chapman's Inquest, *The Daily Telegraph*, 27/9/1888 from Chisholm, Di Grazia and Yost, *News from Whitechapel*, p.70
181. Fishman, *East End 1888*, p.168; Gray, *London's Shadows*, p.67
182. Sugden, *The Complete History of Jack the Ripper*, p.100
183. Edwards, I. *Jack the Ripper's Black Magic Rituals*, (Penny Publishing,2001)
184. Bell, *Capturing Jack the Ripper*, p.148
185. Begg, *Jack the Ripper: The Definitive History*, p.151
186. Sugden, *The Complete History of Jack the Ripper*, pp.77–8
187. Rumbelow, *The Complete Jack the Ripper*, pp.39–41
188. Bell, *Capturing Jack the Ripper*, p.151
189. Begg, *Jack the Ripper: The Definitive History*, pp.98–9
190. Annie Chapman's Inquest, *The Daily Telegraph*, 27/9/1888 from Chisholm, DiGrazia and Yost, *News from Whitechapel*, p.76
191. *East London Observer*, 29 September 1888
192. Begg, Fido & Skinner 'The Jack the Ripper A–Z' (1996), pp.347–350
193. Frayling, 'The House that Jack Built'
194. *Reynolds's Newspaper*, 16 September 1888
195. For example, not all accounts concur, the *Daily News* on Monday, 17 September 1888 has the man at 5 foot 3 inches tall.
196. *Manchester Times*, 22 September 1888
197. http://www.historic-uk.com/HistoryMagazine/DestinationsUK/Tower-Subway/ [accessed 10/11/14]
198. One exception is John Carey's 2006 contribution 'Escape Routes: Ripper on the Railway' *Ripperologist*, No. 8/June 2006 (pp.13–14). However, Carey only considers transport on the basis that the killer was not a local man, but a visitor to the area, something we believe is unlikely.
199. Kellett, J. R. *The Impact of Railways on Victorian Cities*, (London: Routledge, 1969)
200. *The Times*, 16 April 1842

201. Seaman, L. C. B. *Life in Victorian London,* (London: B. T. Batsford Ltd, 1973), pp.58–59

202. Barker, T. C. and Robbins, M. *A History of London Transport: Volume One – The Nineteenth Century,* (London: George Allen & Unwin, 1975), pp.98–99

203. Barker and Robbins, *A History of London Transport,* p.116

204. Olsen, D. J. *The Growth of Victorian London,* (Harmondsworth: Penguin Books, 1976), p.319

205. *Daily News,* 10 January 1863

206. *Pall Mall Gazette,* 3 January 1885

207. Gray, *London's Shadows,* p.215

208. *See* Short, K. R. M. *The Dynamite Wars: Irish-American Bombers in Victorian Britain,* (Dublin: Gill & MacMillan, 1979) 209.

209. Barker and Robbins, *A History of London Transport,* p.188, p.196

210. Seaman, *Life in Victorian London,* pp.64–5

211. Trow, M. J. *The Thames Torso Murders,* p.46

212. Ibid, p.54

213. *Birmingham Daily Post,* 6 October 1888

214. Trow, *The Thames Torso Murders,* p.55

215. Trow notes that Dr Bond reported at the inquest that there were signs of pleurisy present, but Dr Hebbard had not noted this at the post-mortem. Trow, *The Thames Torso Murders,* p.53

216. *Reynolds's Newspaper,* 30 September 1888

217. *The Star,* 5 October 1888

218. http://www.british-history.ac.uk/survey-london/vol25/pp65-71#h3-0008 [accessed 15 June 2018]

219. Gordon, *The Horse World of London,* p.184

220. *The Pall Mall Gazette,* 4 October 1888

221. *The Freeman's Journal and Daily Commercial Advertiser,* 3 October 1888

222. *The Star,* 4–5 October 1888

223. *The Star',* 7 August 1888

224. *Liverpool Mercury,* 23 October 1888

225. Flanders, J. *The Invention of Murder: How the Victorians Revelled in Death and Detection and Created Modern Crime,* (London: Harper Press, London, 2011)

226. Hutchinson, P. *The Jack the Ripper Location Photographs: Duffield's Yard and the Whitby Collection,* (Stroud: Amberley Books, 2009), pp.54–5

227. Magellan, *By Ear and Eyes,* p.63

228. *See* for example, *Murder by Decree* (Bob Clark, 1979) and *From Hell* (The Hughes Brothers, 2001)

229. MEPO 3/140 (Inspector Abberline's report)

230. Begg, *Jack the Ripper: The Definitive History*, pp.182–3

231. Elizabeth Stride's inquest, *The Daily Telegraph*, 6 October 1888 in Chisholm, DiGrazia and Yost, *News from Whitechapel*, p. 122

232. Weather Conditions for the Nights of the Whitechapel Murders, (https://www.casebook.org/victorian_london/weather.html), [last accessed 15/9/18]

233. Elizabeth Stride's inquest, *The Daily Telegraph*, 6/10/1888 in Chisholm, DiGrazia and Yost, *News from Whitechapel*, pp.120–1

234. Ibid, pp.122–3

235. Police Code at the time stated that any persons seen carrying a suspicious package after sunset were to be stopped and searched. PC Smith did not stop and search the man he saw, however, but perhaps he considered doing so, and therefore retained a clear description of him. Our thanks here to Neil Bell for his advice.

236. Loftus, E. F. 'Leading Questions and the Eyewitness Report', *Cognitive Psychology*, 7, (1975), pp.560–572; Loftus, E. F and Zanni, G. 'Eyewitness Testimony: The influence of the wording of a question', *Bulletin of the Psychonomic Society*, 5 (1) (1975), pp.86–88

237. Begg, et al, *The Jack the Ripper A–Z*, (London: Headline Book Publishing, 1996); Anderson, Sir R. *The Lighter Side of My Official Life*, (London: Hodder and Stoughton, 1910)

238. Begg and others have acknowledged that here, as with many aspects of the case, the accuracy of witness testimony is problematic. With Schwartz there are several ways to read his evidence, and when we take into consideration that he gave slightly different versions of it, via a translator, to the police and *The Star* newspaper, and that Swanson's recollection was several years later and not first-hand, it leaves plenty of room for doubt. Begg, Bennett and Jones, *Jack the Ripper*, pp.88–9.

239. Hannaford, S. 'Anderson and the Swanson Marginalia' *Casebook: JTR* [last accessed 23/5/17]

240. Sugden, *The Complete History of Jack the Ripper*, pp.168–9

241. Ibid, p.173

242. Begg, *Jack the Ripper*, p.178

243. Stubbings Shelden, N. *The Victims of Jack the Ripper*, (Knoxville, Tn.: Inklings Press, 2007), p.23

244. Begg, Bennett and Jones, *Jack the Ripper*, p.84

245. Begg, *Jack the Ripper: The Definitive History*, p.192; Begg, Fido, and Skinner, *The Complete Jack the Ripper A to Z*, p.158. Incidentally, the shawl so famously described as the key to the mystery by Russell Edwards is now considered by some to be merely a piece of cut-down table cloth – albeit a nice one.

246. Catherine Eddowes's inquest, *The Daily Telegraph*, 5 October 1888 in Chisholm, DiGrazia and Yost, *News from Whitechapel*, p.168; *see* also Rubenhold, *The Five* for a suggestion that not all of the Whitechapel victims were, as had always been assumed, sex workers.

247. Sugden, *The Complete Jack the Ripper*, p.237

248. Edwards, R. *Naming Jack the Ripper New Crime Scene Evidence, A Stunning Forensic Breakthrough, The Killer Revealed*, (Basingstoke: Pan MacMillan, 2014)

249. Stubbings Sheldon, *The Victims of Jack the Ripper*, p.36

250. Lawende's description was not given at the inquest at the request of the City Solicitor, Mr Crawford. Instead it was printed in the *Police Gazette* on 19 October: 'age 30, height 5ft 7 or 8 in., complexion fair, moustache fair, medium build; dress, pepper-and-salt colour loose jacket, grey cloth cap with peak of same material, reddish neckerchief tied in knot; appearance of a sailor'. Catherine Eddowes's inquest, *The Daily Telegraph*, 12 October 1888 in Chisholm, DiGrazia and Yost, *News from Whitechapel*, p.180

251. Ibid, p.179

252. *See* plate section for an artist's impression of what Mitre Square looked like when Eddowes' body was discovered there.

253. For a useful essay on the nature of street lighting in Mitre Square, and what it tells us about the killer's actions that night, *see* Neil Bell 'Jack by Gaslight', in Begg, P. (Ed), *Ripperology*, (New York: Barnes & Noble, 2006). Bell argues that the killer would have had enough light to carry out his purpose.

254. We are grateful to Neil Bell for clarifying contemporary police procedure here.

255. Begg, *Jack the Ripper: The Facts*, p. 178

256. MEPO 3/140 3B-6

257. Quoted in Sugden, *The Complete Jack the Ripper*, pp.176–7

258. Ibid, p.244

259. Bell, *Capturing Jack the Ripper*, p.176

260. Rumbelow, *The Complete Jack the Ripper*, pp.125–6; HO144/221/A49301C ff. 162–70; *See* Begg, Fido, and Skinner, *The Complete Jack the Ripper A to Z*, pp.186–8 for a detailed discussion of the graffito.

261. Begg, *Jack the Ripper: The Definitive History*, p.197

262. Bell, *Capturing Jack the Ripper*, pp.177–8

263. Knight, *Jack the Ripper: The Final Solution*, p.177

264. Begg writes that 'it seems to mean that the Jews were not the people who would tolerate being blamed for something they didn't do', or the murderer may have 'intended it to indicate that he was responding to some real or imagined offence to his race or religion', Begg, *Jack the Ripper*, p.197

265. Sugden, *The Complete History of Jack the Ripper*, pp.256–7

266. Rowlands, G. 'Jack the Ripper: The Writing on the Wall', *Criminologist*, Vol. 17, No. 2, (Summer 1993)

267. Dew, W. *I Caught Crippen: Memoirs of Ex-Chief Inspector Walter Dew, CID of Scotland Yard*, (London & Glasgow: Blackie & Son Ltd, 1938), p.137

268. Extra men were brought in throughout the autumn. MEPO3/141 ff.136–137, 161–166

269. Smith, H. *From Constable to Commissioner; the story of sixty years, most of them misspent*, (London: Chatto & Windus, 1910)

270. In an early essay on the Goulston Street evidence, Paul Begg argued that it would be 'highly improbable that [the murderer] would have reached home, then ventured out to the vicinity of the murder scene to dispose of an incriminating piece of evidence that he could have burned on the fire.' Paul Begg, 'Eddowes' Apron', in Begg, *Ripperology*, p.19. If he'd been 'nabbed' before getting home, however, being sidetracked by another potential victim perhaps, this might explain things that night.

271. Recently it was has been suggested that the Whitechapel murders were an elaborate and preconceived attempt at spreading anti-Semitism in London. This is certainly an interesting angle on the case and the Goulston Street grafitto in particular. *See* Stephen Senise, *False Flag* (Acorn Independent Press, 2018)

272. Letter from Thomas Gribton, 11 November 1888 HO144/221 A49031C (pp.204–205)

273. There are two excellent resources for those interested in examining the correspondence the police received. Stewart Evans and Keith Skinner's *Jack the Ripper: Letters from Hell* (Stroud: Sutton Publishing, 2001) offers a detailed analysis of the letters, while the National Archives has a Teachers' Resource Pack, which researchers may find useful: https://www.nationalarchives.gov.uk/documents/education/jacktheripper.pdf [last accessed 24/7/18]

274. White, J. *London in the Nineteenth Century: 'An Awful Wonder of God'* (London: Jonathan Cape, 2007), pp.378–9

275. Friedland, *The Trials of Israel Lipski*

276. Griffiths, D. *Fleet Street: Five Hundred Years of the Press* (London: British Library, 2006), pp.92–4

277. Simpson, A. E. (ed), Stead, W. T., *The Maiden Tribute of Modern Babylon* (Lambertville, NJ:True Bill Press, 2007)

278. Raw, *Striking a Light*

279. *Terror and Wonder: The Gothic Imagination*, The British Library (2014–2015)

280. Sugden, *The Complete Jack the Ripper*, p.260
281. Begg, *Jack the Ripper: The Definitive History*, p.222
282. Cornwell, P. *Portrait of a Killer: Jack the Ripper – Case Closed*, (London: Little, Brown, 2002)
283. 27 September1888, London E. C. in Evans and Skinner, *Jack the Ripper: Letters from Hell*, pp.218–219
284. We have used Sugden's version (p.264) of the letter but Begg's has slight differences: he transcribes it as 'I may send you a bloody knif that I took it out', p.223. The letter has been missing since 1888 and only a photo (taken by the police) remains.
285. Reported in *The Times*, 19 October 1888
286. Quoted in Begg, *Jack the Ripper*, p.225
287. Warren, N.P., 'A Postal Kidney', *The Criminologist* 13(1), Spring 1989
288. *Jack the Ripper: The First Serial Killer*, Atlantic Productions (Channel 5), 2006
289. *Jack the Ripper: The First Serial Killer*
290. Begg, Fido, and Skinner, *The Jack the Ripper A–Z*
291. Marriage Certificate, *John Arant/Catherine Scott*, St. Thomas's Church, Bethnal Green, 7 April 1883
292. It was founded by Canon Samuel Barnett at 28 Commercial Street, with its stated mission to 'educate citizens in the knowledge of one another, to provide teaching for those willing to learn and recreation to those who are weary.' Weinreb, B. and Hibbert, C., *The London Encyclopaedia* (London: Book Club Associates, 1983), p.880
293. *Jack the Ripper: Killer Revealed*, Atlantic Productions (2009). Screened 11 October 2009 and 24 November 2013
294. Knight, *Jack the Ripper: The Final Solution*
295. Matters, *The Mystery of Jack the Ripper*,
296. Weston-Davies, W. *The Real Mary Kelly* (London: Blink Publishing, 2015)
297. Williams with Price, *Uncle Jack*
298. Sugden, *The Complete History of Jack the* Ripper, p.308
299. *The Daily Telegraph*, 13 November 1888
300. Begg, *Jack the Ripper: The Facts,* p.267
301. Walter Dew later wrote that he knew her quite well by sight and that she was 'aged between 20 and 25 and quite attractive'. Dew was the first policeman to enter the room where her body was found. Dew, *I Caught Crippen*, p.86
302. Quoted in Begg, *Jack the Rippers: The Facts*, p.279
303. Mary Kelly's inquest, *The Daily Telegraph*, 13 November 1888, Chisholm DiGrazia and Yost, *News From Whitechapel*, p.215
304. Dew, *I Caught Crippen*, p.143
305. Magellan, *By Ear and Eyes*, p.132

306. Paley, B. *Jack the Ripper: The Simple Truth* (London: Headline, 1995)

307. Davis, J. 'The London Garotting Panic of 1862: A Moral Panic and the Creation of a Criminal Class in mid-Victorian England', in V. A .C. Gatrell (ed), *Crime and Law: The Social History of Crime in Western Europe since 1500* (London: Europa, 1980)

308. Gray, *London's Shadows*

309. Begg, *Jack the Ripper: The Facts*, p.297

310. *The Daily Telegraph*, 13 November 1888

311. MEPO 3/141 ff.150–157 (Letter from Thomas Bond)

312. Sugden, *The Complete History of Jack the Ripper*, p.318

313. Smith, *From Constable to Commissioner*

314. *The Daily Telegraph*, 13 November 1888

315. Begg, *Jack the Ripper: The Facts*, p.282

316. It is odd that this was not clarified by the police in Hutchinson's statement, after all the Queen's Head was listed as a public house. Again, our thanks to Neil Bell for raising this point.

317. MEPO 3/140 ff. 227–229 (George Hutchinson's statement)

318. Sugden, *The Complete History of Jack the Ripper*, p.336

319. Statements of George Hutchinson, 12 November 1888, MEPO 3/140. Ff.227–9 and 13 November 1888, *Star* 14 November

320. He also waited three days to give his evidence to the police and there is a suggestion that he invented the suspect and that he was later being paid by police to 'patrol' the area to see if he could see him again. Begg, Bennett and Jones, *Jack the Ripper*, p.121

321. *The Daily Telegraph*, 13 November 1888

322. *East London Observer*, 31 March 1888

323. Shelden, *The Victims of Jack the Ripper*, p.43

324. *Daily News*, 13 November 1888

325. Bell, *Capturing Jack the Ripper*, p.198

326. Begg, *Jack the Ripper: The Facts*, p.264

327. *Reynolds's Newspaper*, 25 November 1888

328. *See,* for example, the conflicting descriptions in the *Evening News*, 21 November 1888.

329. Not something that was unusual in itself in the late 1800s, but perhaps less understandable in the midst of a serial killer's actions in late 1888.

330. Federal Bureau of Investigation report on 'Jack the Ripper' (1988 – SSA John E. Douglass), [last accessed 18/3/16]. https://vault.fbi.gov/Jack%20the%20Ripper/view

331. MEPO 3/140 ff.2 and 1B

332. Anderson, *The Lighter Side of My Official Life*, p.137

333. *The Daily Chronicle*, 29 December 1888

334. For a detailed and recent examination of Mylett's death *see* Arif, D. and Clack, R. 'A Rose By Any Other Name: The Death of Catherine Mylett, 20 December 1888', *Ripperologist*, 108, (November 2009)

335. Given that he missed the beginning of the Whitechapel murder series due to his enforced leave of absence, and found the C.I.D. in a state of demoralisation on his return, Anderson may have been fairly determined to contain any idea that the police had failed to catch 'the Ripper'. In his memoirs he is confident that the killer was a 'Polish Jew' who escaped trial because his fellow Jews were not prepared 'to give up one of their number to Gentile Justice'. He disregarded all other murders in the series after Kelly's because of this, believing the real killer was under watch, in an asylum, or dead. Anderson, *The Lighter Side of My Official Life*, pp.137–8. However, we should take Anderson's memoirs (written very many years after the event) with a large pinch of salt.

336. *The Star*, 24 December 1888

337. Brown, B. 'Inspector Spratling's Pass' *Ripperologist*, 29 June 2000 (*Casebook* Dissertations)

338. According to the records she was last admitted on 20 January 1888, leaving again on 9 March. Poplar and Stepney Sick Asylum Admission and Discharge Book, March 1885 to March 1886 (SA/M/1/12), from Arif and Clack, 'A Rose By Any Other Name', p.18

339. Baptism entry, St Matthew's Church, Bethnal Green, 13 November 1859; GRO Birth certificate, James Hardiman, Whitechapel, 1859, vol 1c p.378, no. 439

340. http://www.st-matthews.co.uk/history/

341. Gray, *London's Shadows*, p.125

342. Census records, Marriage & Death Certificates 1851–1901 (ancestry.com)

343. GRO Death Register, Whitechapel, Samuel Hardiman, July 1873, Vol 1C, p.239, No. 116

344. Edward Hardiman died aged 43 in 1880 when James was 20. GRO Death Register, Whitechapel, January 1880, vol 1C, p.244, no. 442

345. *Lloyd's Weekly*, 16 September 1888

346. *The Daily Telegraph*, 11 September 1888

347. Sugden, *The Complete History of Jack the Ripper*, p. 82; GRO Death Certificate, *Sarah Hardiman*, Whitechapel, 1885, vol 1c p 200, No. 301

348. 1881 Census, (ancestry.com)

349. Hills, R. & Stockton, A. 'Cousin Jack', *Ripperologist, No.68*, June 2006; GRO Marriage Certificate, *James Hardiman/Sarah Scott*, Bethnal Green, 1876, No. 478

350. Hutchinson, *The Jack the Ripper Location Photographs*, p.38

351. Ibid, p.20

352. GRO, Death Certificate, *Sarah Hardiman*, Whitechapel, 1885, vol 1c p 200, No. 301

353. Baptism Registry, Christ Church, Spitalfields, *Harriet Maria Hardiman*, 3 July 1887 (ancestry.com)

354. London Hospital Patient Admissions Register, *Sarah Hardiman*, 18 June 1888

355. GRO, Death Certificate, *Sarah Hardiman*, Whitechapel, 1888, vol 1c p 216, No. 338. The age given on certificate as 29, although a likely entry for her birth in the registers (Birmingham, March 1860, vol 6d p. 152) would suggest the lower figure.

356. Government of Western Australia, Department of Health, ww2.health. wa.gov.au/~/media/Files/Corporate/general%20documents/Tuberculosis/ PDF/Policy%204.3_TB_and_pregnancy.pdf (last accessed 15/11/18).

357. MSD Manual (Professional Version), Congenital Syphilis, https:// www.msdmanuals.com/professional/pediatrics/infections-in-neonates/ congenital-syphilis (last accessed 15/11/18); The Free Dictionary by Farlex, Congenital Syphilis, https://medical-dictionary.thefreedictionary. com/maternal+to+Fetal+Infections (last accessed 15/11/18); MSD Manual (Professional Version), Congenital Tuberculosis, https://msdmanuals.com/ en-gb/professional/pediatrics/infections-in-neonates/perinatal-tuberculosis-tb (last accessed 15/11/18); Victoria State Government (Australia), Department of Health and Human Services, Neonatal TB, https://www2health.vic.gov.au/ hospitals-and-health-services/patient-care/perinatal-reproductive/neonatal-handbook/infections/tuberculosis (last accessed 15/11/18); Government of Western Australia, Department of Health,ww2.health.wa.gov.au/~/media/ Files/Corporate/general%20documents/Tuberculosis/PDF/Policy%204.3_ TB_and_pregnancy.pdf (last accessed 15/11/18).

358. National Institute of Neurological Disorders and Stroke, Transverse Myelitis Factsheet, https://www.ninds.nih.gov/Disorders/Patient-Caregiver-Education/Fact-Sheets/Transverse-Myelitis-Fact-Sheet#3 (last accessed 15/11/18).

359. Chung, M-F. 'A Study of Thirty-Four Cases of Rapidly Developing Syphilitic Paraplegia', Archives of Dermatology and Syphilology, 14/2, August 1926; *see* also the pioneering work of Henry C. Bastian (1837–1915) a neurologist who wrote on syphilitic paraplegia in his 1893 book *Various forms of Hysterical of Functional Paralysis. See* Pearce, J. M. 'Henry Charlton Bastian (1837–1915): Neglected Neurologist and Scientist', *European Neurology*, 63/2 (February, 2010)

360. Government of Western Australia, Department of Health, ww2.health. wa.gov.au/~/media/Files/Corporate/general%20documents/Tuberculosis/ PDF/Policy%204.3_TB_and_pregnancy.pdf (last accessed 15/11/18).

361. *Who Do You Think You Are?* (Martin Freeman), Season 6 Episode 11 (Dir. Mark Bates), Wall to Wall Television (2009)

362. Ibid

363. GRO, Death Certificate, *James Hardiman*, Whitechapel, 1891, vol 1c p 378, no. 370

364. GRO, Death Certificate, *Sarah Hardiman*, Whitechapel, 1888, vol 1c p 216, no. 338

365. Weinreb and Hibbert (eds), *The London Encyclopaedia*, p.138

366. Royal College of Surgeons (biographical entry – John Astley Bloxham), https://livesonline.rcseng.ac.uk/biogs/E000907b.htm [last accessed 22/6/16]

367. Bettley, J. 'Post Voluptatem Misericordia: The Rise and Fall of the London Lock Hospitals', *The London Journal*, 10/2 (1984)

368. Federal Bureau of Investigation report 'Jack the Ripper'

369. Census 1871

370. Census 1881

371. As the author of the 'Dear Boss' letter wrote in late September 1888. Evans & Skinner, *Jack the Ripper*, p.218

372. Hills, 'Cat's Cradle'

373. Hill's source is the Wandsworth Nominal Prison Registers, held at the London Metropolitan Archives. XO20/403-ACC/3444/PR/01/009-010, page 00231-00232. Register No. 4815. Committed 26 Nov '80 Southwark – released 25 Nov '81. 12 months hard labour for theft/embezzlement (James Alf Hardiman). Hills, 'Cat's Cradle', *Ripperologist No. 75*, Jan. 2007. A previous article, 'Cousin Jack' by Hills, R. and Stockton, A. (*Ripperologist No. 68*, June 2006) covers his initial suspicions about Hardiman and Wandsworth prison.

374. Census 1871

375. Hills, 'Cat's Cradle'

376. Rule, *The Worst Street in London*, p.138

377. Begg, *Jack the Ripper: The Facts*, p.325

378. Quoted from a report in the *Acton, Chiswick, and Turnham Green Gazette*, 5 January 1889 by Sugden, *The Complete History of Jack the Ripper*, pp.382–3

379. Mcnaghten memorandum (1894), MEPO 3/141 ff.177–183

380. Begg, *Jack the Ripper: The Facts*, p.321

381. Frayling, 'The House that Jack Built'; Paul Begg has also stated that Mcnaghten cannot be regarded as a reliable source. In comparing the draft (Aberconway

Papers) and the final (Mcnaghten) report, Begg noted that the latter 'reads like an informed police opinion, whereas from the notes it is clear that much [of it] was Mcnaghten's own. Possibly the most important deletion [Mcnaghten made, and he made several according to Begg] is the claim in the notes that against the three named men "the police held very strong suspicion". In the Report Mcnaghten merely says that any one of the three men was "more likely than Cutbush to be the killer". This deletion poses the question whether or not the police did have strong suspicions – or any suspicions at all – about the three men'. Begg, *Jack the Ripper: The Uncensored Facts*, p.171

382. *Hull Daily Mail*, 4 June 1889

383. *Reynolds's Newspaper*, 9 June 1889

384. Begg & Bennett, *Jack the Ripper: The Forgotten Victims*, p.156

385. Trow, *The Thames Torso Murders*, p.59

386. Begg & Bennett, *Jack the Ripper: The Forgotten Victims*, p.159

387. Gordon, *The Horse World of London*

388. MEPO 3/140 (Dr Hebbert's report, 16/9/89); *see* also Trow, *The Thames Torso Murders*, p.62 who refers to Hebbert's own analysis of the case (C. Hebbert, *An Exercise in Forensic Medicine*, 1888); and Arif, D. 'The Murder of Elizabeth Jackson' Casebook: JTR https://casebook.org/victims/jackson.html [last accessed 15/4/17]

389. *Hull Daily Mail*, 7 June 1889

390. Sergeant Badham was closely involved with the Whitechapel murder case having taken Chapman's body to the mortuary and given evidence at the inquiry into her death, attended at the scene of Mary Kelly's murder, and taking the extraordinary statement of George Hutchinson. Begg, Fido, and Skinner, *The Complete Jack the Ripper A to Z*, p.41

391. MEPO 3/140 (Sergeant Badshaw's report, 16 July 89)

392. MEPO 3/140 (Arnold's report, 17 July 89

393. Hamm, J., 'The Broken Pipe' Casebook: JTR from Evans, & Skinner, The Ultimate Jack the Ripper Sourcebook. https://www.casebook.org/dissertations/brokenpipe.html [last accessed 26/5/16]

394. MEPO 3/140 (Margaret Franklin's statement, 22 July 1889; Elizabeth Ryder's statement, 22 July 1889)

395. Report of Dr Bond, MEPO 3/140, ff. 259-262385

396. MEPO 3/140 (Dr Phillip's report, 22 July 1889)

397. Report of Dr Bond, MEPO 3/140, ff. 259–262

398. Begg, Fido, and Skinner, *The Complete Jack the Ripper A to Z*, p.59

399. Begg & Bennett, *Jack the Ripper: The Forgotten Victims*, p.178

400. Anon. *The History of the Whitechapel Murders: a full and authentic narrative of the above murders with sketches.* (New York, 1888)

401. *Sunderland Daily Echo and Shipping Gazette*, 17 July 1889

402. *The North-Eastern Daily Gazette*, 18 July 1889

403. *The Sheffield & Rotherham Independent*, 18 July 1889

404. Ripper Letter 58895/H, ff. 380-2 from Evans and Skinner, *Jack the Ripper: Letters from Hell*, p.280

405. Trow, *The Thames Torso Murders*, p.77

406. MEPO 3/140 (Dr Hebbert's report, 16 July 1889)

407. MEPO 3/140 (Monro's Report, 11 September 1889)

408. Gordon, R. M., *The Thames Torso Murders of Victorian London*, (Jefferson, NC: McFarlane & Company, Inc., 2002), p.151

409. Shorter, E., 'Old Pump House, 19–20 Hooper Street' Survey of London https://surveyoflondon.org/map/feature/1010/detail/ [last accessed 22/7/17]

410. Begg & Bennett, *Jack the Ripper: The Forgotten Victims*, p.197

411. Ibid, p.194

412. Dunlop, J. Casebook: JTR Forum 'John Arnold – Pinchin Street Torso'. https://www.jtrforums.com/showthread.php?t=22868 [last accessed 13/2/16]

413. Hills, 'Cat's Cradle'

414. MEPO 3/140 (Monro's report)

415. Arnold or Cleary may have been dismissed a little too easily in some accounts. Begg, Fido and Skinner, *The Complete Jack the Ripper A to Z*, p.32

416. *Yorkshire Post*, 2 June 2006

417. MEPO 3/140 (19 July 1889)

418. MEPO 3/140 (Monro's Report, 11 September 1889)

419. MEPO 3/140 (Monro's Report, 11 September 1889). Monro does acknowledge that the police were stretched at this time due to 'the pressure for men in Whitechapel just now' and so PC Pennent was covering part of the beats of two other men in addition to his own.

420. Begg and Bennett, *Jack the Ripper: The Forgotten Victims*, p.201

421. MEPO 3/140 (Superintendent Arnold's report)

422. Ibid

423. Ibid.

424. 'Frances Coles', Casebook: JTR (accessed 15/3/16), https://www.casebook.org/victims/coles.html

425. Begg, *Jack the Ripper: The Facts*, p.316

426. Sadler himself said that he met Frances (someone he 'ad previously known') at the Princess Alice between 8.30 and 9 that evening. MEPO 3/140

427. Begg and Bennett, *Jack the Ripper: The Forgotten Victims*, pp. 212–3

428. MEPO 3/140

429. MEPO 3/140 (Superintendent Arnold's report)

430. Begg & Bennett, *Jack the Ripper: The Forgotten Victims*, p.234

431. The C.I.D. report rather forlornly notes that on his release Sadler was whisked away by reporters from *The Star* newspaper, and that 'cheers were raised by the crowd'. MEPO 3/140 (daily report of Inspector Moore, 3 March 1891)

432. Begg and Bennett, *Jack the Ripper: The Forgotten Victims*, p.204

433. Apparently one of the detectives most involved on the case, Edmund Reid, was prepared to countenance that Frances had been killed by the same man that he had been chasing since August 1888, as he told the *Police Review* in 1903. Gordon, R. M. *The Poison Murders of Jack the Ripper: His Final Crimes, Trial, and Execution* (Jefferson, NC: McFarlane & Company, Inc., 2008) p.33

434. Federal Bureau of Investigation report 'Jack the Ripper'

435. Ibid

436. MEPO 3/141 Dr Bond's report on the murders, 10 November 1888; *see also* Bonn, S., 'Criminal Profiling: The Original Mind Hunters' *Psychology Today,* 4 December 2017 (.https://www.psychologytoday.com/us/blog/wicked-deeds/200712/criminal-profiling-the-original-mind-hunters [last Accessed 8/7/17]

437. von Krafft-Ebing, R. F., *Psychopathia Sexualis with special references to Contrary Sexual Instinct: A Medico-Legal Study* (Trans. Chaddock, C.G.) (Philadelphia, Pa.: F. A. Davis Company, 1924), p.64

438. Aggrawal, A., *Necrophilia: Forensic and Medico-Legal Aspects* (2011), in Griffiths, M. D., *Life on a Knife Edge*, 'Psychology Today' (Jan 2015), accessed 9/4/2016

439. Keppel, R.D. et al, *The Jack the Ripper Murders*, 'Journal of Investigative Psychology and Offender Profiling' 2, (2005), p. 15

440. Ibid, pp. 17–19.

441. Ibid, pp.18–19

442. Myers, W. *Juvenile Sexual Homicide* (2002), in Griffiths, M.D., *Life on a Knife Edge*, 'Psychology Today' (Jan 2015)

443. Federal Bureau of Investigation report 'Jack the Ripper'

444. Aggrawal, *Necrophilia*

445. Ibid

446. Geberth, V. *The Anatomy of Lust Murder*, 'Law and Order' (1998), in Griffiths, M. D., *Life on a Knife Edge*, 'Psychology Today' (Jan 2015)

447. von Von Krafft-Ebing, *Psychopathia Sexualis*, p.64, pp.66–67

448. Griffiths, *Life on a Knife Edge*

449. Von Krafft-Ebing, Psychopathia Sexualis, p.68

450. Geberth, *The Anatomy of Lust Murder*
451. Ibid
452. Dew, *I caught Crippen*, p.161
453. Revenge, for something, was certainly considered by those involved in investigating the case at the time. Dr Thomas Bond suggested that the killer's 'homicidal impulse may have developed from a revengeful or brooding condition of the mind', along with other explanations for his behaviours. MEPO 3/141 ff.150–157
454. Bailey, J. A., 'The Art of Profiling an Historical Case: The Whitechapel Murders', in Begg (ed), *Ripperology*, pp.230–231
455. For a detailed history of the rise of the Victorian and modern press *see* Griffiths, *Fleet Street*
456. Woods, P. & Baddeley, G., *Saucy Jack: The Elusive Ripper* (Hersham, Ian Allen Publishing, 2009), pp.114–115
457. Hills, R. 'Jack a Knacker?' *True Detective*, December 2004
458. Flanders, *The Invention of Murder*, pp.62–66
459. Ibid, pp.258–260
460. Ibid, pp.387–394; Vale, V. *The Woman Who Murdered Babies for Money: The Story of Amelia Dyer* (London: Andre Deutsch, 2011)
461. https://en.wikipedia.org/wiki/Francisco_Guerrero_(killer), [last accessed 28/7/2018]
462. Starr, D. *The Killer of Little Shepherds: The Case of the French Ripper and the Birth of Forensic Science* (New York: Simon & Schuster, 2012)
463. Michaud, S. G. and Aynesworth, H. *Ted Bundy: Conversations with a Killer* (Authorlink, 2000); Amirante, S. L and Broderick, D. *John Wayne Gacy: Defending a Monster*; Guillen, T. and Smith, C. *The Search for the Green River Killer: The True Story of America's Most Prolific Serial Killer* (Open Road Media, 2017); Whittle, B and Ritchie, J. *Harold Shipman – Prescription For Murder: The true story of Dr Harold Frederick Shipman* (Hachette, 2009); Sounes, H. *Fred And Rose: The Full Story of Fred and Rose West and the Gloucester House of Horrors* (Hachette, 2011); Burn, G. *Somebody's Husband, Somebody's Son: The Story of the Yorkshire Ripper* (Faber & Faber, London, 2011)
464. Canter, D. *Criminal Shadows: Inside the Mind of the Serial Killer* (London: Harper Collins Publishers, 1994
465. Canter, *Criminal Shadows*, p.101
466. Map ii, in Canter, *Criminal Shadows*, p. 102 & Canter, D. *Mapping Murder – The Secrets of Geographical Profiling* (London: Virgin Books, 2007), p.131
467. *Jack the Ripper: The First Serial Killer*, Atlantic Productions (Channel 5), 2006

468. English, W. 'Jack the Ripper', https://www.wesleyenglish.com/geoprofile/ infamous-cases/jack-the-ripper [last accessed 22/10/2015]

469. Trow, *Thames Torso Murders*, pp.147–8

470. *Missing Evidence: Jack the Ripper* (Blink Films, 2014)

471. Along with the numerous Harrison, Barber yards there were also hundreds of smaller, private slaughterhouses in late-Victorian London. In 1897 there 'no less than 497'. *Municipal Slaughterhouses* (Fabian Tract no.92, 1899) London Collection Pamphlets, P2556. Bishopsgate Library & Archives, p. 2.

472. Bell, *Capturing Jack the Ripper*, p.91

473. The road was named, however, after an Astronomer Royal rather than the businessman.

474. *Jack the Ripper: The First Serial Killer* (Atlantic Productions, 2006)

475. *The New York Herald*, 11 September 1889

476. Federal Bureau of Investigation report 'Jack the Ripper'

477. MacCarthy, F. *The Simple Life: C.R. Ashbee in the Cotswolds* (London: Lund Humphries, 1981), p.36

478. Census 1891; *Mapping the Practice and Profession of Sculpture in Britain and Ireland 1851–1951)* [online source]

479. MacCarthy, *The Simple Life*, p.8, p.338

480. Ibid

481. GRO, Death Certificate *William Hardiman*, Whitechapel vol.1c p. 163, no. 457

482. Thompson, M. K. *The Shadow of the Ripper: The Evolution of the Ripper Mythology*, Unpublished PhD thesis The Australian National University, (February 2017), p.259

483. Odell, R. *Ripperology: A Study of the World's First Serial Killer and a Literary Phenomenon* (Ohio: Kent State University Press, 2006)

484. Thompson, *The Shadow of the Ripper*

485. Diamond, M. *Victorian Sensation: Or, the Spectacular, the Shocking and the Scandalous in Nineteenth-Century Britain.* (London: Anthem Press, 2004), p.184

486. Anon., *The History of the Whitechapel Murders: a full and authentic narrative*

487. Matters, *The Mystery of Jack the Ripper*

488. Robinson, T. *The Whitechapel Horrors. Being an authentic account of the Jack the Ripper Murders* (Manchester, *c.*1920). Bishopsgate Institute library, LCP D8. 1a/80/17

489. Robinson, *The Whitechapel Horrors*, p.4

490. Sugden, *The Complete History of Jack the Ripper*, pp.105–6

491. Curtis, *Jack the Ripper and the London Press*, p.115

492. Oldridge, 'Casting the spell of terror', pp. 46–55

493. Odell, *Ripperology*, p.17

494. Frayling, 'The House that Jack Built', pp. 13–28

495. Dimolianis, S. 2010. *Jack the Ripper and Black Magic: Victorian Conspiracy Theories, Secret Societies and the Supernatural Mystique of the Whitechapel Murders*. Jefferson: McFarland & Company, p.6

496. Dimolianis, *Jack the Ripper and Black Magic*, p.161

497. Monk, C. 'Optograms, Autobiography, and the Image of Jack the Ripper', *Interdisciplinary Literary Studies: A Journal of Criticism and Theory*, Volume 12 (1) Fall 2010. p.95

498. Begg, *Jack the Ripper: The Definitive History*, p.259

499. Thompson, *The Shadow of the Ripper*, p.209

500. Marriott, *Beyond the Tower*, p.152

501. *The Star*, 24 September 1888

502. Quoted in Frayling, 'The House that Jack Built', p.24

503. Walkowitz, J. R., 'Narratives of sexual danger', in Warwick and Willis (eds.), *Jack the Ripper: Media, Culture, History* (Manchester: Manchester University Press, 2007), p.191

504. Odell, *Ripperology*, p.251

505. All traces of Flower and Dean Street were virtually eradicated between 1891 and 1894 in a slum clearance programme.

506. Stead, W. T. 'The Maiden Tribute of Modern Babylon: The Report of the Secret Commission', *Pall Mall Gazette*, (4–10 July 1885); *see also* Walkowitz, *City of Dreadful Delight*, pp. 81–120

507. Besant, W. *All Sorts and Conditions of Men: An Impossible Story* (London: Chatto & Windus, 1882); Octavia Hill, *Homes of the London Poor*, (London: Macmillan, 1883); Mearns, *The Bitter Cry of Outcast London*

508. Frayling, 'The House that Jack Built', p.25

509. London, *The People of the Abyss*

510. Bloom, C. 2013. *Victoria's Madmen: Revolution and Alienation* (Basingtoke: Palgrave MacMillan, 2013), p.149

511. http://www.casebook.org/suspects/jill.html [last accessed 10/4/18]

512. Bloom, C. 'The Ripper writing: a cream of a nightmare dream', in Warwick and Willis (eds.), *Jack the Ripper: Media, Culture, History* (Manchester, Manchester University Press, 2007), p.105

513. Colville, C. and Lucanio, P. *Jack the Ripper: His Life and Crimes in Popular Entertainment.* (Jefferson: McFarland & Co., 1999)

514. Smith, C. *Jack the Ripper in Film and Culture: Top Hat, Gladstone Bag and Fog* (Basingstoke: Palgrave MacMillan, 2016)

515. Colville and Lucanio, *Jack the Ripper*, p.9

516. Thompson, *The Shadow of the Ripper*

517. Smith, *Jack the Ripper in Film and Culture*, p.6

518. Walkowitz, 'Narratives of sexual danger', p.183

519. *Terror and Wonder: The Gothic Imagination*, British Library, 2014–15

520. Moore, A. & Campbell, E. *From Hell: Being a Melodrama in Sixteen Parts.* (Marietta, GA; Top Shelf Productions, 1989)

521. Sinclair, *White Chappell*; Ackroyd, P. *Dan Leno and the Limehouse Golem* (London: Minerva, 1995)

522. Lonsdale, K. 'Rounding up the Usual Suspects: Echoing Jack the Ripper' in Krueger, C. L. (ed). *Functions of Victorian Culture at the Present Time*, Athens: Ohio University Press, 2002), p.104

523. Gray, *London's Shadows*, p.237

524. Lonsdale, 'Rounding up the Usual Suspects', p.98

525. Bloom, *Victoria's Madmen*, p.201

526. Colville and Lucanio, *Jack the Ripper*, p.8

527. Wood, A. 'Gore Peddlers?' *The Ripperologist*, 145 August 2015

528. Bradshaw, K. 'Jack is a feminist issue', *The Ripperologist*, 145 August 2015. Kate sadly passed away in 2018 and is much mourned by the Ripperology community.

529. Walkowitz, 'Narratives of sexual danger', p.190

530. Quoted in Cameron, '"That's Entertainment?" Jack the Ripper and the Selling of Sexual Violence', in Radford, J. and Russell, D. E. H. *Femicide: The Politics of Woman Killing.* (New York: Twayne Publishers, 1992) p.186

531. Walkowitz, 'Narratives of sexual danger', p.193

532. Warwick, and Willis (eds.), *Jack the Ripper: Media, Culture, History.* Manchester: Manchester University Press, 2007), p.9

533. Hayward, C. Review Essay, 'Waxworks and Wordless Women: The Jack the Ripper Museum'. *The Public Historian*, Volume 39 (2) May 2017, p.52

534. Monk, 'Optograms, Autobiography, and the Image of Jack the Ripper', p.94

535. Hayward, 'Waxworks and Wordless Women', p.54

536. Cameron, '"That's Entertainment?"', p.185

537. Thompson, *The Shadow of the Ripper*, p.283

538. Cameron, '"That's Entertainment?"', p.187

539. Evans, R. J., *In Defence of History* (London: Granta Books, 1997), p.79

540. Evans, *In Defence of History*, p.79

541. Sugden, *The Complete History of Jack the Ripper*, p.183

542. Rumbelow, *The Complete Jack the Ripper*, pp.60–62

543. Begg, *Jack the Ripper: The Facts*, pp.182–3

544. Partner, N. 'Historicity in an Age of Reality-Fictions', in *A New Philosophy of History,* eds. Ankersmit, F. and Kellner, H. (Chicago, 1995), p.23, quoted in Evans, *In Defence of History,* p.80

545. Gray, *London's Shadows,* p.4

546. Hills, 'Cat's Cradle'; Hills & Stockton, 'Cousin Jack'

547. The term was first coined in 1972 and then used in a derogatory way. We are not using the term derogatively but as it is used today, as a way of identifying students of the case. Begg, Fido and Skinner, *The Complete Jack the Ripper,* p.438

548. Begg, *Jack the Ripper,* pp.417–8

549. Conan Doyle, A. *The Sign of Four* (London: *Strand Magazine,* 1890), ch.6

550. Begg, *Jack the Ripper,* p.385

551. www.casebook.org

BIBLIOGRAPHY

Archival sources

Municipal Slaughterhouses, (Fabian Tract no.92, 1899) London Collection Pamphlets, P2556. Bishopsgate Library & Archives

Kelly's Post Office Trades Directory (1889)

London Hospital Patient Admissions Register (1888)

Mcnaghten memorandum (1894)

MEPO/3/140

PP.1884–5 Royal Commission on the Housing of the Working Classes

Newspapers and periodicals

All the Year Around

Birmingham Daily Post

Daily Chronicle

Daily Express

Daily News

Daily Telegraph

Devon and Exeter Daily Gazette

East End Observer

East London Advertiser

East London Observer

Essex County Chronicle

Essex Newsman

Essex Standard, West Suffolk Gazette, and Eastern Counties' Advertiser

Essex Times

Evening News
Freeman's Journal and Daily Commercial Advertiser
Hansard
Hull Daily Mail
Illustrated Police News
Liverpool Mercury
Lloyd's Weekly Newspaper
Manchester Times
Morning Post
New York Tribune
North-Eastern Daily Gazette
Northern Echo
Pall Mall Gazette
Penny Illustrated Paper and Illustrated Times
People
Reynolds's Newspaper
Sheffield & Rotherham Independent
Sheffield Daily Telegraph
Standard
Sunderland Daily Echo and Shipping Gazette
The Times
Yorkshire Post

Works printed before 1910

Anon. *The History of the Whitechapel Murders: a full and authentic narrative of the above murders with sketches.* (New York, 1888)

Acton, William. *Prostitution considered in its moral, social and sanitary aspects in London and other cities, with proposals for the mitigation and prevention of its attendant evils,* (London, 1857–70)

Anderson, Sir Robert. *The Lighter Side of My Official Life,* (London: Hodder and Stoughton, 1910)

Besant, Walter. *All Sorts and Conditions of Men: An Impossible Story,* (London: Chatto & Windus, 1882)

—— *East London* (London: Chatto & Windus, 1902)

Booth, Charles. *Labour and Life of the People Volume 1: East London* (London: Williams and Norgate, 1889)

Fox, George Henry. *Photographic Illustration of Cutaneous Syphilis* (1891)

Goldsmid, H. J. *Dottings of a Dosser: Being the Revelations of the Inner Life of Low London Lodging Houses,* (London: T. Fisher Unwin, 1886)

Gordon, William John. *The Horse World of London*, (London: David & Charles Reprints, London, 1893/1971)

Haslam, John. *Observations on Madness and Melancholy: including practical remarks on those diseases*, (London, 1809)

Hebbert, C. *An Exercise in Forensic Medicine*, (London, 1888)

Hill, Octavia. *Homes of the London Poor*, (London: Macmillan, 1883)

London, Jack. *The People of the Abyss*, (London: Macmillan, 1903)

Mayhew, Henry. *London Labour and the London Poor: A cyclopaedia of the condition and earnings of those that will work, those that cannot work, and those that will not work, Vol. III* (London, 1851)

Mearns, Andrew. *The Bitter Cry of Outcast London: An Inquiry into the Condition of the Abject Poor*, (London, 1883)

Morrison, Arthur. *Child of the Jago*, (Oxford: Oxford University Press, this edition 2012)

Smith, Henry. *From Constable to Commissioner; the story of sixty years, most of them misspent*, (London: Chatto & Windus, 1910)

Stead, W. T. 'The Maiden Tribute of Modern Babylon: The Report of the Secret Commission', *Pall Mall Gazette*, (July 4–10 1885)

Books and articles

Ackroyd, Peter. *Dan Leno and the Limehouse Golem*, (London: Minerva, 1995)

Aggrawal, A. *Necrophilia: Forensic and Medico-Legal Aspects* (2011), in M. D. Griffiths, *Life on a Knife Edge*, 'Psychology Today' (Jan 2015)

Archer, John E. *The Monster Evil: Policing and Violence in Victorian Liverpool* (Liverpool: Liverpool University Press, 2011)

Arif, Debra and Robert Clack. 'A Rose By Any Other Name: The Death of Catherine Mylett, 20 December 1888', *Ripperologist*, 108, (November 2009)

Arrizabalaga, Jon, with John Henderson & Roger French. *The Great Pox: the French Disease in Renaissance Europe*, (New Haven & London: Yale University Press, 1997)

Barker, T. C., and Michael Robbins. *A History of London Transport: Volume One – The Nineteenth Century*, (London: George Allen & Unwin, 1975)

Bartley, Paula. *Prostitution, Prevention and Reform in England, 1860–1914*, (London: Routledge, 2000)

Begg, Paul, with John Bennett and Richard Jones. *Jack the Ripper* (Bournemouth: Future Publishing Ltd, 2017)

Begg, Paul. *Jack the Ripper: The Definitive History*, (London: Routledge, 2013)

Begg, Paul & John Bennett. *Jack the Ripper: The Forgotten Victims*, (London & New Haven: Yale University Press, 2013)

Begg, Paul with Martin Fido and Keith Skinner. *The Complete Jack the Ripper A to Z*, (London: Blake Publishing Limited, 2010)

Begg, Paul (Ed. *Ripperology*, (New York: Barnes & Noble, 2006)

Begg, Paul. *Jack the Ripper: The Facts*, (London: Robson Books, 2004)

Begg, Paul, *et al. The Jack the Ripper A–Z*, (London: Headline Book Publishing, 1996)

Begg, Paul. *Jack the Ripper: The Uncensored Facts, a Documented History of the Whitechapel Murders of 1888*, (London: Robson Books, 1988)

Bell, Neil R. A. *Capturing Jack the Ripper In the boots of a Bobby in Victorian London*, (Stroud: Amberley Books, 2014)

Bettley, James. 'Post Voluptatem Misericordia: The Rise and Fall of the London Lock Hospitals', *The London Journal*, 10/2 (1984)

Bloom, Clive. *Victoria's Madmen: Revolution and Alienation*, (Basingtoke: Palgrave MacMillan, 2013)

——. 'The Ripper writing: a cream of a nightmare dream', in Warwick, Alexandra and Willis, Martin (eds.), *Jack the Ripper: Media, Culture, History*, (Manchester, Manchester University Press, 2007)

Bradshaw, Kate. 'Jack is a feminist issue', *The Ripperologist*, 145 August 2015

Briggs, Asa. *Victorian Cities*, (Berkeley. Ca.: University of California Press, 1993)

Brown, B. 'Inspector Spratling's Pass' *Ripperologist*, 29 June 2000

Brown, K., R. Keppel, J. Weis and K. Welch. 'The Jack the Ripper Murders: A *Modus Operandi* and Signature Analysis of the 1888–1891 Whitechapel Murders', *Journal of Investigative Psychology and Offender Profiling*, Vol 2, 2005

Cameron, Deborah. '"That's Entertainment?" Jack the Ripper and the Selling of Sexual Violence', in Radford, Jill and Russell, Diana E. H. *Femicide: The Politics of Woman Killing*. (New York: Twayne Publishers, 1992)

Canter, David. *Mapping Murder – The Secrets of Geographical Profiling*, (London: Virgin Books, 2007)

—— *Criminal Shadows: Inside the Mind of the Serial Killer*, (London: Harper Collins Publishers, 1994)

Carey, John. 'Escape Routes: Ripper on the Railway' *Ripperologist*, No. 8/June 2006

Chisholm, Alexander, Christopher-Michael DiGracia & Dave Yost. *The News from Whitechapel; Jack the Ripper in the Daily Telegraph*, (Jefferson, N C: MacFarland & Co, 2002)

Chung, Mon-Fah. 'A Study of Thirty-Four Cases of Rapidly Developing Syphilitic Paraplegia', *Archives of Dermatology and Syphilology*, 14/2, August 1926

Colville, Gary and Patrick Lucanio *Jack the Ripper: His Life and Crimes in Popular Entertainment*. (Jefferson: McFarland & Co., 1999)

Cornwell, Patricia. *Portrait of a Killer: Jack the Ripper – Case Closed*, (London: Little, Brown, 2002)

Cullen, Tom. *Autumn of Terror*, (London: Bodley Head, 1965)

Curtis, Lee Perry. *Jack the Ripper and the London Press*, (London & New Haven: Yale University Press, 2002)

Davies, Andrew. *Gangs of Manchester*, (Wrea Green: Blake Publishing Limited, 2009)

——.'Youth gangs, masculinity and violence in late Victorian Manchester and Salford', *Journal of Social History*, (Winter, 1998)

Davis, Jennifer.'The London Garotting Panic of 1862: A Moral Panic and the Creation of a Criminal Class in mid-Victorian England', in V.A.C. Gatrell (ed), *Crime and Law: The Social History of Crime in Western Europe since 1500*, (London: Europa, 1980)

Dew, Walter. *I Caught Crippen: Memoirs of Ex-Chief Inspector Walter Dew, CID of Scotland Yard*, (London & Glasgow: Blackie & Son Ltd, 1938)

Diamond, Michael. *Victorian Sensation: Or, the Spectacular, the Shocking and the Scandalous in Nineteenth-Century Britain*. (London: Anthem Press, 2004)

Ditmore, Melissa Hope (Ed). *Encyclopedia of Prostitution and Sex Work, Volume 2*, (Santa Barbara, Ca.: Greenwood Publishing Group, 2006)

Eddleston, John J. *Jack the Ripper: An Encyclopaedia* (London: John Blake Publishing Ltd, 2010)

Edwards, Ivor. *Jack the Ripper's Black Magic Rituals*, (Penny Publishing, 2001)

Edwards, Russell. *Naming Jack the Ripper*, (Guilford: Globe Pequot Press, 2014)

——. *Naming Jack the Ripper New Crime Scene Evidence, A Stunning Forensic Breakthrough, The Killer Revealed*, (Basingstoke: Pan MacMillan, 2014)

Emsley, Clive. (*The English Police: A Political and Social History*, (London & New York: Longman, 1991)

Evans, Richard J. *In Defence of History*, (London: Granta Books, 1997)

Evans, Stewart, and Keith Skinner. *The Ultimate Jack the Ripper Sourcebook*, (London: Robinson, 2001)

——. *Jack the Ripper: Letters from Hell*, (Stroud: Sutton Publishing, 2001)

Fishman, William J. *East End 1888*, (London: Gerald Duckworth, 1988)

Flanders, Judith. *The Invention of Murder: How the Victorians Revelled in Death and Detection and Created Modern Crime*, (London: Harper Press, London, 2011)

Frayling, Christopher. 'The House that Jack Built', in A. Warwick & M. Willis (eds), *Jack the Ripper: Media, Culture, History*, (Manchester, Manchester University Press, 2007)

Friedland, Martin L. *The Trials of Israel Lipski: A True Story of a Victorian Murder in the East End of London* (New York: Beaufort Books, 1984)

Geberth, V. *The Anatomy of Lust Murder*, 'Law and Order' (1998), in Griffiths, M. D., *Life on a Knife Edge*, 'Psychology Today' (Jan 2015)

Gordon, R. Michael. *The Poison Murders of Jack the Ripper: His Final Crimes, Trial, and Execution*, (Jefferson, NC: McFarlane & Company, Inc., 2008)

——. *The Thames Torso Murders of Victorian London*, (Jefferson, NC: McFarlane & Company, Inc., 2002)

Gray, Drew D. *Crime, Policing and Punishment in England, 1660–1914* (London: Bloomsbury, 2016)

Gray, Drew. 'Gang Crime and the Media in Late Nineteenth-Century London: The Regent's Park Murder of 1888', *Cultural and Social History*, 10, 4 (2013)

Gray, Drew D. *London's Shadows: The Dark Side of Victorian London*, (London: Bloomsbury, 2010)

Griffiths, Dennis. *Fleet Street: Five Hundred Years of the Press*, (London: British Library, 2006)

Hall, Lesley A. 'Venereal diseases and society in Britain, from the Contagious Diseases Acts to the National Health Service', in Roger Davidson and Lesley A. Hall (eds), *Sex, Sin, and Suffering: Venereal Diseases and European Society since 1880*, (Basingstoke: Macmillan International Higher Education, 2012)

Harrison, Shirley, & Michael Barrett, *The Diary of Jack the Ripper*, (London: Smith Gryphon Books, 1993)

Hayward, Claire. Review Essay, 'Waxworks and Wordless Women: The Jack the Ripper Museum'. *The Public Historian*, Volume 39 (2) May 2017

Hempel, Sandra. *The Strange Case of the Broad Street Pump: John Snow and the Mystery of Cholera*, (Berkeley, Ca.: University of California Press, 2007)

Hills, Rob. 'Cat's Cradle', *Ripperologist* No 75, Jan. 2007

Hills, R. & A. Stockton, 'Cousin Jack', *Ripperologist*, No.68, June 2006

Hills, Robert. 'Jack a Knacker?' *True Detective*, December 2004

Humphries, Stephen. *Hooligans or Rebels? An Oral History of Working-Class Childhood and Youth, 1889–1939*, (Oxford: Oxford University Press, 1981)

Hutchinson, Philip. *The Jack the Ripper Location Photographs: Duffield's Yard and the Whitby Collection*, (Stroud: Amberley Books, 2009)

Jackson, Lee. *Dirty Old London: The Victorian Fight Against Filth*, (New Haven and London: Yale University Press, 2014)

Keating, P. J. 'Fact and Fiction in the East End' in Jim Dyos & Michael Wolff (eds.), *The Victorian City: Images and Realities Volume 2* (,London & New York: Routledge, 1973)

Kellett, J. R. *The Impact of Railways on Victorian Cities*, (London: Routledge,1969)

Keppel, R.D. et al, *The Jack the Ripper Murders*, 'Journal of Investigative Psychology and Offender Profiling' 2, (2005)

Knight, Stephen. *Jack the Ripper: The Final Solution*, (London: Grafton Books, 1976)

Laite, Julia. *Common Prostitutes and Ordinary Citizens: Commercial Sex in London, 1885–1960*, (Basingstoke: Palgrave Macmillan, 2012)

Loftus, Elizabeth F. 'Leading Questions and the Eyewitness Report', *Cognitive Psychology*, 7, (1975)

Loftus, Elizabeth F. and Guido Zanni, 'Eyewitness Testimony: The influence of the wording of a question', *Bulletin of the Psychonomic Society*, 5 (1) (1975)

Lonsdale, Kate. 'Rounding up the Usual Suspects: Echoing Jack the Ripper' in Krueger, Christine L. (ed). *Functions of Victorian Culture at the Present Time*, Athens: Ohio University Press, 2002)

MacCarthy, F. *The Simple Life: C. R. Ashbee in the Cotswolds*, (London: Lund Humphries, 1981)

Macilwee, Michael. *Gangs of Liverpool. From the Cornermen to the High Rip: The Mobs that Terrorised a City* (Wrea Green: Blake Publishing Limited, 2006)

McNeill, William H. *Plagues and Peoples*, (London: Penguin, 1976, 1994)

Magellan, Karyo. *By Ear and Eyes; The Whitechapel Murders Jack the Ripper and the Murder of Mary Jane Kelly*, (Derby: Longshot Publishing, 2005)

Matthew, Colin (ed.) *The Nineteenth Century: The British Isles, 1815–1901*, (Oxford: Oxford University Press, 2005)

Matters, Leonard. *The Mystery of Jack the Ripper*, (Arrow Books, 1929, 1964)

Monk, Craig. 'Optograms, Autobiography, and the Image of Jack the Ripper', *Interdisciplinary Literary Studies: A Journal of Criticism and Theory*, Volume 12 (1) Fall 2010

Moore, Alan & Eddie Campbell, *From Hell: Being a Melodrama in Sixteen Parts*. (Marietta, GA; Top Shelf Productions, 1989)

Morley, C. J. 'Jack the Ripper: A Suspect Guide' (E-book, 2005)

Myers, W. *Juvenile Sexual Homicide* (2002), in Griffiths, M.D., *Life on a Knife Edge*, 'Psychology Today'

Odell, Robin. *Ripperology: A Study of the World's First Serial Killer and a Literary Phenomenon*, (Ohio: Kent State University Press, 2006)

Oldridge, Darren. 'Casting the spell of terror; the press and the early Whitechapel murders,' in A. Warwick & M. Willis (eds), *Jack the Ripper: Media, Culture, History*, (Manchester: Manchester University Press, 2007)

Olsen, Donald J. *The Growth of Victorian London*, (Harmondsworth: Penguin Books, 1976)

Paley, Bruce. *Jack the Ripper: The Simple Truth*, (London: Headline, 1995)

Pearce, J. M. 'Henry Charlton Bastian (1837–1915): Neglected Neurologist and Scientist', *European Neurology*, 63/2 (February, 2010)

Pearson, Geoffrey. *Hooligan: A History of Respectable Fears* (Basingstoke: MacMillan, 1983)

Quétel, Claude. *History of Syphilis*, (trans. Judith Braddock and Brian Pike), (Cambridge: Polity Press, 1990)

Raw, Louise. *Striking a Light: The Bryant and May Matchwomen and their Place in History*, (London: Bloomsbury, 2009)

Robinson, Tom. *The Whitechapel Horrors. Being an authentic account of the Jack the Ripper Murders*, (Manchester, c.1920)

Rowlands, Gary. 'Jack the Ripper: The Writing on the Wall', *Criminologist*, Vol. 17, No. 2, (Summer 1993)

Rubenhold, Haille. *The Five: The Lives of Jack the Ripper's Women*, (London: Houghton Mifflin, 2019)

Rumbelow, Donald. *The Complete Jack the Ripper: Fully Revised and Updated*, (London: Penguin Books, 2004)

Rule, Fiona. *The Worst Street in London* (Hersham: Ian Allen Publishing, 2008)

Samuel, Raphael. *East End Underworld: Chapters in the Life of Arthur Harding*, (London: Routledge, 1981)

Seaman, L.C.B. *Life in Victorian London*, (London: B. T. Batsford Ltd, 1973)

Senise, Stephen. *False Flag*, (Acorn Independent Press, 2018)

Shelden, Neal Stubbings. *The Victims of Jack the Ripper*, (Knoxville, Tn.: Inklings Press, 2007)

Short, K.R.M. *The Dynamite Wars: Irish-American Bombers in Victorian Britain*, (Dublin: Gill & MacMillan, 1979)

Showalter, Elaine. *Sexual Anarchy: Gender and Culture at the Fin de Siècle*, (London: Virago, 1992)

Siena, Kevin P. *Venereal Disease, Hospitals and the Urban Poor: London's 'Foul Wards', 1600–1800*, (Rochester, NY: University of Rochester Press, 2004)

Simpson, Antony E. (ed), W. T. Stead, *The Maiden Tribute of Modern Babylon*, (Lambertville, NJ:True Bill Press, 2007)

Sinclair, Iain. *White Chappell, Scarlet Tracings* (London: Penguin Books,1987)

Smith, Clare. *Jack the Ripper in Film and Culture: Top Hat, Gladstone Bag and Fog*, (Basingstoke: Palgrave MacMillan, 2016)

Starr, Douglas. *The Killer of Little Shepherds: The Case of the French Ripper and the Birth of Forensic Science*, (New York: Simon & Schuster, 2012)

Stedman Jones, Gareth. *Outcast London: A Study in the Relationship Between Classes in Victorian London*, (Oxford: Oxford University Press, 1971)

Storch, Robert D. 'The Policeman as Domestic Missionary: Urban Discipline and Popular Culture in Northern England, 1850–1880', *Journal of Social History*, 9:4 (1976)

Sugden, Philip. *The Complete History of Jack the Ripper, New Edition* (London: Constable & Robinson, 2002)

Sweet, Matthew. *Inventing the Victorians: What we think we know about them and why we're wrong*, (New York: St Martin's Press, 2001)

Tarn, John N. *Five Per Cent Philanthropy: An Account of Housing in Urban Areas between 1840 and 1914*, (Cambridge: Cambridge University Press, 1973)

Taylor, Howard. 'Rationing Crime: The Political Economy of Criminal Statistics since the 1850s', *Economic History Review*, 51 (1998)

Trow, M. J. *The Thames Torso Murders*, (Barnsley: Wharncliffe Books, 1988)

Vale, Alison. *The Woman Who Murdered Babies for Money: The Story of Amelia Dyer*, (London: Andre Deutsch, 2011)

von Krafft-Ebing, Richard Freiherr. *Psychopathia Sexualis with special references to Contrary Sexual Instinct: A Medico-Legal Study*, (Trans. C.G. Chaddock) (Philadelphia, Pa.: F. A. Davis Company, 1924)

Walkowitz, Judith. 'Narratives of sexual danger', in Warwick, Alexandra and Willis, Martin (eds.), *Jack the Ripper: Media, Culture, History*, (Manchester: Manchester University Press, 2007)

Walkowitz, Judith R. *City of Dreadful Delight: Narratives of Sexual Danger in Late-Victorian* London, (London: Virago, 1994)

——. *Prostitution and Victorian Society: Women, Class, and the State*, (Cambridge: Cambridge University Press, 1980)

Warren, N. P. 'A Postal Kidney', *The Criminologist* 13(1), Spring 1989

Warwick, Alexandra and Martin Willis (eds.), *Jack the Ripper: Media, Culture, History*. Manchester: Manchester University Press, 2007)

Weeks, Jeffrey. *Sex, Politics and Society: The Regulation of Sexuality after 1800*, (London: Longman, 1981)

Weinreb, Ben and Christopher Hibbert. *The London Encyclopaedia*, (London: Book Club Associates, 1983)

Westcott, Tom. *The Bank Holiday Murders: The True Story of the First Whitechapel Murders*, (Crime Confidential Press, 2013)

Weston-Davies, Wynne. *The Real Mary Kelly*, (London: Blink Publishing, 2015)

White, Jerry. `*London in the Nineteenth Century: 'An Awful Wonder of God'*, (London: Jonathan Cape, 2007)

——. *Rothschild Buildings. Life in an East End Tenement Block, 1887–1920* (London: Routledge & Kegan Paul, 1980)

Williams, Tony with Humphrey Price, *Uncle Jack*, (London: Orion Books, 2005)

Wood, Adam. 'Gore Peddlers?' *The Ripperologist*, 145 August 2015

Woods, Paul & Gavin Baddeley, *Saucy Jack: The Elusive Ripper*, (Hersham, Ian Allen Publishing, 2009)

Unpublished Thesis

Thompson, Matthew Keith. *The Shadow of the Ripper: The Evolution of the Ripper Mythology*, Unpublished PhD thesis The Australian National University, (February 2017)

Websites

www. ancestry.com
www.casebook.org
www.policemagistrate.blog
www.wesleyenglish.com

Documentary

Jack the Ripper: The First Serial Killer, Atlantic Productions (Channel 5) 2006
Who Do you Think you Are? (Martin Freeman) season 6, episode 11 (Director Mike Bates). Wall to Wall Television (2009)

INDEX

'A must-have... The only thing wrong with this book is that you come to the end of it.' PAUL BEGG, *Ripperologist*

Capturing Jack the Ripper

In the Boots of a Bobby in Victorian London

NEIL R. A. BELL